# All
# of a
# Sudden
# Things that Matter
# in Contemporary Art

Jörg Heiser

*Sternberg Press*

Jörg Heiser

All of a Sudden

Things that Matter in Contemporary Art

Publisher: Sternberg Press

First published as *Plötzlich diese Übersicht: Was gute zeitgenössische Kunst ausmacht*
© by Ullstein Buchverlage GmbH, Berlin. Published in 2007 by Claassen Verlag

Translator: Nicholas Grindell
Copy editor: Courtney Johnson
Design: Miriam Rech, Markus Weisbeck, Surface, Berlin/Frankfurt am Main
Printing and binding: Brandenburgische Universitätsdruckerei und Verlagsgesellschaft Potsdam
ISBN 978-1-933128-39-9

Sternberg Press
Caroline Schneider
Karl-Marx-Allee 78, D-10243 Berlin
1182 Broadway #1602, New York, NY 10001
www.sternberg-press.com

# Table of Contents

# Introduction

## Good Cop, Bad Cop

Since the mid-1990s, contemporary art has been booming like never before. There is more of everything—more artists, more collectors, more galleries, more art fairs, more museums, more biennials, more interest, more industry, more pop, more hype. And even with the looming prospect of an economic downturn, there's little reason to believe that this "more" will simply evaporate. Faced with all this, some art professionals reach for the revolvers of cultural pessimism: Mass Stupidity Is Killing Great Art! Others (often the same people a short while later) defect with all the greater abandon to the alleged enemy. The entrenched battle between defenders of art's autonomy and champions of its merging with entertainment culture continues. There is more of everything, with one exception: criteria with which the art of the moment can be understood, judged, praised and, if need be, damned—without getting bogged down in this eternal trench warfare. Is the artificial sun installed by the Danish artist Olafur Eliasson in Tate Modern's gigantic turbine hall in 2003 automatically bad because it drew millions of visitors? Are the young Leipzig painters with their finely brush-stroked visions automatically good because American collectors scramble to buy them? What do rising auction prices say about the value of a work? And what, more importantly, do they not say?

Talking about art in terms of nothing but hard numbers and soft personal preferences is not only unproductive but also, in the long term, tedious. Can I at least fall back on art history's canon of beauty and truth? If only it were so easy. But the canon is constantly being revised, from decade to decade, from era to era. Quantity and quality form a Gordian Knot; I can only cut through it once I have ignored it for a while. Instead, I must come to terms with a major, fundamental paradox: any judgment on art ultimately remains arbitrary and subjective—and for precisely this reason, it must be all the more solidly and verifiably argued. In this book, I state which currents, artists, and works do and do not carry contemporary art forward, and I give reasons.

This is something of a presumption, of course. My point of view is inevitably limited. Any attempt to encompass *all* relevant artists and artistic movements of today would not only be practically impossible within the confines of a single book—even a single head—but also ignorant of the subtleties of cultural situatedness on a global scale. (In other words, I'm looking forward to reading a similar kind of book written from a non-Western perspective.) Some prominent artists are not discussed in this book—for example, Jeff Koons, Andreas Gursky, Ai Wei Wei, and Damien Hirst. The reason they are not included is not that I felt they were irrelevant to the course of contemporary art (or that they don't merit the wide public recognition they already enjoy), but that it would have felt forced to include them in my line of argument. This book is not about providing a gazetteer of names and movements in contemporary art—though it does provide a critical mass of examples—but about identifying some central ideas and artistic methods that seem important for understanding what fuels art's progress into the future. These are the "things that matter in contemporary art," while other factors—say, the sociology of art's reception, or the machinations of the art market—are discussed here only in terms of their repercussive effects on these very ideas and methods.

How can I recognize structures where a cheerful or oblivious hodgepodge seems to prevail? Should I talk instead about how artists became what they are—about their biographies? That says plenty about the artists, for sure, but it often says too little about their work, for as soon as they go out into the world, like teenagers going out and meeting other teenagers, artworks begin to live a life of their own. Perhaps, then, I should try an approach based on medium—on painting and sculpture, photography and video? Such attempts are touchingly anachronistic, as the mangy mongrels sired at the borders between media and genres during the twentieth century cannot simply be whistled back into classical categories. The composer Hanns Eisler once said: "If you only know about music, then you don't know about music either." (For "music," please substitute the name of any other artistic discipline.) But this does not mean that media and genres can simply be treated as one big undifferentiated mass: materials and techniques are governed by distinct rules.

The painter or sculptor in a picturesquely trashy studio is still a popular motif for photo features in glossy magazines. This reveals much about a nostalgic yearning for bohemian lifestyles harbored by today's cultural and economic elite. And it reveals little about what distinguishes the art of the present from the art of past eras. For in contemporary art, the emphasis has shifted from biography and medium to method and situation.

In 2002, Mexico City-based Belgian artist Francis Alÿs realized a work that illustrates this very clearly. A gawky guy buys a pistol, releases the safety catch, steps out of the gun shop, and walks unhurriedly through the busy streets. His right hand swings around as if he were carrying a shopping bag, not a gun. No one seems to take any notice, until, after eleven minutes—as we see from the time code on the video camera that follows him—a police car draws up alongside him. The man tries to run away, but not decisively enough, and the officers have no trouble apprehending him, bundling him into the car, and speeding off.

The gawky guy is the artist himself. He wanted to find out how long one can walk around the streets of Mexico City with a gun before being arrested. But this is not merely a test of courage; it is a test of reality. After his arrest, he persuaded the officers to recreate the whole scene with him, exactly the same, for a second shoot. This then became the actual video work entitled *Re-Enactment*. In exhibitions, the first version is projected alongside the second, which differs from it only in a few cuts and close-ups.

The "original" suddenly appears infected with doubt: What if the authentic, risky action was not authentic, but also contrived? Conversely, the second version still seems dangerous enough: What, for instance, if a passerby not aware that the scene was staged were to try to stop the armed man by force? Either way, the idea of the artist risking his life for art is swallowed up by the logical vacuum between fact and fiction. What we are left with is neither the artist's biography—no, Francis Alÿs is not a gun fanatic—nor the medium. Is it video? Is it performance? It's neither and both at the same time. What we are left with is the situation (man goes for stroll with gun) and the method (repetition).

This work by Alÿs is not just a good example because he uses the modern media of performance and video. It's not a matter of evaluating contemporary art by upholding anything conceptual, performative, or digital against the "old stuff" of painting and sculpture. Alÿs also works with painting and sculpture. Painters and sculptors diligently continue to make paintings and sculptures, and much of what they produce is rubbish. But the same can be said of the endless rehashing of theatrical putting-the-world-to-rights and the "disturbance of perception" by "interventions in reality" that often show how out of touch with reality those involved are.

Sigmund Freud wrote about jokes and their link to the unconscious, and about the pleasure derived from the surprising resolution of contradiction. Sergei Eisenstein spoke of "intellectual montage," the cut as a collision between different film images that produces meaning not present in either of these images in their own right. The four chapters of this book deal with four central relationships within contemporary art that articulate conflicts derived from an engagement with historical precursors. Examining these conflicts cannot mean falsely reconciling them within a unity or silencing them within a clear-cut dualism.

In the first chapter, pathos is pitted against ridiculousness, and slapstick is the method by which to operate under the radar of stiff seriousness. Beginning in the year 1913, with Marcel Duchamp, Charlie Chaplin, and newspaper cartoons, sculpture proves to be the key medium, made to resonate by the new experience of moving images, right up to the present day. Why is the deadly earnest of the avant-garde only one side, and why is it still about more than just telling a few funny stories?

In the second chapter, bodiless elegance confronts pungent physicality: flattened two-dimensionality versus three-dimensional volume. It is painting (not without guest appearances by photography, cartoons, and installation) where these opposites lock horns in exemplary fashion: a painting of decisions, in which social relations are acted out both symbolically and in the material. Gerhard Richter, Maria Lassnig, and Sigmar Polke are the seminal figures here, in relation to whom younger painters like Glenn Brown, Dana Schutz, Gillian Carnegie, and Laura Owens develop their own approaches. What's behind the mock battles over the thousandfold death of painting? And what could replace the endless, now unhelpful contrasting of abstraction and figuration, of hot expressivity and cool copying?

In the third chapter, illusion is pitted against anti-illusion: multi-part film and video projections, set within exhibition architectures, duplicate and subdivide this contrast until it explodes. An odd trailblazing trio is formed by the film pioneer of the early Stalin years, Dziga Vertov, and the designers-in-chief of postwar America, Charles and Ray Eames. From the 1960s, in the work of Dan Graham or Anthony McCall, the pictures become three-dimensional, to the point where, in the projection spaces of Doug Aitken, Marcel Odenbach, and Eija-Liisa Ahtila, they are rhythmicized and orchestrated in new ways. What happens to the viewers in these spaces? Do they become independent flaneurs in a picture paradise, or helpless mice in the labyrinth of the spectacle—or neither of these?

And finally, in the fourth chapter, autonomy is pitted against the market, deferred gratification against immediate gratification. Starting with the work of Robert Barry and Douglas Huebler, "unseizable gratification" appears as an effect achieved by works that keep art in a state of suspension by withdrawing from the usual conditions of production and consumption. The putting-into-circulation of information, objects, actions, or rumors is conceptually situated somewhere between rule and chance. In various ways, the work of Tino Sehgal, Aleksandra Mir, and Roman Ondák poses the question of whether there may be something beyond a choice between the "*J'accuse*!" of an emphatically critical art that considers itself above the "impure" sphere of the market and counts on later recognition in the academic and museum milieu, and the "Jacuzzi!" of an emphatically affirmative art that luxuriates in the warm jets of money and hype.

In contrast to the cheerfully arbitrary stylistic mix of the postmodern, all these chapters focus on collisions between ideas, attitudes, and methods. At first, the opposites appear irreconcilable, but at a deeper level they are closely linked, without merely canceling each other out in a zero-sum game. Bizarre entities emerge, split like Jekyll and Hyde between reason and madness, commonality and peculiarity—and it's as if the closer we come to recent contemporary art, the more these opposites finally stop merely disowning and fighting each other, joining instead to form teams of good cops and bad cops to put the screws on all the charming dogmas and stupidities of the present day.

But before we examine this development in terms of real live artworks, the question remains: Why am I saying all this anyway? Because art is more than just a randomly chosen cultural field of activity in which to acquire a little specialist knowledge with which to show off. When it's good, art hits where it hurts, striking at the heart of an ossified status quo by which it itself was brought forth. Perhaps this is something that much important art since Modernism has in common with slapstick. Instead of just aiming to shock and outrage, it shows authority losing its grip. Instead of inflating itself, it deflates the pompous in the name of art.

# Pathos *versus* Ridiculousness Art With Slapstick

## Art Lore

Let's suppose that contemporary art, with all its quirks and peculiarities, has become socially accepted once and for all. Its last real enemies have given up or died. Some people use it to adorn themselves; others study it attentively. Some expect it to look good; others expect it to be critical. The former find the latter too highbrow; the latter find the former too lowbrow. But apart from that, everything's okay. I'm okay, you're okay. It's all over before it's even begun and everyone goes home.

This, of course, is not the case. Contemporary art has not been accepted once and for all, and where it is accepted, then only on a fragile basis. But even if all of the above were true, there would still be the question of whether art is actually what people think it is. Do we miss out on something when we reduce art to tales of fearless studio heroes and enigmatic exhibition beauties? Yes, we do. Among other things, we miss out on slapstick. So can we just replace the heroic legends and beautiful poses with anti-hero legends and comic poses? No, we cannot. Because art is not a story.

For all the innovations of the avant-garde, literature, theater, and film are still essentially narrative forms. But in art—as in music—this is not the case. Art is essentially anti-narrative. This fact is easily obscured by two things. First, it has long been the case that all manner of media (films, texts, comics, etc.) are admissible in artistic production. But the more a work of art makes itself at home in these narrative media, the more it might perhaps be better placed within the discipline in question—or worse placed, considering the competition it would face there. And second, much writing about art tends to move on as quickly as possible to anecdote-spiked biography of the artist, as if the anti-narrative core of art were a black hole that needed to be given the widest berth possible. Pollock's drinking, van Gogh's ear, Picasso's underpants—these and a myriad of other yarns about artists and their lives can be spun without even touching on the actual impact art has on ourselves, and on the world.

In principle, there's nothing wrong with good old-fashioned art lore. Bring on the legends of flamboyance and stubbornness! The tales of asceticism and delirium! As long as they don't obscure the fact that art (which in this respect resembles the natural sciences) has distanced itself more thoroughly than other fields of culture from the task of telling stories, be it to help you sleep or to scare you stiff. In other words, art produces stories as a by-product, the way NASA produced Teflon pans. When someone says an artwork is about this or that, or stands for this or that view, they've said next to nothing about its quality as a picture, object, concept, gesture, or act. This is true to a certain extent of any cultural form, but in the case of art, it's the central point. With works of art, it's less about *what* than about *how*. Not about the story itself, but about what set the story in motion, what interrupts it, what gives it rhythm, or what jumps out of the story like a frog out of a pond.

All this can be very frustrating. There we were, thinking contemporary art was the sort of culture that could tell us a story about a better life, or at least about better home decoration, and what do we find? Nothing but a black hole—nothing but embarrassing pauses, comic stumbling blocks, silent intermezzos. But if we don't turn away bored or flee into feigned approval, then something happens.

Which almost brings us to the theme of this chapter: slapstick in art. But first, we must quickly deal with one more problem.

It's not about art taking the content of slapstick on board like a vessel. The theme of slapstick alone does not make a good work of art. It's not about comedies that have mistakenly ended up not on stage, or on screen, or between the covers of a book, but in art. Above all, it's not about the kind of market "synergy" in whose name unimaginative curators and critics—and the artists who play their game—pounce on other cultural arenas and their financial potential, only to tack them on with an ampersand, like generously tolerated favorites at the court of the regal discipline of art: art & theater, art & football, art & armpits.

Instead, it's about slapstick as a *method*. Slapstick as a technique, attitude, or approach: as something that gets to the heart (or is it the dark, empty core?) of making and looking at art itself. Slapstick is not a clown interlude, a bit of light relief in the revered and prestigious art circus, a secondary aspect. It's a central triggering mechanism, both a premeditated trick and a spontaneous idea—a *déclic*, as Walter Benjamin called it—that's responsible for bringing art into being and making it go somewhere. It is thus worth taking a closer look at the early days of modern slapstick and of modern art.

# Crash! Bang! Wallop!—Biff! Bang! Pow!

In his book *Comedy is a Man in Trouble*, Alan Dale defines slapstick as staging a "collapse of the hero's dignity"—either by attack from outside or of its own accord. A poke in the eye, a boot to the rump, a brick to the head, a banana skin. The tragicomic boom-bash as fates entwine and bodies collide. Why is this funny, even the thousandth time? One well-known reason is schadenfreude. Another is the exact opposite: empathy and a feeling of solidarity in moments of misfortune. Slapstick as a sudden jolt in a smooth sequence, an absurd attack of hiccoughs in everyday life and world events, allowing us to catch glimpses of the truth about ourselves and our relations with others. There's something liberating about this, and something moving.

Thus far, slapstick could be placed within the history of theater and literature, from Aristophanes to Miguel de Cervantes to Alfred Jarry. But a closer look at slapstick in the medium of *film* reveals qualities that suggest an elective affinity with art—that is, the way it tells funny little stories as a guise through which to render storytelling itself absurd, by repetition of motifs (running gags), chaotic montage, and overindulgence in certain medium-specific effects. "Crash! Bang! Wallop!" and "Biff! Bang! Pow!" For a good gag, slapstick will gladly dispense with narrative logic, plot, and characterization.

The fast cuts and absurd contrasts of slapstick had their roots in the quick-paced reviews of vaudeville and in the cartoon strips of early twentieth-century newspapers. In film, from 1910, camera and editing technology reinforced them

1a

1b

1c

2

1a-c     **Franz West,** Laocoön's Bouncing Head
(Lessing Study), 2002
2         Franz West and Janc Szeni with Adaptives
by **Franz West** in front of the Wittgenstein
House in Vienna-Erdberg (late 1970s)

and gave them a central role. At the time, this prompted critic and slapstick apologist Gilbert Seldes—in his eulogy *The Seven Lively Arts* (1924)—to oppose attempts at explaining slapstick purely in terms of historical precursors. Slapstick, he claimed, is camera angle, technical tricks, editing, projection; without these factors it would forfeit its tempo and rhythm, or become mere acrobatics.

Both slapstick and art, then, have a tendency toward the anti-narrative, and both aim to use the mechanisms of the media in which they are situated to achieve something that would not be possible without them.

# Lessing's Bouncing Head: Franz West

What suggested this idea of a link—beyond connections merely in subject matter—between slapstick and art? First: the observation that contemporary sculpture often deliberately sets the scene for an embarrassing event. Charles Baudelaire is supposed to have said that sculpture is something you trip over when you stand back to look at a painting. The quotation is also variously attributed to painters Barnett Newman and Ad Reinhardt, or Pop artist Claes Oldenburg. Whoever originally came up with this bon mot, it vouches for the preferential treatment of painting and its flights of the imagination over the blunt presence and earthly heaviness of sculpture—the type of naked physical presence of which the style-conscious dandy poet and the bourgeois intellectual grappling for composure would rather not be reminded.

But the real irony of such disparaging attitudes to sculpture is that from the early twentieth century—and increasingly right up to the present—art has developed a fondness for the situation comedy of tripping over stuff that gets in the way. Not always literally, of course, but in a certain sense. Let's take an example: A shapeless papier-mâché lump, the size of a bison's head, part of it sprayed pink, sits atop a steel spring. The spring is mounted on a white plinth. This object was made by Viennese artist Franz West. What on earth is it meant to be? Where's the story? It's not written anywhere; we have to tell it ourselves.

A closer look, then, and a little patience. The white plinth is open on one side, so it could also be a lectern. And there's a shelf with a small book. Can I leaf through it? Normally, you're meant to keep your fingers off the art, but since the lectern bears clearly visible traces of use—like printers ink and grease from the hands of a speaker gripping its edges—I feel authorized to touch.

So I pick up Gotthold Ephraim Lessing's *Laocoön, An Essay on the Limits of Painting and Poetry*, written in 1766. In it, Lessing makes a distinction that was to remain influential until far into the twentieth century: art is a static medium, literature a time-based one. Writing has rhythm and progression, whereas art is a frozen moment. At the Vatican in Rome there is proof of this: the marble Laocoön fighting two serpents that are after him and his two infant sons. For more than two thousand years, he has been frozen in a moment of imploring the heavens for pity. Right, I think, as I lean forward to put the book back on the shelf, and—ouch!—bang my head on the lump of papier-mâché. Thanks to the steel spring, it starts to sway gently back and forth like the head of a nodding dog in the back of a car. Lessing is refuted. Art does move in time and space after all.

When, in 2002, Franz West placed this amorphous object on a white plinth-cum-lectern and called it *Laocoön's Bouncing Head (Lessing Study)*, he might also have had in mind that, together with the lectern, the comical bulbous head becomes a speaker with a reddened face, trying to exude authority and wobbling his head out of sheer nervousness. The object is already a parody in its own right. West has a reputation for helping people loosen up in the face of over-blown theatricality. As a young man, he was present in 1968 at the notorious event by the Vienna Actionists that came to be known as the "university mess." In front of a packed lecture hall, Actionist spiritual leader Otto Mühl swung his whip and urinated into Günter Brus's mouth, when the latter was not whistling the Austrian national anthem while masturbating and smearing himself with his own excrement. During all this, Oswald Wiener stood at the blackboard and delivered a lecture. As the action neared its close, the audience was asked if anyone wished to comment on the whole ballyhoo, a question answered with stony silence by all three hundred people present. Whereupon Franz West went to the front, politely thanked the performers, and asked for some applause. Silence gave way to mirth as West treated the great, fearless breach of taboo as no more than an edifying lecture event—unlike the state authorities, who handed down prison sentences of several months to the Actionists for denigrating national symbols.

With his *Lessing Study*, too, West feigns a fool-like naïveté, since there is more going on here than just a clumsy oaf refuting Old Lessing by bumping his thick skull against some swaying thing that recalls a flustered lecturer. That really would be no more than a funny story. What makes it really interesting is that contemporary art achieves this effect by laying out books as bait, so that I pick them up although I really should know better. By making plinths that are not plinths but lecterns with grubby fingerprints. By having titles that give me a hint, a punch line, but also a puzzle about the status of the artwork: Is it just a self-sufficient object in space like some extraterrestrial apparition, designed for rapt contemplation? Or is it there to be used, even if only for some potential, imagined purpose? In a word: instead of constantly emphasizing its unity, its inapproachability, its autonomy—like the tabernacle of some sacred idea—interesting art does the exact opposite and throws itself without restraint into the arms of my perception. It leaves me with the joyous dirty work of thinking and criticizing. It doesn't tell stories; it generates them.

The true genius of this strategy of self-diffusion—of the "open work," as Umberto Eco first called it—is the paradoxical way it leaves art's autonomy as a form of expression intact. After all, describing reality, looking good, and, if necessary, being critical are all things other forms of expression can do just as well, often better.

For West, it all began with the *Adaptives* (since 1974). These twisted, limb-like forms made of plaster over a metal core challenged viewers to take them in their hands and to use them as a cross between Uncle Albert's crutch and Aunt Bertha's brassiere, to pose with them or to play with them. The only question is: Who adapts to whom here, me to the object or the object to me? We don't want to look too foolish fiddling around with these crooked things, and if no one is watching we only end up chuckling all the more foolishly.

These objects, then, tested the border between "fine" and "applied" art—there was certainly some applying going on here, but what was its purpose? West would not be West if he didn't give this testing of borders a mercantile twist. And it was in the 1990s that he became more widely known with his chairs and armchairs. These items, produced by West and his assistants with the diligence of any small-scale furniture manufacturer, proved very popular with museums and collectors who could offer a seat to visitors with a casual "that's a West." But those who boast of such ownership too proudly get their comeuppance. The chairs have crudely but precisely built steel frames, upholstered with robust fabrics, but it's hard to make up one's mind whether or not they are actually comfortable. In search of the best sitting position, one ends up switching back and forth between sagging slump and ramrod straight, which raises the suspicion that West imagined a sitter forever alternating between blind drunk and terminally uptight.

When, in exhibitions, West then demonstratively places his chairs in front of sculptures or paintings by himself or other artists, it becomes obvious (if further proof was needed) that all this comfortable-uncomfortable stretching and shifting enacts bourgeois art-viewing and art-collecting as a sketch—at the same time as taking it very seriously: What do people *really* do with art? How do they live with it, and how does it figure in the irksome, embarrassing, irritating earthly heaviness of their everyday life? As with the *Adaptives*, the notion of "becoming one" with the cathartic experience of the sublime or artistic beauty turns into a comedy number, and we are the ones acting it out.

# The Year 1913 and What Came Before

West's Laocoön head, which developed out of his *Adaptives* and chairs, shares a central quality with a famous work by Marcel Duchamp. In 1913, Duchamp mounted the front wheel of a bicycle on a stool; *Bicycle Wheel* is the simplest imaginable collage of two otherwise unaltered objects, and as in West's piece, a moving object is mounted on a static one. In both works, it is movement which knocks the dignified off balance. Duchamp's bicycle stool was no good for sitting on, and any attempt to do so would have resulted in a pratfall. Apropos of 1913: this was the year Charlie Chaplin signed his contract with Keystone, where, beginning in 1914, he churned out a steady stream of short slapstick films. The year 1913 also saw the successful newspaper cartoon duo *Mutt and Jeff*—a tall thin guy and short fat guy, both totally crazy—hit American cinema screens as an animated cartoon. And George Herriman's *Krazy Kat*—that peculiar cartoon cat in love with a mouse who keeps hurling bricks at her head, while she spurns the advances of a policeman who tries to protect her from this abuse—was first published in a daily newspaper.

Brick plus cat's head: a slapstick answer to Cubism's concept of collage. In 1912, Braque and Picasso had begun to include pieces of wallpaper, scraps of tablecloth, and newspaper clippings in their still lifes. Admittedly, the period immediately preceding World War I was fairly bursting with cultural and technological upheavals, but in spite of this, the simultaneous emergence of modern slapstick à la Chaplin and the modern art object à la Duchamp cannot be purely coincidental.

3      **Marcel Duchamp**, Bicycle Wheel, 1913
4      **George Herriman**, Krazy Kat, 1913
5a+b  **Bud Fisher**, Mutt and Jeff, 1913

# When Gestures Come Unstuck

In 1900, the philosopher Henri Bergson wrote *Laughter: An Essay on the Meaning of the Comic*. So what is comical? For Bergson, laughter is a reaction to "a certain mechanical inelasticity," when human movements resemble automatic mechanisms. He gives the example of a man running along a street who stumbles and falls, triggering the impulse to laugh in those looking on. Timeless as this may sound—even Neanderthal man fell flat on his face occasionally—this statement is very much of its time, as the turn of the last century bore witness to an historically unprecedented wave of industrialization and mechanical acceleration in all areas of life. Perhaps Bergson had seen the short film made by the Lumière brothers in 1895 entitled *The Gardener, or, The Sprinkler Sprinkled*, one of the first ever "acted" films and a prototypical piece of slapstick: man waters garden, young rascal appears behind him, steps on hose, baffled man examines suddenly dried up nozzle, and—of course!—gets a soaking.

Laughter is an ambivalent reaction: relief at deviation from the norm but also a mocking reprimand to return to it. The norm in question here involved adapting to the new industrial society and using its achievements with confidence (including running water coming out of a garden hose), even if the society in question was still largely mired in a pre-industrial mindset of strict relations of rank and kin. The laugher, Bergson writes, behaves like "a stern father" who "at times may forget himself and join in some prank his son is playing, only to check himself at once in order to correct it." We see before us the classic image of a late-nineteenth-century bourgeois paterfamilias attempting to shore up his dwindling authority with postures of dignity and authoritarian intimidation.

Slapstick and the comic feed on the failure of such attempts, when gestures come unstuck, when unintended movements and mishaps torpedo the bourgeois individual's controlled stasis inspired by the soldierly pathos of the nineteenth century. For Germany, Norbert Elias has fittingly dubbed this fatal tendency the "Wilhelmine society of satisfaction," where the model for engagement was not the interplay of free expression but the strictly regulated, pitiless duel. The corresponding type of sculpture is meant to demonstrate military might and imperial grandeur, from the "Monument of the Battle of the Nations" in Leipzig (inaugurated in 1913) to the gigantic Germania watching over the Rhine near the Loreley.

For Bergson's France, a comparable phenomenon might be termed "Napoleonic pseudo-meritocracy." The bourgeoisie opposed the aristocracy's heredity-based elites by forming its own based on competence and capability. But it was obliged to gloss over its own establishment and perpetuation of privilege over generations by working itself up into the Napoleonic pathos of the Grande Nation as a bulwark against the rising tide of barbarism and weak-mindedness. As far as Victorian Britain is concerned, suffice it to recall that table legs were covered up as a precaution against sexual connotations; the opposite theory, that it was less about sex than status and that a table's legs were covered up above all when the workmanship did not match the class of its owners, makes no fundamental difference—both are expressions of social inhibition.

It was in America that immigrants representing all these backgrounds and attitudes met up with those who had fled from them to the New World. And above all, it was in the America of the 1910s and 1920s that slapstick and art collided directly for the first time. Marcel Duchamp embarked for America in 1915, having come to know France's pseudo-meritocracy only too well.

# Duchamp's Slapstick: The Year 1913 and What Came Next

In 1912, Duchamp submitted his painting *Nude Descending a Staircase, No. 2* to the Salon des Indépendants in Paris. Inspired by Etienne-Jules Marey's first photographic portrayals of sequences of motion, his "chronophotographs" of pole vaulters or birds in flight, Duchamp represented motion in space by multiplication. Within the sequence, the naked female figure was broken down. But the ideological guardians of Cubism's purity—not the true innovators Picasso and Braque, but the group centered on Jean Metzinger and Albert Gleizes—sensed an affront. Firstly, the picture smacked of the enthusiasm for motion and technology displayed by Italy's Futurists (though Duchamp later claimed he was unaware of them at the time), the rival movement preferring accelerated action over Cubism's motionless forms, and excitement over contemplation. Whether or not Duchamp tried to link the two, either way he violated Cubism's freshly installed dogma that called for crystalline stasis, a frozen array of simultaneous perspectives. But the graver problem, so it seems, was the picture's title: a naked woman moving mechanically and, what's more, coming downstairs instead of obeying the dictates of decency by staying in her boudoir. Why couldn't Duchamp just paint wine glasses, pipes, and guitars like Cubists were supposed to?

The Cubist ideologues suspected mocking parody—*blague*, as it was called in Paris. This *blague* was an attitude of permanent irony, the playful, *modern*, enlightened bourgeois aloofness that had emerged in bohemian and student milieus of the nineteenth century. The general public, too, had long since developed its own parodies of the artistic avant-garde. On the vaudeville stage and in newspaper caricatures, Cubism was ridiculed as puffed up, self-important charlatanry. The mocking question posed by many caricaturists and humorists was: Can you see the face hidden in the picture? This question is echoed in Martin Kippenberger's Cubist farce from 1984 with its hopelessly tangled, slapdash brushstrokes of gray and red and its eloquent title *Ich kann beim besten Willen kein Hakenkreuz erkennen* (With the best will in the world, I can't see a swastika). That the painting should end up in the collection of Mick Flick, as a fig leaf to criticism of the collector's position regarding the origin of his family's fortune (Flick-owned companies benefited from forced labor during the Nazi period), was a hostile takeover against which the late Kippenberger could no longer defend himself.

Irritation and paranoia, then, were the reactions of the "offended party" to Duchamp's supposed transgressions. He was called on to at least change the painting's title. Adding insult to injury, this ultimatum was delivered by Duchamp's two older brothers, Jacques Villon and Raymond Duchamp-Villon. Duchamp avoided a scandal and withdrew the picture. But the humiliation spurred him on to a radical move, a threefold gesture of one-upmanship: You don't want this painting? I want nothing more to do with painting. You want charlatanry? Then I'll show you what charlatanry is. Paris? New York!

In 1913, *Nude Descending a Staircase, No. 2* caused a sensation and a scandal at the Armory Show in New York, where 1,250 works by more than three hundred modern artists were shown to the American public for the first time. The critic for the *New York Times* derided the painting as "an explosion in a shingle factory" and one Chicago newspaper advised its readers to "eat three welsh rarebits, smoke two pipefuls of 'hop' and sniff cocaine" before trying to understand the picture. At the time of this unexpected triumph, however, Duchamp was still in France, playing around in his studio with the first version of his *Bicycle Wheel*—which, as he noted in an interview of the 1960s, he understood as something "pleasant," something "to have in my room the way you have a fire, or a pencil sharpener, except that there was no usefulness." Nonetheless, it was the prototype for what, two years later, were to be called the *Readymades*. Meanwhile, Gertrude Stein was having newspapers featuring the *Krazy Kat* cartoons sent to her in Paris and translating them for her friend Picasso during his Sunday visits.

The most famous film star in France at the time was a certain Max Linder, a smug bon vivant with a top hat and a pencil moustache, for whom no gag was too foolish. He was the first great slapstick star of short silent films, and Chaplin later called him his "professor." In *Max Plays The Hero* (1910), for example, he is the hero of a deadly dull stage drama. When the audience starts falling asleep out of sheer boredom, he wakes them up by squirting them with a hose.

When Duchamp left for Manhattan, did his baggage include a knowledge of such films? One thing we know for sure is that he was very impressed by the radical absurdity of Alfred Jarry. And according to Duchamp expert Francis M. Naumann, Chaplin was the artist's favorite film personality during the early American years.

On arriving in the United States, Duchamp began by upbraiding the group of artists around Alfred Stieglitz for not yet having taken as subjects the very things that characterized their country: that is, the machines and the skyscrapers. But Duchamp's friend Francis Picabia, now also in the New World, had long since begun to make machine pictures that translated slapstick—the gleefully vulgar allusions to body parts, the pure mechanical mishap—into the language of hydraulics and motors. In *Parade amoureuse* (1917), simply rendered pistons and drive wheels creak and groan in absurd self-referentiality, and his "machine portrait" *Ici, c'est ici Stieglitz*, featured in one issue of *291* magazine (published by photographer and gallerist Stieglitz himself), shows a camera whose bellows is not connected to the lens, a gear stick in neutral, and an engaged handbrake.

The first Cubist exhibition on American soil took place at Gimbels department store in New York. With World War I still raging, a hard-drinking, liberal-minded crowd of artists and well-heeled citizens partied in the city, as vividly described by Duchamp biographer Calvin Tomkins. At the soirées given by the Arensbergs, a collector couple, Duchamp was the focus of attention—due not least to the sensation surrounding *Nude Descending a Staircase, No. 2.*

*Du Cubisme*, the book published in 1912 by the movement's ideologues-in-chief Gleizes and Metzinger, was a verbose attempt to affirm Cubism's seriousness in the face of conservative skepticism. It was, they claimed, about evoking beauty via the development of taste; Cubists, too, were "realists" and only their belief in beauty gave them the requisite strength. Five years after the rejection of

PARADE AMOUREUSE

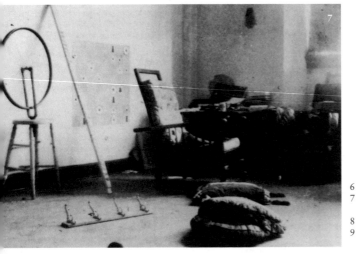

6    **Francis Picabia,** Parade amoureuse, 1917
7    **Marcel Duchamp,** Duchamp's studio at
     33 W. 37th Street, New York
8    **Charlie Chaplin,** A Woman (film still), 191
9    **Man Ray,** Marcel Duchamp as Rrose Sélav
     1920

his "mechanical nude," and for all his interest in Cubism, Duchamp had no interest whatsoever in this kind of rhetorical humbug. "Beauty" and "good taste" are highly suspect categories of supposed incorruptibility—shaped as they are by the ongoing play of social influences and opinion-mongering. And it was on precisely these categories that Duchamp played his trick of reversal. You want good taste, you want beauty? I'll give you not even tastelessness, not even ugliness, but the pure absence of taste and beauty in the indifferent choice of a banal, industrially manufactured object.

And so, in New York in the spring of 1917, he pseudonymously entered a urinal entitled *Fountain* to the exhibition of the Society of Independent Artists. This inevitably provoked the question: Does he mean this seriously or is he joking? The answer would have been: both at once, of course. Ironically, Duchamp was a founding member of the society in question, the declared aim of which was to facilitate the open and free showing of contemporary art—an aim which he now put to the test. According to the legend, a hurriedly convened conference decided against exhibiting the urinal and Duchamp resigned from the committee, without revealing his authorship. It must have felt like déjà vu, except that he had brought it about deliberately. The great and enduring misconception, then, is to believe that the transferal of the urinal into an exhibition context in itself constituted the artwork. In fact, the work only acquires its full significance in the light of the specific exhibition context in question—one that explicitly and emphatically defined itself as free and open. As in the prototypical slapstick movement of falling from the vertical into the horizontal, the surviving photographs show the urinal laid on its back. And it is marked—very plainly, in large letters—with the year and artist's signature: "R. Mutt." This, too, was no random choice. Mott was the name of the urinal manufacturer, "But Mott was too close," Duchamp recalled in 1966. "So I altered it to Mutt, after the daily cartoon strip *Mutt and Jeff* which appeared at the time, and with which everyone was familiar. Thus, from the start, there was an interplay…"

Bud Fisher's cartoon was originally called *A. Mutt* ("A" for Augustus). Mutt, with its shabby canine associations, is a reference to the lanky horserace fanatic's status within his family; in 1908, in an insane asylum, Mutt meets Jeff, who becomes his small, fat sidekick. The comic paradigm of the odd couple was familiar from vaudeville, and it is striking how well the description fits the odd couple of Duchamp and Francis Picabia, his best artist friend at the time: the tall one with the high forehead and the French manners—elegant, friendly, elusive, sardonic—and the chubby one with the cigar and the funds from his Cuban parents, full of *joie de vivre* and intrigue.

Duchamp combines the French attitude of the *blague* with the Anglo-American attitude of *deadpan*, the comic technique where hilarious lines are delivered with a fixed, emotionless expression ("pan" was a slang expression for face, and although the technique was practiced long before, "deadpan" entered common parlance in the 1920s as Buster Keaton became its great master). With *deadpan blague*, then, Duchamp rose above the pitched battle between Cubism's bigoted critics and its almost equally bigoted ideologues.

# The Bullshit Detector: Duchamp's New York Studio

Somewhere between 1912 and 1917, this idea of deadly serious hilariously comical art matured in Duchamp's mind. This was also the first golden age of slapstick. A coincidence? Perhaps. There are no explicit references to movie slapstick in Duchamp's works. So can we ignore this link when considering the ideological battle over the status of the Cubist avant-garde? Absolutely not. Duchamp was never one to willingly name every single source of inspiration. What goes into an artist's work consists not only of "influences," but also of what art historian Thierry de Duve, writing on Duchamp, has called "resonances." The crucial thing is whether these resonances become "audible" in the work itself.

In slapstick cinema, movement as physical misadventure and movement as moving image come together. Of course, there had been clownery and buffoonery long before, but only by playing with the possibilities of film did slapstick's specific form of heave-ho comedy with its chopped rhythms emerge. In Duchamp's work, the mechanical movements of film and of the new industrial machines figure as a "slap stick" with which to stir up the stagnant debate on the avant-garde.

At first it was "only" a practical experiment with ideas, just as games are experimentally played through in chess, a passion of Duchamp's. One photograph of his New York studio shows the readymade of a small coat rack—four hooks on a board—lying on the floor, redeployed as a *Trap*, the work's English title. In French, it is called *Trébuchet*, the word for a medieval siege catapult, a type of bird-trap, and a specialist term in chess for a trap laid for one's opponent. It also contains *trébucher*, to stumble. In the background, we see the *Bicycle Wheel*. In another picture, a snow shovel hangs from the ceiling. This readymade is titled *In Advance of the Broken Arm:* before slipping while shoveling snow—not that breaking an arm is funny, but exaggerated portrayals of physical injury have never got in the way of slapstick.

What for Duchamp initially seemed like no more than a pastime—the readymades as an eccentric plaything in the artist's studio—became the thing that truly revealed a fundamental shift in art in modern times. Thanks to the principle of industrial production and technical duplication, art as a realistic medium of representation has been rendered nostalgic. In this situation, rather than invoking the artist's privileged access to visuality, vitality, beauty, and good taste, "salvation" lies in accepting the challenge and appropriating the forms of industrial culture oneself, turning them against the implacable logic of utility value—as demonstrated by the best slapstick in comics and movies.

Duchamp touched a raw nerve that is still twitching today. In the increasingly anonymous public sphere of major cities, the artistic avant-garde was torn between a longing for influence and defiant self-referentiality. This resulted in attempts to form schools and dogmas. Interesting art and interesting artists have a built-in bullshit detector that resists this tendency toward the pathos of the coterie by throwing wild punches. Duchamp's reaction was the slapstick of the readymade.

Conditions may have changed—publics now constitute themselves in ways that are both more globalized and more decentralized, within a delicately structured fabric of urban agglomerations, the Internet, the media, and low-budget air travel. But the tension in art between the drive for recognition and the tendency to navel-gaze has not been resolved; it has merely become similarly globalized, decentralized, and delicately structured. The current prosperity of the art market and the dubious pleasure of seeing culture elevated to the status of a critical economic factor cannot obscure this. Consequently, there is still a need for bullshit detectors and slapstick to break into the routines both of forming schools and cadres and of narcissistic self-satisfaction. The odd couple of pathos and ridiculousness is still relevant. But before we come to the present, we must further trace the line that leads from Duchamp and early slapstick to where we are now.

# Chaplin's Aunt: Dada, etc.

Where Dada and Surrealism are concerned, we can pick up the thread with the constellation of Duchamp and Chaplin. There is one striking parallel: from 1920, Marcel Duchamp adopted a female alter ego, Rrose Sélavy. The famous portrait by Duchamp's friend Man Ray shows her carefully made-up, wearing a hat in the geometrical fashion of the day, elegantly holding her fur collar in place with an affected gesture. Five years previously, Chaplin had shot the short comedy *A Woman*: in it, Charlie shaves off his beard and dresses as a woman to trick a pair of angry rivals, both of whom promptly start courting him. Incidentally, 1915 also saw the release of a silent film version of the British stage farce *Charley's Aunt*, with Oliver Hardy.

Rrose Sélavy's getup clearly resembles Chaplin's in *A Woman*. Here, at the very latest, we see how physical slapstick with its "innocent" exaggeration of violence (brick to head, stick to seat of pants) is embroiled in the sexual play of dressing up and pretending. At the same time, cross dressing is a way of covering up male insecurity, overplaying the sexual with the comical. Less amusingly, this also meant that even female comic roles were often left to men, in both art and film.

At a notorious Dada review in Paris in 1920, organized largely by the Rumanian writer Tristan Tzara, the rumor of an appearance by Chaplin was circulated to mobilize the masses, but eventually, his non-appearance was made up for by brawling, joyful pandemonium, and heartfelt chants of "Vive Napoléon! Vive Chaplin! Vive Tzara!"

Erwin Blumenfeld—a Jewish photographer from Berlin who trained as a dressmaker in 1920s and then opened a boutique in the Netherlands—may have been the only Dadaist who actively sought to identify himself with the great star Chaplin: "Bloomfeld, President-Dada-Chaplinist" is written on a photocollage from 1921 featuring Blumenfeld's head stuck onto the graceful pose of a female nude. A typical comic motif of this period is bearded men in tutus dancing *en pointe*, as featured in René Clair and Francis Picabia's film *Entr'acte* (1924), which also features Duchamp, though not in a female role. Instead, he plays chess with Man Ray until a jet of water sweeps away pieces and players alike. A mourning party leaps along in slow motion behind a hearse pulled by a camel; the hearse breaks free of the camel and the people start running after it. Mourning, translated into pathos and piety, comes unstuck. A legless man, a

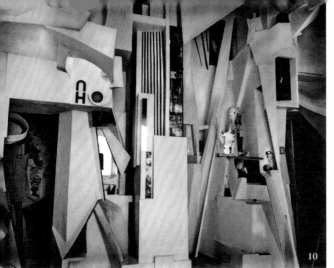

10    **Kurt Schwitters,** Merzbau (detail), 1933
11    **Richard Artschwager,** Counter I, 1962
12    **John Baldessari,** (film still from) Title, 1972
13    **Piero Manzoni,** Artist's Shit, 1961

war veteran, brings up the rear, dragging himself along on a tray with wheels; then he has legs again and jumps up to join in the chase. All of this is like one big case of Tourette's syndrome, a neurological disorder first described in the nineteenth century, typical symptoms of which include uncontrollable twitching and sudden exclamation of obscenities. Dada finished off the already dented top hat on the head of a bourgeois culture discredited by war and destruction, a culture that still believed itself to be in the nineteenth century.

The playful, anti-narrative romp with the specific possibilities of film in *Entr'acte* was pioneering at the time. Considered together, however, all these attempts to present urban bourgeois culture as a madhouse, whether in films or reviews, have one problem in common: as a movement, then as now, Dada exudes a false sense of superiority over the masses. This may be helpful as a step in personal development—countless punk bands were founded by adolescent Dada fans—but to experience oneself as an active agent of opposition, one should not get stuck in the triumph of the initiated putting themselves above those who don't get it.

John Heartfield and Rudolf Schlichter's *Preussischer Erzengel* (Prussian Archangel), from 1920, is a soldier hung under the ceiling, with a pig's face, labeled as follows: "To fully understand this artwork, drill daily for twelve hours with a heavily packed knapsack in full marching order on Tempelhof Field" (a military training ground in Berlin). "MERDE" ("shit") wrote Richard Huelsenbeck on a postcard addressed to Tristan Tzara with a picture of the Monument of the Battle of the Nations in Leipzig. These are striking examples of courageously satirical, politically engaged rebellion against the undying militarism of the post-World War I establishment. But they also point to the way the Dadaists as a school ran the risk, as they fixed their gaze on the political *what,* of slipping into merely routine repetition of their artistic *how*—the satirical collages, the tumultuous performances, the slapstick aspect. The unmasking of convention as a routine that forgets itself in its own gesture.

Duchamp was a harder to figure out. In spite of his sometime links to Dada, he is anything but a Dadaist. Kurt Schwitters, too, can be excluded from this criticism: his *Merzbau*, on which he worked from 1920 through 1936, proliferated throughout his apartment in Hanover as a work that was unfinished out of principle. He gave the strict geometry of Constructivism a turn toward Gothic angularity. In the resulting nooks and corners, he created little "grottos" commemorating heroic Modernists such as the Russian Constructivist El Lissitzky, the Dutch De Stijl pioneer Theo van Doesburg, and the Swiss Dadaist and later Constructivist Sophie Taeuber-Arp. There was also a love grotto. White mice could crawl through tunnels built specially for them, activating light switches as they went.

An alternative title for the *Merzbau* was *Cathedral of Erotic Misery*, and while its builder thus outed himself as frustrated, this also poked fun at a weak point of slapstick itself—that is, the abovementioned overplaying of the sexual with jokes. The *Merzbau* was an "installation" long before this term existed in art; and it was a monument to the anti-pathetic, as the protracted process of continual rebuilding undermined any sense of pathos. Slapstick and the grotesque are part of the crazy structural balance of the *Merzbau* in the form of constant instability.

Today, Dada as a whole has become folklore, a staple of tired routines. Alternatively, purged of the unpredictable element of humor, it is portrayed in retrospect as a heroic political rebellion. Considered as a whole, this folklore has something gimmicky about it. Unlike in Duchamp's work, its *blague* is mostly paired not with the corrective sobriety of the deadpan, but with a theatrical, vociferous begging for attention. In the spirit of Dada, the Fluxus movement of the 1960s celebrated the humoristic frustration of audience expectations during performances and actions, and in its weaker moments it suffered from a similar problem. Here, too, important individual works and actions by artists including Nam June Paik, Yoko Ono, Dieter Roth, Ben Vautier, and Robert Filliou are exempted from this criticism.

# Silence Into Music, Shit Into Gold: John Cage, George Brecht, Yves Klein, Piero Manzoni

The Duchamp of the Fluxus movement is the composer John Cage. In his work too, the comedy does not lie in theatrical gestures. His famous silent piece *4'33"* can of course be read as a prayer-like focusing of attention on silence and the audience's discomfort with it. On closer examination, however, the deliberate situation comedy of the pianist is hard to ignore. According to the score, the piece consists of three parts, all *tacet* (silence), adding up to four minutes and thirty-three seconds. At the premiere in 1952, pianist David Tudor marked these divisions by shutting and opening the keyboard lid. This is the slapstick of obstruction, of paralyzed hesitation, of *embarrassing* silence. But the humor is minimalist, structural, manifesting itself in the notion of subdivided silence, reducing the conventions of written music to absurdity. Cage does not write anything like "open and shut the lid." As with Duchamp, it is not the kind of humor that aims for easy laughs—at the premiere, the dominant reaction was one of annoyance. For all its wittiness, it would be wrong to consider *4'33"* a mere joke. Slapstick in art does not just push seriousness, pathos, and theatricality aside (as if that were even possible!), but also infiltrates their core: the mechanisms of instating and stabilizing authority—authority of speech, of gesture, of action.

George Brecht was perhaps Cage's cleverest student. Years before Fluxus became a movement, his teacher helped him understand that the score of a composition is nothing other than an instruction that tells you what to *play*. Why not an instruction that tells you what to *do*? The idea for the *Events* was born. Duchamp turned objects into readymades; Cage did the same with sound; George Brecht did it with actions.

The starting point was to be nothing more than a text, as brief as possible—a haiku. As in the case of *A Play* (1963), it could be just: "A Play: Act I (smoke), Act II (handshake), Act III (stool)." The proximity of this mini-drama to situation comedy is obvious. Here, though, it is not acted out, but simply proposed. In 1982, Brecht did make a work that spells out this sense of situation comedy with a reference to one of its virtuoso pioneers: *Karl Valentin strolling through the English Garden on a nice (but foggy) spring day*, a title suggesting the sight of Germany's most important twentieth-century comedian strolling through Munich's grand park, while consisting of nothing but a monochrome gray surface mounted in an ornate gold frame.

Like George Brecht, Yves Klein created situation comedy using voids. Beginning in 1959, he produced *Zones of Immaterial Pictorial Sensibility*, for which he issued certificates in exchange for a few grams of gold. In 1962, a buyer was obliged to burn the certificate immediately, in front of witnesses, and Klein threw half of the gold into the Seine. There are echoes here of alchemy and the Midas touch, the whole mythical garbage of the artist genius, but in the photographs documenting the event, the more serious Klein looks, the more he resembles Buster Keaton. The transaction between artist and collector as value creation through value destruction successfully transforms economic dependence into chutzpah.

THE SLAPSTICK POTENTIAL OF MINIMAL ART    37

Turning shit into gold was the logical step taken by Pierro Manzoni. His *Artist's Shit* (1961)—ninety tins, each filled with thirty grams of his own excrement—was sold for the equivalent value of thirty grams of gold. The easiest reproach leveled at the avant-garde—"it's nothing but pretentious arty crap"—is gratefully accepted, canned, signed, and returned to the philistines with best regards. Meanwhile, those still unable to abandon the notion that true inspiration comes from the guts of the artist were catered to with corresponding visceral products.

The authority and authorship of the artist; the collector as connoisseur and patron; the worst fears of the conservative public—nothing is spared here. But as with related Fluxus fun and games (a sense of smug cabaret jokiness shows through here) a well-calculated pun will always remain dependent on its subject: dopey punters are used as a foil to set off the mischief. Such is the logic of many hoaxes to this day.

# The Slapstick Potential of Minimal Art

One cannot blame the pioneers of Conceptual and Minimal art for believing that only a demonstration of absolute seriousness would give them a chance against the growing trend toward alchemy and buffoonery. At last, no more need for such a palaver, no more grand gestures! New York artist and critic Donald Judd spoke the language of a new sobriety and clarity that seemed to match the age of industrial serialization. In a programmatic text from 1965, he referred to his abstract hybrids of sculpture and painting as "specific objects." What in Judd's confident tone sound like sober constructions from the drawing board actually look in many cases like things sedimented out of a strange daydream. His abstract geometrical formations in wood and metal are often plunged in a gaudy cadmium red; the viewer takes a psychedelic plunge into amber Perspex, glaring purple, or candy-colored metallic green.

This is only natural: something so closely accompanied by a rhetoric of pragmatically unambiguous sobriety cries out for delirium and craziness in the guise of precisely this sobriety. From the front, a headache pill; from the back, LSD. Robert Smithson thought this out in his texts, not least with concepts like that of the "impure-purist surface" of Minimal art. The work of Richard Artschwager gives a taste of what later generations, from Rosemarie Trockel to Tom Burr and Monica Bonvicini, would bring forth: artists who adopted the formal idiom of Minimalism and charged it up with precisely the dose of play, politics, sex, and comedy that seemed to have been so thoroughly driven out of it.

In a certain sense, the objects of classical Minimal art actually lend themselves to this. Ordinary industrial building materials (wood, metal, Perspex) are factually present in the exhibition space as fabricated constructions. But at the same time, they are fetishes; taken out of some other context, they are capable of attracting all manner of wishes and projections. Like a drug experience that not only reverses the categories of strangeness and familiarity but also short circuits them, Minimalist objects produce a kind of oxymoron, a paradoxical loop of meaning. Exposed to this as visitors to a gallery, we may be unsettled at first, but we also sense that it wouldn't take much to turn these objects into props for an absurd comedy of stumbling and bumped knees. The core of their theatricality is like someone being pushed out onto an open stage. One is in the spotlight, but without a play to perform. At this moment, the only thing that prevents the artwork from being merely a cruel instrument for the intimidation of its audience is a form of comic tension or, better still, tension and relief in one. Something "inappropriate" that interrupts and dissolves the labels and status of all involved for a moment, an accident—provided the artwork itself "shares" the embarrassment, and provided it undermines the possible pedagogical intimidation that says, "Hey there, educated viewer, you'd better not mess up your homework, make sure you interpret me correctly!"

# Richard Artschwager's Question Mark

Richard Artschwager was perhaps the first to place the Minimalist object under this kind of tension, sidestepping the strict notion of Minimal art before it even properly began to take shape. The "pure" Minimal artists made the utmost effort to avoid any allusion to everyday objects or illusionary effects. By contrast, Artschwager made a piece called *Counter I* (1962), an object that looks like the abstracted form of a cash register standing on tall, thin legs with wheels. It's painted black and the upper surface is covered with a pale, strongly grained veneer into which several rows of wooden circles are inlaid, like buttons without a function. If one were to try to push them, the object would roll away slightly every time, provoking an absurd shoving game recalling failed attempts to get close to someone.

"Disinterested pleasure" is what Kant called the desirable absence of ulterior motives when enjoying art. In its mechanized chaos, slapstick ruins the possibility of any such motive. As a result, the notion that nothing should cloud such disinterested pleasure collides head-on with the "disinterested" monotony of alienated labor. Artschwager's object alludes to this through its absurd form.

There is a provocatively modest cheerfulness in Artschwager's decades-long refusal of grandeur. The price he paid for this, of course, was to be viewed for a long time as just some strange character who made obscure objects. He does not produce thigh-slapping guffaws; his marksmanship is as silent as it is accurate. He is the Jacques Tati of Geometric Abstraction. His oeuvre is too extensive to be dealt with in all its glory here, but let's take as another example the works in which question marks, inverted commas, or exclamation points become objects. One enters a room and is welcomed by a man-size *Exclamation Point* (1995) as a huge object made of nylon bristles, freestanding and three-dimensional in the space: the dot lies on the floor, the vertical stroke hangs by a thread from the ceiling. It is as if an "Uh!" or "Oh!" has tumbled from the mouth of some massively inflated ego, materializing in a form that bears a striking resemblance to a toilet brush. The exclamation point mockingly echoes the viewer's reverence before the object (behold!); the question mark does the same with regard to the viewer's perplexity. The coded signs of written language become physical slapstick with surface (scratchy, shaggy) and volume (standing about in the room, puffed up or embarrassed). According to the narrow definition, slapstick is a form of comedy that works with bodies and objects only, not with language. But what if the joke consists precisely in treating language as a physical body? Artschwager's punctuation mark objects demonstrate this. And they demonstrate his independent artistic trajectory between Pop, Minimal, and Conceptual art.

# The Slapstick Potential of Conceptual Art

In rhetorical terms, the dogmatists of Minimal and Conceptual art may have been even more cunning than their ancestors, the ideologues-in-chief of the early avant-gardes, but ultimately they were just as stubborn. (Even today, artists feel a need to resist their fantasies of tidy separations and clear-cut boundaries, but without rejecting all of their smart approaches.) Donald Judd's attempt to define the only true interpretation of Minimal art is topped only by Joseph Kosuth's manifestos of Conceptualism.

Born in 1945, Kosuth aimed to establish a competitive advantage in the struggle within the New York art world of the late 1960s in order to succeed Andy Warhol as the hot kid on the block, not only by affecting a cool air with blond hair and dark glasses, but also by penning precocious manifestos of a new art. His *Art After Philosophy* (1969) claimed not only that art takes philosophy as its model, but also that it is the heir to philosophy as the cradle of ideas.

Kosuth's own art was of course the prototype for this model. In his famous work *One and Three Chairs* (1965), an ordinary chair is grouped with a photograph of itself and a dictionary definition of "chair." The supposed tautology—a chair is a chair is a chair—flirts with the frustration of the viewer who feels duped: as if I didn't know what a chair was, not to mention being made to look at three tedious versions of it. It is the same frustration focused on in the tradition of analytic philosophy: no, you don't know what a chair is—at least not exactly how knowledge of what a chair is constitutes itself in the first place.

The whole thing tried to create the impression that with the help of Duchamp and Wittgenstein, Conceptual art could be invented by one man as a kind of linguistic lesson to purge art of its fetish character, its formalism, and other remnants of magical thinking. Art is defined as radically self-referential. What art has in common with logic and mathematics is its tautological character—the fact that the artwork can be constituted and perceived as an artwork without the need for verification outside the art context. According to Kosuth, true art refers only to itself and thus ultimately tries to control one thing above all: what can be read into it. The audience is permitted to comprehend this controlled reading. It goes without saying that such a position cannot go unopposed.

# John Baldessari's Stone With Dog

As an artist from America's West Coast, John Baldessari was not really part of the plan for this New York endgame of art as tautology, and this may have given him more freedom to pull the chair out from underneath the dogmatic version of Conceptual art. Baldessari was born in 1931, the year when the Russian film giant Sergei Eisenstein first published his theory of "intellectual montage:" the film cut as a collision of pictures that produces meaning not contained in any of these pictures on their own—semiotic slapstick. If there was anyone who really took Eisenstein's observation to heart, then it was Baldessari—not as a film director, but as an artist.

Haters of Conceptual art will find no comfort in Baldessari. Duchamp duped the dogmatists and their enemies in one fell swoop, and he does the same. At the time, painter Al Held deprecatingly stated that "all Conceptual Art is just pointing at things." Conceptual art appeared to be bringing semiotics, the theory of the relationship between the signifier and the signified, into art. What Held meant with his accusation was something like: "Signifying? Anyone can do that."

Baldessari treated this description as an encouraging appeal to make art. He took photographs of an index finger pointed at everyday items—a pile of pills, a broken piece of wood trim, a rotten banana—and commissioned a series of amateur painters to recreate the resulting images in photorealistic detail (*Commissioned Paintings*, 1969). Underneath the pictures, sign painters—people specialized in making nice legible signs announcing the price of vegetables—wrote the name of the artist in each case: "A painting by…." But wasn't Baldessari the artist? That was precisely the point: the pointing finger led the viewer astray in more than one way. The pejorative "just" in Al Held's statement was refuted by the slapstick technique of the overly literal following of an instruction. At the same time, the work also did a handsome disservice to Kosuth: instead of heroically supplying definitions of art—this is art because I say it's art—there was an element of everyday casualness. The pile of pills, the broken wooden trim, and the rotten banana do not cease to be in the world just because someone points at them in the name of art; on the contrary, their presence in the world is testified to in the most wonderfully banal way.

Pomposity really gets Baldessari going, and by the early 1970s, it had long since spread from the dogmatic variants of Conceptual art to Performance art. This called for ridicule. In the video *I Am Making Art* (1971), Baldessari sits like someone recovering from surgery, limply raising first one arm, then the other, etc., proclaiming all the while, in a sedated tone of voice, that these gestures of his are art. In *Baldessari Sings LeWitt* (1972), mockery turned to homage. Like a lay preacher, he singsongs Sol LeWitt's manifesto-like *Sentences on Conceptual Art* (1969) to the tune of evergreens including "Cheek to Cheek" and "Old MacDonald Had a Farm." The seriousness with which he keeps this up for a full quarter of an hour makes it clear that he would not begrudge theories like "rational judgments repeat rational judgments" or "illogical judgments lead to new experience" a broad popularity.

In New York, the Conceptual art elite seemed to demonstrate that it takes a handful of leading figures to do something innovative and generate a new benchmark for the art world. Baldessari, on the other hand, seemed to be saying: "Making art, having ideas, is not so difficult—give it a try yourself!" An attitude that speaks of almost excessive modesty, since every third or fourth of his works contains an idea that would have kept other artists going for an entire career. Whereas Kosuth tries to tautologically close the game to allow him to lay down clear definitions, Baldessari opens it up in a clash of pictures and meanings.

Baldessari lives in Los Angeles and he has Hollywood's conventions of image production and storytelling at his doorstep. But he's interested in what happens when one refuses to tell stories. In 1972, for instance, he made a short film whose title is "Title," as the opening credits promisingly announce, before the stars and costars are presented to us in a first sequence of separate, short shots—a stone, a chair, a dog, and a man (the young painter David Salle). The second sequence combines the stone and the dog in the same shot (an encounter! a story is getting underway!), then the stone and the man (this is getting exciting!). Whereas some people still delight in throwing off conventional narrative structures in favor of Structural film, Baldessari made both look foolish. Stone meets dog—the heave-ho logic of Krazy Kat as a way to escape all such constraints.

# Ed Ruscha's Crackers (Feat. Mason Williams, Andy Kaufman)

In January 1963, the young Baldessari took a ride from Los Angeles to Santa Barbara in the passenger seat of a red sports car, photographing the backs of all the trucks the car overtook on the way. Sounds like a way to kill time for a bored teenager hungry for experience. The previous year, Ed Ruscha had done something similar. He photographed twenty-six gas stations on the drive from Los Angeles to Oklahoma City—the city where he grew up—and published the results in a book, with twenty-six pages, called *26 Gasoline Stations*. The title really did say it all.

The book medium is usually about telling stories, about information, and, if necessary, in coffee table format, about visual appeal. All this hits a historical all-time low in Ruscha's book. Dry-as-bones documentation of the banal, which frustrates any expectation of edification, is injected with a mute quick-witted-ness purely by virtue of repetition. These are visual counting rhymes of a new way of seeing. With works of this kind, the Californians issued their manifesto of Minimal Pop art: no soup cans or Marilyns à la Warhol, no, just plain old trucks and gas stations, one after the other, mile after mile, page after page.

Typography and topography become one. The advertising slogans on the buildings one cruises past and the trucks one overtakes become vehicles for road movie longings, for what Klaus Theweleit has called *Lustserien*, or series of desire.

Slapstick as a method—not just as a quotation—only became really apparent in Ruscha's work with two books he made with Mason Williams, a teenage friend from Oklahoma City and sometime roommate in LA. In the mid-1960s, Williams became one of the main writers for the successful Smothers Brothers Comedy Hour on CBS—hosted by Dick, the swinging bachelor, and Tom, his deceased brother who stands by his side as a reformed guardian angel. With their combed and parted hair, the duo parodied the immaculate exteriors of the 1950s, but the show featured music by bands like The Who and The Doors and, more than once, Vietnam War propaganda was subjected to mockery.

This same Williams, then, played an important part in Ruscha's *Royal Road Test* (1967), a book documenting how Williams threw an old, mechanical, Royal-brand typewriter out of a car driving at ninety miles per hour. A few pictures of a car in the desert, plus commentary in a tone somewhere between a consumer advice service and the district attorney's office: "Piece of Ribbon and Frame Shift Assembly (found furthest from point of impact)." The comedy lies in the absurdity of the action due to the predictability of its result. The mechanical typewriter, a myth of writerly existentialism, is treated like a dumb block of stone.

In Ruscha's book *Crackers* (1969) things finally do "go crackers." This comes as no surprise due to the renewed participation of Mason Williams. In 1969, probably at the behest of President Nixon, the Smothers Brothers Comedy Hour was taken off the air, and the same year Williams wrote the script for Ruscha's book. The totally absurd short story bearing the programmatic title *How to Derive the Maximum Enjoyment from Crackers* is printed on the inside back flap and reads like a recipe for deeply neurotic playboys: organize a date with a beautiful woman, take her to a cheap motel room and persuade her to get into bed with "several pounds of fresh ripe tomatoes, cucumbers, celery, olives, green onions, and so forth." Then proceed to souse the lady with five gallons of her stated choice of salad dressing. You then realize you've forgotten an important supplement to the salad: the crackers. Drive away, buy some, check into the luxury hotel suite you booked earlier, get into bed, turn out the light and, munch munch munch, nibble away at the crackers one by one in the dark! Ruscha faithfully recreated this instruction as a photo story. In 1970, a short film was also made with the title *Premium*—the brand of crackers used.

Most writing on Ruscha, incidentally, makes no mention of his work with Williams. In this light it's no surprise that although the legendary comedian Andy Kaufman is the subject of a Hollywood biopic (*Man on the Moon*, 1999, with Jim Carrey as Kaufman), he has not received serious recognition in the art context, although his actions far outdo many art performances in their conceptual sophistication, audacity, and wit. Thus he not only promises to read an assembled audience the whole of *The Great Gatsby*, he actually does it, on into the wee small hours, when only a very few listeners remain. Or, after a performance at Carnegie Hall, he has the entire audience of 2,800 people transported by twenty buses to the promised feeding with milk and cookies. Or, on the David Letterman Show, he incites a famous pro wrestler to punch him, even though he's wearing a neck brace, only then to abuse him all the more furiously with an onslaught of words that are banned on TV and throw coffee in his face—all without the slightest trace of a smile, all arranged in advance. Kaufman's humor always plays on the borderline of credibility and of insult, a line it most often crosses.

## Sex and Tackle, Gender and Gear: Lee Lozano

In *Crackers*, manliness reduces itself to absurdity. But, for all the de-heroicization of the male, the female remained in the background, an object. Lee Lozano was perhaps the artist in 1960s New York who gave the most original expression to her discontent with this state of affairs, as a painter of polymorphously perverse pictures and as a hippie Conceptualist. Initially, she worked in oil, pencil, or wax crayon: clamps hook up with hammers, hammers with spanners; vaginas become power sockets; nipples become penises. In the 1980s and 1990s, the slapstick-like collision of sex and tackle was turned into sculpture, as in the work of Georg Herold or Sarah Lucas. But in painting at that time, it was not the done thing, Abstract Expressionism and Hard Edge were still the dominant modes. All Lozano shares with early Pop art is the cartoon simplification. Of her contemporaries, only the drawings of Claes Oldenburg or the assemblages of Ed Kienholz reveal a similar pleasure in libidinously charging up simple everyday objects—with Picabia's machine pictures as a historical precursor, as in his simple outline drawing of a sparkplug entitled *Portrait d'une jeune fille américaine dans l'état de nudité* (Portrait of a young American girl in the nude, 1915). In 1964, Lozano painted a single screw, spread over two canvases almost five meters wide, whose tip bends toward the viewer like a curious worm. But Lozano doesn't focus exclusively on surreal sex capers. She paints effects of light and shadow on pipes and cones that fill the entire canvas, almost slipping into tidy geometricality—only to puncture the canvas with circular holes in unexpected places.

Lozano died, forgotten, in 1999. She was only rediscovered in the years that followed, initially as the artist who in 1971—as a concept—announced her withdrawal from the art world, moved to Texas, and was never seen again. And who at roughly the same time—also as a concept—broke off all contact with women, not even wishing to be served by them when she went shopping. If one imagines this as a sketch, it is bitterly amusing slapstick. Lozano thus underlines both the male dominance in her avant-garde milieu and her disappointment with ineffective resistance—her boycott of women began after an unsatisfactory meeting of the feminist sub-committee of the Art Workers Coalition. She rejected the formation of cadres within the left-wing art world during the period of anti-Vietnam protest; she rejected the idea of the "art worker" in favor of "art dreamer," opposing production with play.

As a result of these positions, the artwork for Lozano becomes an act that intervenes bizarrely in the life of those involved, and above all in the life of the artist herself. The work consists of this act. All that's added are concise reports in the form of handwritten notes in felt pen, mostly on pages torn out of notebooks. *Grass Piece*, for example, which involves the artist getting stoned for six weeks (she has to constantly increase the dose to stay high), immediately followed by the *No-Grass Piece*, also intended to last six weeks (she only lasted six days). Or *Party Piece* (also called *Paranoia Piece*): "Describe your current work to a famous but failing artist from the early '60s. Wait to see whether he boosts (hoists, cops, steals) any of your ideas."

Her *Dialogue Piece* from 1969 manifests itself in the instruction: "Call people for the specific purpose of inviting them to yr loft for a dialogue." The list of artists is long and illustrious, including Robert Smithson, Dan Graham, and Lawrence Weiner. Lozano reveals nothing about the content of the dialogues, but she introduces the notes with a quotation from the obscenity-rich hippie weekly *Screw: The Sex Review*: "It was a congenial meeting & was only occasionally broken by small farts..." Here, it is not the act itself that partakes of slapstick, but the succinctness of the instruction and the subsequent descriptions, the way Lozano pushes the sacred-cum-scientific gravity of Conceptualism into the realm of ridiculousness, paranoia, and the Fabulous Furry Freak Brothers.

# Gordon Matta-Clark Dangles From the Clock Face

With Baldessari, Ruscha, and Lozano in the back of one's mind, certain things look different. Suddenly one notices, in works by pioneers of aesthetic rupture and negation previously treated with solemn seriousness, the hairline cracks of comedy. Gordon Matta-Clark (1943–1978) is considered a prototypical artist of Deconstruction, who with cold brilliance almost literally took apart both architecture and institutions, drilling holes through whole floors of a building, pulling down walls, and revealing structures. In 1974, he sawed an ordinary American single-family house in two, from the roof to the foundations. *Splitting* can be read quite straightforwardly as a bold intervention and as a symbolic marking of the rift that runs through the image of an intact suburban world.

But if one watches the ten-minute film that documents the action, then a more multifaceted picture emerges. First, the artist plays the part of the gruff construction worker who swings the sledgehammer. But then he pretends to hold up the sagging half of the house with his bare hands—Buster Keaton style. In *Clock Shower*, also from 1974, there is even an unveiled Harold Lloyd quotation: Matta-Clark, dressed in black like a pantomime artist, showers and shaves, covering everything in shaving foam in the process, all of this while clinging to the face of the clock on New York's Clock Tower building, before dangling precariously from its hands like Lloyd in *Safety Last* (1926).

# Bruce Nauman Helps the World

In Bruce Nauman's work, too, slapstick is often present in places where it is not dealt with openly. For over forty years, he has touched again and again on a raw nerve in the conditions of artistic production: The narcissistic drama of the individual trying to make something—an idea—out of the supposed nothing of confusion and desperation. Nauman's skill in hitting the mark is legendary. In 1967, he placed a snail-shaped neon sign in the window of his studio in a vacant store: "The true artist helps the world by revealing mystic truths," it stated in a style usually employed to advertise donuts or freshly tapped beer, now extolling the virtues of the artist as a shamanic service provider. Plenty of hippie disciples will certainly have taken it literally. But "helping" and "revealing" are tasks that can only plunge art into either despair or ridicule. This attempt at a pastoral rendering leads right to the core of the guru mania of the New Age era. Anyone who ever doubted Nauman's willingness to make a fool of himself as an artist as a way of opposing this trend should take a look at his drawing *Portrait of the Artist as a Fountain* from the same year. Rather than some young art star with water flowing from his mouth like pure creativity, what we see is a naked parody of a classical statue of an athlete, frozen forever above a tiny basin.

In *Stamping in the Studio* (1968), Nauman stomps round his studio like an angry child who didn't get the new art idea it asked for, at the same time stamping down and measuring out every square centimeter. In *Wall-Floor Positions* (1968), we see him feeling his way between the wall and the floor with his arms and legs, as if trying out uncomfortable sleeping positions. One is immediately reminded of Valie Export nestling against jutting sections of wall and Matthew Barney climbing through the gallery in mountaineering gear—works that gave this same approach a gender charge. In the 1980s, Nauman returned to video drama, this time with actors and an openly slapstick-like aggravation of tensions between the sexes. In *Violent Incident* (1986), a man and a woman meet for dinner, but he pulls the chair out from under her, prompting her to throw her drink in his face. The clash ends with both of them on the floor, knifed to death. In Nauman's miniature choreographies, Samuel Beckett and John Cage meet Stan Laurel and Oliver Hardy, depriving slapstick of comic relief.

# Why Men Long Believed Slapstick Was Theirs and Theirs Alone

The existence of a direct link between slapstick and tensions between the sexes had already been demonstrated by Valie Export and Peter Weibel in central Vienna in 1968. Wearing a suit and crawling on all fours, Weibel was dragged through the streets on a dog's leash by Export. *Aus der Mappe der Hundigkeit* (From the Portfolio of Doggedness) is documented in black-and-white photographs. Theoretically, the work could be taken from an early silent movie. In practical terms, however, it exaggerates fears of threatened manhood into an open game of sexual submission. Male passersby derive comic relief, laughing as a precaution to keep the imagined threat at bay.

In two photographs from 1973 that show him squashed against the wall by a plank, the young Charles Ray doesn't look like much of a superior hero either. In one, the plank presses the backs of his knees against the wall so that he hangs head down, and in the other it presses into his stomach and his arms and legs dangle lifelessly. In both pictures, his face is covered by hanging hair. One cannot help but wonder how these absurd positions were achieved at all—with the help, it should be noted, of a classic slapstick prop, on a par with the banana skin and the custard pie. The work is called *Plank Piece I & II* and a similar length of timber also stars in *The Plank* (1967), a forty-five-minute slapstick film (silent apart from a few grunts) by British comedians Erik Sykes and Tommy Cooper, about two construction workers carrying a floorboard. As a running gag, the board is swung around dangerously, narrowly missing someone each time. By contrast, Ray's encounter with the plank is apparently the result of either a trick or a sporting capacity for suffering.

In much of Minimal art there is a notion of tacit, abstract manliness (artists like John McCracken leaned polished floorboards against the wall like surfboards). In Ray's work, this manliness is body-checked by absurdly tragic slapstick, as if to say: This is what happens when you get "spatially involved" by an art object, as Minimal art once promised in such neutral terms. And for anyone who still didn't get it, at the 1992 Documenta in Kassel, Ray served up solipsism as dryly banal excess: eight naked waxwork-like clones of the artist were arranged in a group sex (or rather group masturbation) session.

We have already touched on this with Duchamp, but by now there's no escaping the suspicion that slapstick has remained a male preserve throughout the twentieth century, like coal mining and the Catholic priesthood. The works by Lee Lozano and Valie Export described above, as well as those by Lynda Benglis and Rebecca Warren (discussed below), are more than just the exceptions that confirm the rule. But, beyond the inequalities that characterize art in general, the impression of male dominance cannot be explained away so easily. There must be structural, historical reasons for it.

In his book *Sudden Glory*, a kind of history of laughing (the title refers to the triumphal laughter of schadenfreude), American author Barry Sanders lists a series of reasons. They could all be subsumed under the heading "patriarchy," but beyond this they bear witness to a historically different—rather than nonexistent—socialization of women where humor is concerned.

Historically, and especially in the European aristocracies of the sixth through seventeenth centuries, access for women to public speaking and education was obstructed, if not denied. This secured male dominance in religious, scientific, military, and political discourse, and thus indirectly in the field of satire and

14     **Gordon Matta-Clark,** Splitting, 1974

15     **Bruce Nauman,** Stamping in the Studio, 1968

16+17 **Charles Ray,** Plank Piece I & II, 1967

comedy relating to it. The locus of female humor was the quick-wittedness of informal speech, and infiltration by word of mouth—the female equivalent of the male-dominated genre of formal joke-telling. This is the source of the traditional male denunciation of female speech as idle talk—the proverbial "washerwoman's gossip" (from the places where women met in public, like the stream, well, or water pump).

In this light it's no wonder that burlesque and satire have historically been fields occupied mainly by men. Attacks on male authority were more readily accepted from men, via physical and linguistic comedy set in male domains like technology, craft trades, and military and political order. This applies in equal measure to the Keystone Cops in Mack Sennett's early slapstick films, featuring a hopeless troop of hooligan policemen who stage public order as chaos, and to Lenny Bruce, the legendary stand-up comedian who by the time of his death in 1966 was banned from performing in almost every state on account of his sharp, intelligent jokes about abortion, about the Ku Klux Klan and the Catholic church, about being Jewish, and about everything in any way connected with sex.

Only once women's fight for the right to vote had been won did it also become possible to parody and caricature women in public. The range of options for actresses in Hollywood rarely extended beyond parodies of female roles—the exaggeration of stereotypes from sex bomb to naive girl next-door—however successfully these were embodied by Mae West or Doris Day. At the same time, the tradition of men in women's clothes continued, from Chaplin's *A Woman* through Billy Wilder's *Some Like It Hot*, and the countless versions of *Charley's Aunt*.

Following on from isolated precursors like Lucille Ball (*I Love Lucy*), the field opened up over subsequent decades—not without setbacks, but still: Whoopi Goldberg, Ellen DeGeneres, Sandra Bernhard, Roseanne Barr, Sarah Silverman in the US; French & Saunders in the UK; Anke Engelke in Germany. Feminism has frequently been branded humorless, often in thigh-slapping jokes of the kind only laughed at by those who tell them. The time was more than ripe for feminist slapstick in art.

# Army Boot, Dildo, Kitchen Knife: Eleanor Antin, Lynda Benglis, Martha Rosler

Eleanor Antin's *100 Boots* consists of fifty-one different postcard motifs in black and white that were simply sent to around a thousand people worldwide between 1971 and 1973. Each card shows one hundred pairs of black rubber boots from navy supplies lined up on their way across the USA: on their way into a village church, for instance; or in a tidy row like ducklings, with ducks coming towards them; and, finally, standing in line outside the Museum of Modern Art in New York. In a Surrealist manner, the boots take on the soldierly-manly character of their absent wearers at the same time as dispelling it, becoming a droll troop of movie extras. But it remained a vision. At the time, actual male de-heroicization was taking place in far more painful form—the Vietnam War was a day-to-day reality

Whereas Antin worked with mocking cuteness, the approach taken by Lynda Benglis was aggressive and grotesque. Until November 1974, she was known above all for her poured latex and pigment floor sculptures that actively flirt with riots of color and allusions to body fluids. Then she placed an advertisement in *Artforum* magazine that made a polarizing impact. A few months earlier, her friend Robert Morris had adopted a gay S&M pose for an exhibition poster, wearing shades, heavy chains, a collar, and a World War II German army helmet. Benglis outdid this look. Naked, oiled up, with pale bikini marks on her otherwise tanned skin, and with spiky hair and sunglasses, she struck a provocative pose holding a large rubber penis between her legs. Porno slapstick. This heightened grotesquerie was not especially well received. The editors of *Artforum* distanced themselves in an aggrieved letter to the publishers; feminists accused Benglis of treason. Such reactions would be unthinkable today and they show how puritanical prudishness was still a contributing factor in the gender issues of the day, with the result that the feminist response to Benglis's advertisement was only superficial.

Martha Rosler's short video performance *Semiotics of the Kitchen* (1975) returns to Lee Lozano's violently comical crossing of gender and gear, this time as a plot. Rosler was known as a committed agitprop artist. In the collage series *Bringing The War Home* (1967–1972), she transplanted GIs and war victims in blackand-white newsprint from distant jungles into the brightly colored, freshly vacuumed bungalow of *Good Housekeeping*. This wasn't funny, or even particularly sophisticated. But it was an exemplary transfer of John Heartfield's technique of undermining authority by means of "revelatory" image montage—Hitler x-rayed to show an esophagus of gold coins—into the political debate of the 1960s.

*Semiotics of the Kitchen* foregrounds seemingly less controversial subject matter. We see the artist in a static black-and-white shot, in the kitchen. Wearing an old-fashioned frilly apron, she demonstrates her arsenal of utensils in alphabetical order, in the style of televised cookery programs. First the juicer: she twists forcefully, as if breaking the necks of freshly hatched chicks. Then she shows us the large kitchen knife, making rhythmic stabbing movements in the air just like Norman Bates in his mother outfit. Her face remains impassive, like RoboCop enforcing culinary order. Her anger at the economic and social constraints and injustices that force female artists—especially those with children—back to hearth and home is channeled into the ritual execution of apple pie coziness. In so doing, she anticipated the slapstick of the murderous housewife and mother only discovered by Hollywood far later in movies like John Waters's *Serial Mom* (1994).

# Rosemarie Trockel: Irony Under Cross-Examination

Since 1987, Rosemarie Trockel has been making sculptures and wall-mounted works in which different constellations of hot plates are set in white enamel surfaces—monuments to the stove, one might say, in the laconic idiom of Minimalism. But it was the "knitted paintings" (from 1984) that were to become her trademark: computerized knitting patterns featuring everything from the Playboy bunny to the Woolmark and the swastika, which captured the zeitgeist in an almost too-perfect illustration of the notion of a postmodern vortex of signs and meanings—the devaluation of all values.

In both groups of works, Trockel managed to weld together the universalism of geometric abstraction and the particularity of kitchen life. This allowed her to underscore astonishing parallels between the traditionally male-dominated sphere of abstract art and the traditionally female-dominated sphere of housework. Both have come to be considered clichés, while stubbornly persisting as actual realities. And both reveal a latent obsession with cleanliness—the objects gleam tidily in white enamel and black hot plate steel; the knitted pictures empty out the symbols and signs, turning them into modish decor.

In the art scene of the Rhineland in the 1980s, the ironic coolness of such work was entirely justified. For Trockel, it was a matter of setting herself apart from the affected intensity and faux-naïf rock 'n' roll machismo of Cologne's *Neue Wilde*, the "wild" Neo-Expressionist painters, but without withdrawing into the reserve of "women's art." Since the 1990s, however, Trockel has increasingly displayed a productive discontent with the restrictions imposed by such maneuvers, a discontent that articulates itself as slapstick.

There is a drawing from 1993 that marks the point where irony turns in on itself: A Wild West lady wearing nothing but a cowboy hat, a bustier, hot pants, and a holster belt holds up her small pistol, ready to fire, her legs in an elegant pose as if she were wearing high heels—whereas in fact there's an egg under each of her heels and she's standing on tiptoe to avoid crushing them. She also has a pair of eggs between her legs. In German, *Eier* ("eggs") is a colloquialism for testicles. Here she comes, then, *Die legendäre Ei-Ronny*—the legendary "I-Ronny," hatching into a Ronald. In other words, a woman's ironic, "post-feminist" playing with clichéd female roles takes an unpleasant turn, like Calamity Jane being forced to do circus tricks to pay the rent. Symbolic display of female empowerment easily becomes a precarious stunt if the factual dependencies still prevail.

On another level, the "egg" as a tired symbol of fertility and reproduction becomes the slapstick joke of the broken egg. In this sense, the drawing is also a self-portrait: *The Legendary I-Ronny* shows that endless ironization leads to a delicate situation, like walking on eggs. Irony reveals itself not as a refined form of slapstick, but as the exact opposite: Slapstick is what happens when irony oversteps a line, when an embarrassing closeness and directness undermines its distancing gesture. Constantly approaching this state, bringing it about again and again, is a form of fearlessness that characterizes Trockel as an artist.

Trockel creates absurdly comical duels between the odd couples of powerlessness and self-empowerment, cliché and the parody of cliché. In her video *The Great Divide* (1994) it's as if Snow White and her wicked stepmother, perpetually asking who's the fairest (or in this case, the best) of them all, have become the same person. Looking down vertically, we see Trockel cross-examining and slapping a seated doppelgänger wearing the same blond wig—horizontal close-ups reveal that Trockel plays both characters. She tries to force the seated version of herself to "reveal" the name of the best artist in the world. The hesitant "culprit" continues to offer artists' names—Frank Stella, Richard Serra, Luc

Die legendäre Ei- RONNY

18      **Eleanor Antin,** 100 Boots Enter the Museum, 1971
19      **Rosemarie Trockel,** Die legendäre Ei-Ronny, 1993
20      **Martha Rosler,** Semiotics of the Kitchen, 1975

Tuymans (almost all men)—and gets punished for not mentioning the "right name," which, it becomes clear, can only be Trockel's own. When finally the "culprit" says it, her "persecutor" mockingly states she has "hit the jackpot," before continuing to slap her as she nevertheless carries on, invoking the Sigmar Polkes and Gerhard Richters of this world. The curious mantra of artists' names is based on the annual ranking of the one hundred most "important" artists of that year, published by the German magazine *Capital*—a list that placed Trockel somewhere in the top thirty at the time and which has accorded her prominent placings since. By using the actual listing as the basis for a slapstick double number, she achieves two things at once: she reveals the patent absurdity of a list that ranks artistic significance in numerical order, blithely cementing male dominance at the same time; and she reveals that this list also provides the perfect battleground for the real psychological war between narcissism and paranoia, both for those omitted (They've denied me recognition!) and those listed (Who knows how much longer they'll give me recognition!).

# Martin Kippenberger: Daffy Duck Shows His Wounds

Martin Kippenberger, an art college dropout, could hardly be accused of not mocking the extent of his own ambitions—which didn't diminish the ambitions. The late 1970s and early 1980s were dominated by Neo-Expressionist painting, with its demonstrative "intensity." West Berlin's art scene was no exception and the young Kippenberger was in the thick of it, without really being a Neo-Expressionist. At the SO-36 concert venue, the bourgeois milieu of artists and intellectuals mixed with young punks who eyed their bustle and their potential access to money and luxury with suspicion. In places like this—brought together by the electrifying noise of punk—middle-class children and their disadvantaged proletarian counterparts met. The former envied the latter's lack of restraint and then got the fucking shit kicked out of them for acting so fucking clever all the time. Brawling was the order of the day, like the mass punch-ups in silent movies.

The fun came to an end when someone like Kippenberger took the teasing too far. During his brief time as the venue's manager, he distanced himself from the consensus-forming habits of the punk scene with incessant humorous turns: He organized aggressively banal slide shows with ordinary family-album-style photographs (long before German stand-up comedy did anything remotely like it), and then performed with a smart-looking band by the name of *Luxus* (German for luxury). Fuck your fucking luxury—a few punks thought the manager was ripping them off at the bar, and one night in 1980 they gave him a kicking with their big boots. A photograph from the hospital shows Kippenberger's head, thickly bandaged and covered in Band-Aids. He used the image for his next show at Achim Kubinski's gallery in Stuttgart, and turned fate around. The invitation card placed the image of the swollen and maltreated head alongside the words: "KIPPENBERGER. Dialog mit der Jugend" (KIPPENBERGER. Dialogue with the youth of today).

A year later, he turned this image into an oil painting with the same title. In it, he successfully recast the real, humiliating business of falling victim to violence as a slapstick triumph—not with pathos, but like Daffy Duck, as if his bandages were sure to have disappeared in the next frame. The thickness of paint corresponds to the degree of swelling in the face. Kippenberger showed his wounds as a derisive offer of therapy to those who caused them: the picture's title built a bridge of understanding between the punk scene's anti-intellectual bluntness and the art scene's highfalutin ideas, only to immediately tear it down again.

Kippenberger was quick to understand that "being intense" was not enough to make good art. He refused to play the game according to which one had to be either bourgeois-intellectual and clever or antisocial and stupid. Instead, his strategy involved switching with unpredictable speed between intellectual astuteness and feigned apathy, negation and affirmation, refinement and bad taste, authoritarian brazenness and self-ironic embarrassment. And if anyone thought it might get embarrassing if the artist decided to deny such embarrassment after all, Kippenberger was ready with the exhibition title "I.N.P.-Pictures" (I.N.P. for Ist-Nicht-Peinlich—"It's Not Embarrassing"—Galerie Max Hetzler, Cologne, 1984).

Kippenberger didn't want to fall into the trap of "being a serious artist" that leads to stony venerability. His punning and dilettantism were a kick in the granite shins of this venerability, symbolically linked with his howls of pain from a broken toe. In the wind shadow of all the titular, theoretical, and temperamental punch lines that wander through his work like headlines through the press—*One of you, among you, with you; Good Idea Today, Done Tomorrow;* or *Please Do Not Send Home*—he was also working on solutions to urgent questions of representation. His breakthrough exhibition in this respect was

"Peter. Die russische Stellung" (Peter: The Russian Position) at Galerie Max Hetzler in Cologne in 1987. Adopting a stance which for Kippenberger was dangerously close to seriousness, it featured a conglomerate of forty-five sculptural stumbling blocks (developed with the active participation of his assistant Michael Krebber). The title referred to "Petersburg hanging" ("salon hanging" in English), the specialist term for filling the walls of an exhibition with a dense array of pictures—not of course without a little puerile innuendo on the word "position." The *Worktimer*, for example, is a metal frame on wheels with the platforms missing but with two briefcases—the soft leather kind reminiscent of the halcyon days of grey flannel suits walking toward zero unemployment—attached to the front as shock absorbers. *Brummisitz* (Trucker's Seat) is a designer toilet with, stuck to its side, a New Wave fashion feature with a certain Riefenstahl touch. And *Modell Interconti* is a genuine monochrome gray painting by Gerhard Richter repurposed as an occasional table with screwed-on chrome legs. Duchamp's notion of the "reciprocal readymade," an artwork repurposed as a banal item for everyday use ("use a Rembrandt as an ironing board!"), was realized at last. The awkward and the embarrassing populate the space with the urgency of an amateur theater company that puts the routines of the professionals to shame.

Such moments could also be found ready made: real-life slapstick. *Psycho-buildings* (1988), for example—a series of 120 black-and-white photographs in a small book, most of them taken in Spain and Brazil—documents oddities of improvised urban architecture. There's a triangle of asphalt stuck onto the curb, its function certainly evident to the local vegetable salesman, but not the mere observer. And a streetlamp that appears to have been designed crooked, leaning out over the avenue like something forgotten at the roadside. Kippenberger took this lamppost motif—already a familiar prop in macho humor from the red light district to the romanticization of alcohol—and turned it into a whole forest of monuments to whoring and drinking. The best known is one with a red bulb that bends over like a drunk, or as if distorted by a drunk's vision (*Laterne an Betrunkene*, Lamppost to Drunks, 1988). But there are also some, shaped roughly in plaster and then cast in bronze, that lack the upper lamp section—sculptural ruins degraded to warped poles. It's as if these objects, barely able to suppress their laughter, are treating the earnest discourse on the status of sculpture in an age of replicas and readymades as a trifling matter of failed street furniture design. This stance gives them a kind of dignity, the pride of the downtrodden; in *Dialog mit der Jugend*, Kippenberger had to use his own body to get the same effect.

Although not far from Rosemarie Trockel in his strategies for humor, Kippenberger had a far more pronounced desire for self-promotion, a drive to shape his social milieu, lived out as an ongoing laboratory test, complete with cruelly comical experiments. In the case of Vienna Actionist Otto Mühl, all this was played out on the mattresses of his commune; the spontaneous vomiting up of the repressive thinking of the parent generation—the enemy!—in excesses of group pressure. Now it was happening in bohemian bars and restaurants, with Papa as a tyrannical joker who liked nothing more than eating pasta and telling macho jokes. Unpleasant is not the word for the way Kippenberger sometimes tried to turn the potential inferiority of his students, his followers, and the women he knew into actual subordination. Childishly emotional, he delighted in the way they played along with his games of hierarchy. Every good comedian has a dictator in him; Chaplin used his for a film, Kippenberger for a never-ending society farce.

Kippenberger can be—and indeed has been—accused of many things. One obituary even claimed he was "not a good human being"—an ethical judgment where aesthetic judgments failed. But one mistake he didn't make was to comfortably set up shop in the rococo of his own oeuvre, swapping intellectual restlessness for "collecting antique prints and living in a nice little palace" (as Kippenberger put it in an interview with fellow artist Jutta Koether).

The question one still asks oneself about Kippenberger more than a decade after his death (he died at age forty-four) is whether he could have been the brilliantly funny artist he was without all the intimidation and cruelty. In an interview, he once told how his father would always give him and his siblings a deutschmark if they could put the right artist's name to paintings during visits to the Folkwang Museum in Essen. Art as a game for smartasses and know-it-alls—there must be more to it than that, young Martin must have thought to himself. He paid back his father, and the world that was carrying on in the same spirit, with scorn and derision.

The fact that Kippenberger left no stone unturned, no invitation card unused, no trick missed, is by no means necessarily an expression of opportunistic market-minded charlatanry. Instead, it is the counterpart to Duchamp's decades of keeping a low profile. Media and style promiscuity is the tactic, slapstick the method, by which to take what you have just asserted and established and, with the very next step, fill it full of holes like a target in a shooting gallery.

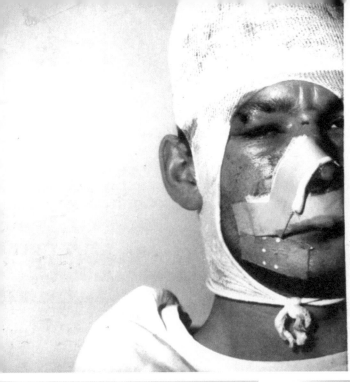

# KIPPENBERGER

## Dialog mit der Jugend

21

23

22

**Martin Kippenberger**
21 Dialog mit der Jugend, 1980
22 Worktimer, 1987
23 Brummisitz, 1987

# Slapstick's Problem Zone: Erwin Wurm, Paul McCarthy, John Bock (*con una entrata in scena positiva di* Francesco Vezzoli; and Finally, Jonathan Meese's Mother)

When this energy-consuming work of constructive self-dismemberment breaks off before it has even begun, then we find ourselves in slapstick's problem zone. Austrian artist Erwin Wurm began very promisingly with works like the video *Fabio Getting Dressed* (*Entire Wardrobe*) (1992), which shows a friend of the artist trying to squeeze into all of his clothes at the same time. The *One Minute Sculptures* (since 1997) remain his most significant contribution to date: a man holds five long, thin rods between his fingertips and the wall; a man stands with a stalk of asparagus hanging out of each nostril; a woman with her legs in the air balances a teacup on each foot. The *One Minute Sculptures* are executed mostly by a single person on the basis of drawings that act as instructions. A video documents the failed attempts and then the "completed" sculpture. This moment of triumph is also isolated in photographs. The great eighteenth-century art historian Johann Joachim Winckelmann's notion that sculptures, even fragments of sculpture, bear within them the dream of eternity, is turned into frozen snapshot slapstick.

The *One Minute Sculptures* stand in the tradition of George Brecht's instruction pieces and West's *Adaptives*. At the same time, they are amusing and light (though sometimes also slightly depressing), while still resonating with cultural history, in terms of Lessing and Laocoön and sculpture and temporariness and reproducibility and performance. Their charm lies in the way all this can be brought into play on an impromptu basis.

Doing the opposite is not wrong in itself; the question is whether it really is the opposite or just the same, only flatter and broader. For some years, Wurm has also been making large-scale works for which he produces caricatures of objects, like *Fat House* (an obese house, literally bursting at the seams, 2004) or *Telekinetically Bent VW Van* (a Volkswagen campervan with a bend in the middle, 2006), painstakingly recreated in actual size. This would be fine if it resulted in something that either laughed at the huge effort involved as an absurd procedure or at least hit the viewer like a forceful honk from a clown's claxon. Neither is the case. It's more "labor of mountain, birth of mouse." The large-scale objects are like an inflated remake of an already-worn vaudeville gag, performed by overzealous set designers. Things are not made any better by the suspicion that all of this is also driven by a view of the art market as a place where the lavishness of a production is a direct yardstick for its recognition. The cynicism of playing the game this way fails to recognize that there are also lavishly produced objects where this is clearly not the case—where lavishness is consistent with the work's concept and addresses the question of production value in an aesthetically and methodologically interesting way.

I'm thinking of the faked remakes produced by Italian artist Francesco Vezzoli: *Trailer for a Remake of Gore Vidal's "Caligula"* (2005) adopts the usual hard-selling narrative style of movie trailers and offers brief glimpses of late-Roman orgy scenes, with guest appearances by Courtney Love and Gore Vidal providing the necessary dose of jaded celebrity glitter. This work was the perfect joke about the notion of "decadence" which linked it to the art-celebrity event in whose midst it had its premiere, the Venice Biennale, with the super-yachts of the super-collectors and their Botox-ridden entourage lying at anchor in the lagoon. Vezzoli has also made a remake of Bruce Nauman's classic *Bouncing Balls* (1969), a nine-minute silent video close-up in which the artist bounces his testicles in slow motion. Instead of this, Vezzoli shows a rear view of a depilated, well-oiled scrotum dangling beneath the buttocks of a professional adult-film actor, who goes through the same motions to the sound of Mozart and against the backdrop of a mountain panorama (2005). Rather than just recreating the original punch line with more effort, the heightening of the original is the actual punch line here.

One possible description of Paul McCarthy's career is that he started with a ketchup bottle and a few sausages and ended up being able to splurge millions of dollars on every installation. Good for him. But here, too, there's a suspicious feeling of the same punch line being repeated, just with greater resources. Since the mid-1970s, McCarthy has been playing the Actionist mucky pup in the belly of America's squeaky clean family entertainment.

In the performance video *Sailor's Meat/Sailor's Delight* (1974), he wears a blond wig and women's underwear. Lying on a hotel bed smeared with raw mincemeat and ketchup, he humps a mayonnaise jar and generally spends a great deal of time (the video is forty-two minutes long) filling his viewers with the mix of loneliness, boredom, and nausea that is bound to be left behind by such a display of solo fetish sex. In *Rocky* (1976) we see the artist punching himself in the face with boxing gloves to the point of exhaustion, all the while clenching his willy between his legs like a little boy who needs to pee, as he prances about like Muhammad Ali. These works counter the inevitable pathos of taboo-breaking with a touching element of oblivion. They feel like slapstick routines that have lost themselves in a trance.

Since 1991, McCarthy has been making large installations in theme-park mode. In *The Garden*, a piece of tranquil woodland is recreated in original size, including a lifelike man with his pants down, energetically copulating with a tree like a hydraulic piston while his young companion does the same to a hole in the ground. In *Cultural Gothic* (1992), it is a father who understandingly lays his hands on his son's shoulders while the latter thrusts into a billy goat from behind. Over the same period, his performances became increasingly elaborate and were recast as video installations. One high point is the sixty-minute farce *The Painter* (1995). In it, an Action painter with a huge lumpy nose and massive rubber hands wears a smock, but no pants, and busies himself with tubes of paint labeled "shit" and "flesh"; a critic sniffs his tail end like a randy dog; and the painter chops off one of his rubber fingers (an arduous business). The comedy is driven by laboriousness, dimwitted clumsiness is taken to grotesque lengths, and the painter is the village idiot of a scene that continues to function nonetheless.

With the active participation of a production crew and of cooperating galleries and museums, McCarthy tries to bring the production values of his installations closer and closer to the family-oriented, Disneyland-style places on which they are based. His enormous, multi-part installation *Pirates* (2005), shown first in Munich and then in London, presents itself as a Dionysian doppelgänger of the Hollywood blockbuster *Pirates of the Caribbean*, with hideously deformed faces, barrels of entrails, severed limbs, and tons of chocolate sauce.

Flogging a joke to death is a legitimate slapstick technique, even when pushed to the level of compulsive repetition. But times have changed. Porno chic, grotesque violence, and parodic de-sublimation have long since entered the standard repertoire of sophisticated cinema and television entertainment. McCarthy's attempt to read the pirate theme as a metaphor for an America under George W. Bush that is trying to colonize the world by military force thus becomes a labored pretext for the $n$th take on the Disney-from-below fairytale.

More than once, German artist John Bock's artistic roots have been traced back to Daddy McCarthy—an obvious genealogy, although in Germany Joseph

24     **Erwin Wurm,** Fat House, 2004
25     **Erwin Wurm,** The Bank Manager in Front of His Bank (from the series "Cahors"), 1999
26     **Francesco Vezzoli,** Trailer for a Remake of Gore Vidal's "Caligula," 2005
27     **Paul McCarthy,** Sailor's Meat/Sailor's Delight, 1975

Beuys is of course also a factor. After all, Beuys too had his comedy moments, including his *ÖÖ-Programm* performances of 1967, in which, at the official matriculation ceremony at Düsseldorf's art academy, he welcomed the new arrivals with an axe and yelled inarticulate sounds into the microphone for ten minutes. Beuys combined comedy with intimidation, but while Bock's installations and performances may be chaotic with eccentric details, they are not megalomaniacal. Unlike McCarthy, he documents his actions in the manageable format of small video productions.

Over the years, one has grown accustomed to Bock's mix of narcissistic, poly-morphous, mad professor and down-to-earth North German farmer. Take, for example, his entry to the Nationalgalerie Prize in 2005, shown at the Ham-burger Bahnhof in Berlin. It begins as a performance with an invited pre-open-ing audience; several hundred people gather round, stretching their necks to catch a glimpse between the busy camera teams filming the event for the video production. Bock blusters about "suppuration of the udder" and waves about the teat cups from a milking machine. Then, without missing a beat, he switches to a childish outburst of rage over whether to order a sushi menu of four or five maki. People are beginning to doze off when suddenly the *coup de grace* is given: an agent provocateur embedded in the audience flings Bock out of the museum gallery through a prepared windowpane. Everyone squeezes through this unexpected breach out into the open, where Bock, covered in fake blood, asks them to follow him to a nearby bridge, from which, after further statements concerning "regression analysis" of the "nutritional value of art welfare," he leaps onto a carefully positioned boat, where he is immediately surrounded by a hired crowd of women waving flags. This is certainly one way of bringing one's own applause.

Bock is an eloquent shredder of language and form. But he doesn't depend on the physical presence of an audience, which merely acts as a filler, not being given even a minor part. His Tom & Jerry slapstick only really comes into its own in the quick cuts of the final video—a dynamism already evident in the pamphlet handed out at the end of the performance, which sums up its shuffling sequence of events in a dozen pithy sentences.

What emerges as a problem in the work of Wurm, McCarthy, and Bock is a kind of preemptive slapstick. It's as if the artwork is saying: whatever possible pathos of authority you may attribute to me, I've already broken it with irony or worked through it with catharsis. It shrugs off the responsibility to which it appears to lay claim—that of remaining methodically experimental.

Which brings us to Jonathan Meese. Does he too not besmirch himself again and again with the same old contaminated, explicitly German, mythological trash? Is he not subject to the same problem? In a word: no. In Meese's work to date, the outcome remains uncertain on account of several decisive factors.

Early on, Meese's image-laden robber's dens were dominated by faces from Malcolm McDowell to Klaus Kinski, hunger for recognition engraved on their frozen, contorted features. But since 1999, more and more space has been given over to Wagnerian Walhalla stuff, the color scheme toned down from bright motley to blackish brown. One example is his sculptural ensemble of Hagen and Siegfried as shop window mannequins (2000). The former has sloppily stuck on chest hair and his helmet has slipped down over his eyes, while the latter has a baggy women's girdle around his loins as an apron that barely conceals a poorly endowed male groin embellished with brown paint. Those who derive even the faintest Nibelungian goose bumps from this will surely delight in a monumental painting from the following year, charmingly titled *Der KOTBART erwacht* (SHITBEARD awakens). The Tristan chord of unresolved contradictions clatters and bangs its way through the tubes of earth-toned oil paint with squealing flatulent cheer. A figure with Jesus-like open arms and Medusa-like shaggy locks is surrounded by a chaotic tumult of painterly head-on collisions.

But the real crux of Meese's oeuvre is in his performances (and hopefully he will not retire to painting and sculpture as his sole media). The first high point of this profuse wallowing in the foul waters of historical power fantasies came in 1999 with a three-hour performance at Cologne's Kunstverein, entitled *Staatssatanismus II Menschenvoodoo* (State Satanism II Human Voodoo): a Stalinist show trial in which Meese himself played the part of the gravel-voiced judge as a mixture of Captain Ahab and G.I. Joe. To the point of total exhaustion, he bombarded the assembled art scene with their own half-digested dreams of anti-pluralism and political elites.

Then, in 2005, he had the great idea of an event in parallel to Bernd Eichinger's six-hour Parsifal production at Berlin's Oper Unter den Linden opera house. The production was transmitted live to the opera house's nearby depot, where Meese allowed its Wagnerian pathos to drown miserably in prolonged low-intensity action, in mechanical gestures repeated for sometimes as long as twenty minutes. In one scene, Meese, in the white face paint and shaggy beard of a second-rate kabuki performer, screamed "jawohl" into the telephone again and again, involuntarily clacking his heels together like personal secretary Schlemmer, the man who continues to say he "had no idea" in Billy Wilder's *One, Two, Three* (1961). All this is accompanied by a mechanical Hitler salute, like Peter Sellers in the war room scene in Kubrick's *Dr. Strangelove or: How I Learned to Stop Worrying and Love the Bomb* (1964).

In 2006, Meese let off steam in Hamburg, the city where he attended art school. In the setting of his show at the Deichtorhallen, with works spanning nearly a decade, he railed against cultural bureaucrats and their endless committees—before staging a kind of talk show during which he was questioned by his seventy-seven-year-old mother in person. She informed him she often found his antics "very hard to stomach" and thanked God he wasn't her only child.

Faced with the knowing, ironic smiles of certain members of the audience, Meese said things like: "You think your anti-pathos will save you," and: "If you want to understand pathos, you have to be full of it." That is the core of the slapstick problem: anyone wishing to empty out staged, pathos-laden, affirmative authority and render it absurd has to study it, instead of congratulating themselves from the outset on having remained untouched.

# Georg Herold: At the Zero Point of Slapstick

Georg Herold, a longtime fellow traveler of Kippenberger, always returns to a handful of particular materials—roofing slats and bricks—so that he appears, superficially at least, to be clinging to a trademark. But this returning to and repeating something that is definitively worn out and exhausted is precisely the point. His works always go to the absolute lowest point: If there's going to be humor, then it's rudimentary humor; if there are going to be building materials, then they're the crudest and least predefined. This is very explicit in *Deutschland in den Umrissen von 1937* (Germany in the borders of 1937), a work from 1985. Crudely nailed together out of roofing slats, the borders of the empire become laughable props cobbled together by a shoddy craftsman who scribbles in "Loreley," "Walhalla," and "Königsberg" with a felt pen as an aid to orientation. Elsewhere, worn-out underpants, plus a few pieces of wire, on coarsely made chipboard plinths, become mountain peaks (*Kleiner Bernhardiner, Brocken* etc., 1985). *For Members Only* (1987) is a dead ordinary cardboard box, raised up on simple wooden supports to such a height that no one can look inside. The interplay of slats, underpants, bricks, and cardboard evokes a certain kind of backwoods mentality that nevertheless exists in suburbia; a worn-out, totally hackneyed picture of oppressive petit-bourgeois conformism.

Some of Herold's sculptures recall the impulse to pull a pair of old underpants over someone's head to take them down a peg or two or just to get a word in edgewise. It's not unusual for his works to feel as if their final form was decided in a fragment of a second—not in the sense of "inspired genius," but more in the sense of a quick-witted gesture that turns out in retrospect to be useful. The ur-scene of the modern comic, George Herriman's *Krazy Kat,* turns up again here. The founding principle of modern narrative as anti-narrative consists in "brick to whatever." That's enough—the confusion of modern life reduced to a simple grotesque gesture whose abruptness and violence evaporate in this reduction and become comical.

In this light, Herold's *X. Baracke* (10th Barrack, 1986) is perhaps his driest and most difficult work, emptying slapstick and taking it to absolute zero. It is a simple brick construction that obstructs the room, with a supporting framework of squared timbers. Inside hangs a photograph taken by Herold in a Belgian church: a tersely worded cardboard sign standing in for the absent tenth station of the cross, the station in which Jesus is stripped of his garments. The religious solemnity of the Stations of the Cross is brought down to earth—Jesus is just being restored. But that's all the humor there is. The shack is not plastered and has no roof, similarly stripped of its clothing, a naked ruin drawing inevitable associations with Auschwitz. With its "out-to-lunch" Jesus, it marks the transition from awe-struck wonder to banal destruction, from religiosity to barbarity. This is more difficult than just making fun of solemnity.

# Sarah Lucas: Kebabs and Corny Puns

Some works by Sarah Lucas show parallels with Georg Herold. The Young British Art of the 1990s, with which her name is always immediately associated, reflected an understanding of art that called for clever one-liners, objects whose thrust could be expressed in a brief description, like Damien Hirst's shark in formaldehyde and Tracy Emin's unmade bed. At their best, the works of this period bespoke a Wildean wit and distain for boredom; at their worst, they emitted the kind of lukewarm zaniness found in certain advertising campaigns.

Let's take two of the best known works by Sarah Lucas: *Two Fried Eggs*

28a+b **Jonathan Meese**, Mamma Johnny—The Geometrical God
(Deichtorhallen Hamburg, 2006)
29 **Georg Herold**, For Members Only, 1987

*and a Kebab* (1992) and *Bitch* (1994). The former places two fried eggs and a kebab on a table in such a way as to make you read them (you have no choice) as a direct rendering of female sexual attributes. But the key operation here is a duplication that is often underestimated: at the far end of the table, a photograph of this same arrangement forms a picture-as-head in which the fried eggs become eyes, the kebab a mouth. The equation of food and sex, then, fixes us again with a soppy, dog-like gaze.

Lucas operates so obviously with these duplications that they are hard to miss as the punch line of the work. Sexist and racist ideas poke fun at themselves. As a result, she has often been accused of overly blatant symbolization. But accusing blatant, deliberate obviousness of being obvious is redundant and misses the point. Lucas is not generally attacking so-called good taste, which has, it's true, long since immunized itself against all manner of sexual clichés. Instead, her work is a specific attack on the demand for "clever allusions" that forms a key criteria in defending privilege. (Can you read the codes? No? Then you're not included!) Rather than following the avant-garde catalogue of standard artistic means, which recommends leaving a gap between artistic representation and the reality it portrays that is wide enough for viewers to make themselves interpretatively cozy and narrow enough to ensure that they follow the predefined path, her point is to make this gap snap shut. Plaster casts of forearms on springs mechanically wave back and forth as a direct rendering of the "wanker" hand signal. Topless pinup wallpaper, beer can penises, cigarette butts—everything is restated in its sad, bare presence. Those who laugh too hard fall into Lucas's trap to at least the same extent as those who find her too obvious.

All the modes of expression, from Duchamp to Nauman—the readymades and the explicit body references—are plunged into the commonplaceness of violence and depression at the so-called "margins of society," at the furthest conceivable remove from art. Admittedly, most of the apologists among critics writing on Lucas merely roll out the same old praise of rebellion and graphicness, and Lucas rides this wave perhaps a little too willingly. But the complaint that puns-as-art are just puns is not new—witness Kippenberger or Fischli/Weiss. A key insight of slapstick is that mechanical repetition to empty something of all meaning is necessary before it can be charged up with new meaning. This insight is in good hands with Sarah Lucas.

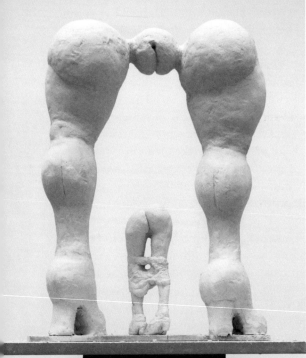

30    **Sarah Lucas**, Two Fried Eggs and a Kebab, 1992
31    **Sarah Lucas**, Bitch, 1994
32    **Rebecca Warren**, Helmut Crumb, 1998
33    **Thomas Schütte**, Mohr's Life, 1988

# Rebecca Warren Meets Helmut Crumb in Pottery Class

There's certainly no lack of sexual graphicness in Rebecca Warren's sculptures. Many of them are made of unfired clay: crudely fashioned, fat female legs, their feet in Daisy Duck shoes, verging on elephantiasis. One of them, its posterior stuck out especially proudly, its heels especially high, is called *Helmut Crumb* (1998). In Warren's works, Helmut Newton's cold elegance and Robert Crumb's sweaty burlesque are dragged into a vortex of imperfectly shaped material. It's not the grotesquerie of appropriated male fantasies in itself that is puzzling here. It's the unfinished quality of the roughly slapped-together figures, the way the various references smack into each other with the heaviness of wet clay—all the while fluttering about like a nervous hummingbird between amorphous, polymorphous, and sexually unambiguous.

Most of the sculptures are placed on "dollies," the kind of wheeled platforms used to shift furniture and artworks; they are movable containers for art-sex complexes, which remain extremely fragile, left unfinished as a constitutive element.

The "impossibility" (impossible in the sense of a lapse of taste) of the faithfully formed figurative female nude is not a matter of prudery or sexism. It is due instead to one of the norms of late modernism: that this is conventional art trash, and it's been done too often, so get rid of it—it's only acceptable, if at all, as an ironic quotation or readymade! As we have already seen, however, friends of slapstick have a special fondness for things that have been declared unfit for service. A heartfelt sympathy with trash.

# Thomas Schütte and the Old Sock Problem

Enter Thomas Schütte. Apparently, the crew of the abandoned Kippenberger mother ship still can't stand him—probably because, like Trockel, his formal inventiveness comes dangerously close, while crossing paths in different, distinctive ways.

The reclining female nude had become degraded, as Schütte puts it, to "small town bank foyer art." This development could not be left to its own devices, and the *Stahlfrauen* and *Bronzefrauen* (Steel and Bronze Women, since the late 1990s, ongoing) are larger-than-life reclining nudes resting on steel tables, hard to digest and packed with contradictions and clichés, like the overflowing cellar of someone you don't find immediately appealing. It's as if Schütte is pushing retired veterans of modernist sculpture like Aristide Maillol or Henry Moore back onto the vaudeville stage of contemporary production. But why? Simply to make defiantly "improper," nude-kitsch sculptures? *Bronzefrau Nr. 13* (Bronze Woman #13, 2003), for example, is a polymorphous combination of voluptuous buttocks and angel wings that look like two pieces of roast pork in fishnet stockings. She crouches there, as if lying in wait for anyone who dares to describe her in such terms. Schütte's steel and bronze women clearly owe much to the insight that conventions and clichés (of both sculpture and gender) return with more and more of a vengeance the more one believes it possible to get rid of them by mere rewording or discrete removal to the depot. As in the case of Lucas or Warren, one automatically suspects that any attempt to quote clichés and the mechanisms of power they conceal ends up perpetuating precisely what it condemns. Schütte's sculptures suggest that the only antidote is to admit fundamentally and unconditionally to inappropriateness and embarrassment: not the kind of embarrassment occasioned by unwelcome public exposure, but a sad and silent glimpse into the mechanisms of self-legitimization. Mechanisms that occupy and torture us all, especially in our most solitary moments. That is true embarrassment, and slapstick is an attempt to find a way out of the attendant depression. In this sense, slapstick-as-art is less about the collapse of heroism and authorities outside than the traces they leave within us. Perhaps this can be seen in Schütte's method: he first designs the bronze works in small ceramic studies, whose momentary slapstick is then faithfully immortalized in large format.

Schütte's part-loving, part-deadly embrace of the idea of the monumental grew not out of a regressive impulse against all the pompous criticism of monumentality brought forth in the name of Conceptual art, but out of vigorous engagement. What, Schütte must have asked himself, happens if a critique of monumentality takes on monumental proportions itself?

The Conceptual notion that "just pointing at things" (or at how things are related) is already art is aptly reduced by Schütte to a familiar everyday problem that even a two-year-old can understand: Where's it gone, the second sock that goes with the first? The old sock problem features in *Mohr's Life* (1988). A small white Plasticine figure in pajamas marvels at a sky full of old socks lined up on an iron stand as if hung out to dry. Whatever allegorical meaning one might ambitiously read into this scene, it will be muffled by the humble presence of the fluffy sock parade. In any case, *Das alte Sockenproblem* (Old Sock Problem, 1989)—a watercolor showing three (not four!) socks on a line—confirms that this might be something worth pondering in pajamas, as if it were the key to understanding the universe. The fact that artists subject themselves to the torture of constant doubt in their search for new ideas and interesting productive possibilities does not automatically make them role models for a new economy that expects just this from its employees. At least not as long as they are working for themselves and the sometimes bizarre objectives of art, and not for the banal and tedious balance sheets of disinterested investors.

# La méthode Fischli/Weiss

Over the past twenty-five years, the Swiss artist duo Peter Fischli and David Weiss have never tired of violating the selfless and pathos-driven work ethic of the full-time artist. Unlike most of Pop art, the two artists appropriate not only the images and themes of the big wide world of everyday life and mass culture, but also and above all its activities. As often as not, this has meant notoriously fogeyish petit-bourgeois hobbies like pottery, woodcarving, handicrafts, amateur photography (lovely flowers in double exposure! airports of the world!), or amateur video (just film everything!). These activities generally involve a huge consumption of time or, to be more precise, working hours. Great. The most striking thing about Fischli/Weiss, and the most puzzling, is the way they potter about in their Zurich environment as if they are just killing time, only to end up realizing a clearly defined project that's as sharp as a knife.

Three truncated gherkins look at a pile of carpets, while a dealer advises them. (Actually, they're not carpets but slices of mortadella and Lyon sausage, and the dealer is a chunk of radish.) Is this a snapshot taken by a drunk looking at the remains of a smorgasbord at four in the morning? No, it's Peter Fischli and David Weiss in 1979, staging and photographing miniature incidents for *Wurstserie* (Sausage Series). What kind of artist does something like that? Who comes up with this kind of mind-expanding silliness?

A thirty-minute film from 1981 provides something of an answer. It's a rat and a bear. Shot on 8-millimeter film blown up to 16-millimeter, *Der Geringste Widerstand* (The Least Resistance) features the two Swiss artists dressed in furry brown rat and panda-bear costumes, roaming a Los Angeles reminiscent of third-rate buddy-cop flicks. Meeting on a bridge over a busy highway, they discuss the latest developments in the art world: "Any work?" "No, but some money." "Interesting, how does that happen?" "Some sources say it's the result of bad vibes between the painter and the viewer. Let's really go to town and cash in for all we're worth, even though we don't have a clue." In the ensuing whodunit, rat and bear come across, among other things, a corpse in a gallery, a sculpture as a murder weapon, and a mansion swimming pool with forensic evidence of recent poolside lounging—the smoking guns being catalogues and magazine spreads featuring Picasso, Mondrian, and Hockney. Here their quest for success in art finds an early answer, as a ghostly voice hovering above the water warbles: "I'm the cultivated life, elegance, you know me well ... but also sleeping late and staying in bed ... I'm beauty, the never-ending garden party. I'm champagne from a lady's shoe ... I'm the least resistance." And so, to cut a long story short, in the fall of 2006, Fischli/Weiss had a major retrospective at London's Tate Modern.

But wait a moment, didn't we begin by saying that art cannot be explained in terms of narrative structures? And now this, a silly plot about the great art success swindle? The subject matter confirms the theory once again: when Fischli/Weiss tell a story, they do so as a way of making fun of storytelling itself, especially stories about artists' careers and blueprints for success. Of course, the narrative content has its entertainment value, too, but it is above all a "pretext" for a further artistic frame of reference, even at the risk of the audience merely finding the narrative content of the works funny and completely missing the conceptual punch lines, which are actually much funnier.

"Plötzlich diese Übersicht" ("All of a sudden, everything becomes clear"), the rat mutters at one point in *The Least Resistance*, continuing with a sleuth's proverb: "Rack your brains with all your might, you'll soon bring the truth to light" (*die Wahrheit kommt sogleich ans Licht, wenn man sich den Kopf zerbricht*). The two artists took this to heart, and the same year they made a series of 200 crudely fashioned clay objects entitled *Plötzlich diese Übersicht* (official English title: *Suddenly This Overview*). Besides managing to reconcile the hitherto separate discourses of Modernist sculpture and amateur pottery, these works point towards an alternative way of framing a panorama of reality. They are slightly rough-cut renderings, with literal titles that describe what you see, of events that have changed the world: vignettes of *Mick Jagger and Brian Jones going home satisfied after writing "Satisfaction,"* or *The Last Dinosaur* standing lonely in a deserted landscape, or a cuddly pet with a bulbous nose and dim eyes clinging to a lamppost (*Mausi's Pissed*).

**Fischli/Weiss,** Sausage Series, 1979

34     At the Carpet Shop
35     In the Mountains
36     Moonraker
37     The Fire of Uster
38     Titanic

Slapstick in exemplary form also features in the staged photographic still lifes of the series *Stiller Nachmittag* (Quiet Afternoon, 1984–1985), each featuring the accomplishment of a precarious balance that must have taken an absurdly large amount of experimental effort to achieve. In one, three tires stand on top of each other, only held in place by small blocks of wood. In another, an empty wine bottle balances on an apple resting in an egg cup, while a plate balances on the cork of the bottle, held in place by the counter-balance of a fish-slice and a ladle, the latter holding a dangling onion in a net. The kitchen utensils appear to have been taken over by the souls of Chinese circus acrobats, except that the combinations are more like some insane mockery of gravity.

*Der Lauf der Dinge* (The Way Things Go, 1987) sets the issue of outwitting gravity in motion. It's an absurd thirty-minute film of triumphant coincidences: car tires, candles, plastic bottles, fire crackers, suspicious liquids, planks, and balloons are all lined up to fall like dominoes (only tinkered with occasionally by a well hidden cut). The mechanism used is one popularized by countless cartoons and slapstick scenes. Here, however, instead of serving to achieve a result that is laughable compared to the effort involved (coffee is poured, burglar gets bucket of water on head), it becomes tautological. At the end, the sequence literally dissolves into nothing, into an undefined mist. The pure physics of chance comes full circle.

*La méthode Fischli/Weiss* involves, firstly, encyclopedic collecting, based on coincidence and memory rather than systematic research, and on images rather than facts—all the funny events in *Plötzlich diese Übersicht* are drawn from memory and association. Secondly, it involves disrupting the hierarchies connected with "serious" scientific and artistic collecting, by sheer weight of numbers, by the media used (major events as crummy clay models), by equalization (major and minor events in the same scale) or inversion (the trivial as important, etc.). Thirdly, it involves the stretching, compressing, or "wasting" of time by laboriously creating a work that can be taken in "quickly" by the eye (as in *Stiller Nachmittag*) or, inversely, by exhibiting real time (as in the video installation with a total of ninety-six hours of footage at the 1995 Venice Biennale that brought together many banal and some beautiful scenes in the style of the Discovery Channel). Fourthly, and perhaps most importantly, it involves the willfully clumsy subversion, highlighting, and exaggeration of the first three methods: evoking an overview where no overview is possible; making a markedly sober approach and markedly neurotic craziness collide; linking banal anonymity with idiosyncratic stubbornness; and deliberately including errors or inconsistencies.

**Fischli/Weiss**

39a+b   The Least Resistance, 1981
40   Mr. and Mrs. Einstein shortly after conceiving their brilliant son Albert (from: Suddenly This Overview, 1981)

The way Fischli/Weiss tend to dim things down to medium intensity is at odds with the demand that art should constantly generate strong stimuli. As a result, they remain below the radar that incessantly scans the art landscape for seriousness, criticality, and controversy.

# Mike Kelley Down in the Basement

Mike Kelley's work deliberately generates stimuli of chaos and overload. But here too, the grotesque is only a mask behind which Kelley operates with a method as carefully considered as that of Fischli/Weiss. He often starts with a pool of material from memory or with things that are not remembered, known in psychological jargon as "repressed" material: the ridiculous, embarrassing, but by no means harmless or irrelevant moments of American adolescence as manifested in youth, underground, and popular culture, and the "dirty" zones of sex, trash, and violence where regression and apathy meet with experimentation and intelligence.

For more than a decade, Kelley has been interested in "repressed memory theory," a pseudo-scientific doctrine popular especially in the United States, according to which many bad things are stored away in the unconscious—things that can be retrieved through therapy decades later, and consisting primarily of things like satanic rituals and child abuse. This is a great trick to keep artistic production running, as critic Steve Stern has remarked: if everything I cannot remember is a trauma, then I can make something out of nothing.

Kelley takes the theory literally. Absolutely everything he cannot remember—like the exact appearance of the basement rooms at Cal Arts in Los Angeles when he was studying there in the 1970s—can only be a sign of the worst kind of repressed experiences. Friendly lecturers on Conceptual art become potential pedophiles, the video editing room becomes Hitler's bunker. As a reflection of the cruel fantasy that shimmers through in repressed memory theory, the slapstick aspect here is forced upon the viewer, who must literally get down on his or her knees to get to the bottom of this dark business.

*Sublevel* (1998) requires visitors to crawl through a wooden tunnel that ends in an aluminum box. From the outside, it looks like a Minimalist monolith, and from the inside it looks like a cross between *The Silence of the Lambs* and *Killer Klowns from Outer Space*. Two metal sinks, clinically clean, plus a closed glass cabinet with a small dildo collection (including a plastic cob of corn and a thick felt pen) line up to make a small skyline of pornographic strangeness. In the center, as a joke that's almost too good, is a small nativity scene made of glass.

In another astute observation, Steve Stern calls Kelley's work "screwball forensic"—fast-paced, innuendo-laden Hollywood comedy meets the diligent investigation of corpses and crime sites. But Kelley has also been known to do without direct sex and shock effects, as in his relatively early video piece *Banana Man* (1983). Here he attempts to fathom the "psychology" of a character from a children's TV series that he recalls only from the accounts of his classmates, a guy who always pulled long things from his many pockets (toy trains or strings of sausages), always accompanied by his only verbal utterance: "Uuuuh!" Plainly enough, psychological profiling collides here with its comedy-phallic negation.

In the dialogue series from 1991, the setup could not be simpler: take the absurdist possible dialogue that may also contain fragments of intellectual brilliance when it comes to making fun of the concept of "dialogue." Record it with ludicrous squeaky or mumbling voices and then play it back on an ordinary tape player set up next to a crocheted picnic blanket. On the blanket, arrange two soft toys from a car boot sale as if they were having a chat. And, lo and behold, they start talking. It's astonishing how automatically one identifies the pretentious talk with the cuddly soft toys; there's not even any need, as there was with Fischli/Weiss's rat and bear, for even the most superfluous of plots. At the same time, however, there emerges from this talk the theme of the embarrassment of physical presence: "The body of a famous critic came to our class the other day. Now we don't believe its writings anymore … And the presence of all that flesh made us think of all the things the writings didn't speak of… It's so sad—it makes you think of money, of prostitution. We would never make that mistake."

# Slapstick Now: A Whistle-Stop Tour

One could imagine slapstick in the art of recent years as an illustrated catalogue or as an exhibition to be walked through. But the artists included are not "slapstick artists" in the sense that such a description could do justice to their work as a whole. It's more a matter of particular artworks and the methods expressed in them. One might think of *The Way Things Go* by Fischli/Weiss, then, as a jumble of artistic approaches to sculpture and performance and their transposition into film, video, or photography, generating absurd concatenations.

The task of "translating" all this into stories and narratives is left to the viewer (or to some critical proxy, as in this book). This procedure is sometimes intimidating, sometimes disarmingly self-ironic. Sometimes, one is pushed out onto an empty stage, and sometimes one is baffled to note that the artwork itself is already drenched with the very feeling of embarrassment one has occasionally felt oneself during sustained attempts to move confidently in social, cultural, and discursive circles.

# Steve McQueen, Martin Gostner, Marko Lulic: Panorama, Paradise, Partisan

Let's begin with a concrete reference. In the video *Deadpan* (1997), British artist Steve McQueen reenacts a famous Buster Keaton scene. The comic steps out of a house whose front facade falls over in such a way that a window frame fits exactly around him and he is not hurt. McQueen repeats the scene several times—with a grave look on his face, as if he were steeling himself for the next test of courage—thus deliberately stripping it of its original comedy, which consisted in the fact that the man doesn't know what's happening to him. Here, then, in addition to its usual meaning of "poker-faced," the word deadpan is also broken down into "dead" and "pan," a panoramic camera shot looking death coldly in the eye.

In his wonderful piece *After my Death* (2003), Austrian artist Martin Gostner gives a frank answer to the maudlin question of what, in art and life, will leave an impression in the long term: my ass. A shallow silicon cast of the artist's buttocks is repurposed as a watering hole and bath for songbirds, symbolically present as decorative decoys in the work's Perspex plinth. "After my death I would like to be a paradise for birds," is written in white letters on the glass. While the artist's butt may give refreshment to birds of paradise in the remote future, his brain in the present is continually inventing new hybrids of solemnity and self-ridicule.

For Marko Lulic, who was born and grew up in Vienna with Croatian roots, the de-heroicization of monuments is a central motif, be it Yugoslavian Modernist partisan memorials or Mies van der Rohe's Berlin memorial to Rosa Luxemburg and Karl Liebknecht, which was destroyed by the Nazis. The replicas he builds are faithful neither in terms of scale, nor material, nor form—but that's not the point, anyway. Instead, as Lulic says, the point is a "fond scratching at the material and content of these monuments"—plywood instead of concrete, for the moment rather than eternity. The humor of this trivialization is marshaled behind a serious question: What remains of Modernism if the heroism is subtracted? This is perhaps best summed up in his series of photographs entitled *Reactivation (Circulation in Space)* (2002/2004), showing the artist draped in the Olympic rings of a sculpture outside Belgrade's museum of modern art, which was created by Vojin Bakić in the 1970s. Lulic "reactivates" the outdoor sculpture by taking its title *Circulation in Space* literally as an instruction, testing all manner of poses from performance art through war memorial, from silly contortions through sporting experiments. Awkward physical presence in polished abstraction. A Chaplinesque pietà.

# Werner Feiersinger, Monica Bonvicini, Tom Burr: Stumbling Block, Love Swing, Latrine

For Werner Feiersinger (to take another artist from Vienna), referring to Modernist architecture and Geometrical Abstraction is not an end in itself. It's more a matter of taking the dogmas that once drove these movements forward, while at the same time hollowing them out completely. What once indicated transparency sinks into the shadows; what was at pains to achieve factuality and pure presence suddenly appears hopelessly laden with meaning. For example: a small, unspectacular painted bronze (*Untitled*, 1992) sits on the floor. Although no clear function can be attributed to this thing, it does not seem autonomous, but rather like some kind of aid—as if someone has made a plinth or podium by using an elongated flowerpot with rounded ends as a mold and then turning the hardened contents out like jelly. The colors seem improvised: at one point, an inadequately opaque white is covered by an irregularly applied red rectangle, as if to mark some damage. At this point, if not before, any attempt to classify the piece under the art-historical term of "negative space"—in the sense of Bruce Nauman's *Space Under My Steel Chair* (1965–1968)—falls apart. The "negative space" suddenly becomes a "positively" present stumbling block. One is reminded of the above-mentioned quip about sculpture being something you trip over when stepping back to look at a painting.

This sense of collision is more explicit in the work of Monica Bonvicini, an Italian artist living in Berlin since the 1980s. Here it's as if words and sentences

After my death
I would like to
be a paradise
for birds

41

42

43a

43b

41     **Martin Gostner,** After my death I would like t
       a paradise for birds, 2003
42     **Mike Kelley,** Sublevel, 1998
43a+b  **Marko Lulic,** Reactivation (Circulation in Spa
       2002/2004

are materializing, on the wall, in the dust, solidified into clumps of letters, and, conversely, as if what she has made is soaking up syntax and vocabulary. But the result reads not like a neat set of operating instructions, but as a dirty (or at least dusty) joke. For *Plastered* (1998), visitors to the private view looked at the exhibits, and sank with an alarmingly quiet creaking sound into the floor, which was laid out with untreated drywall boards. One moment they're casually demonstrating their urbanity in small talk, and the next they're stalking about like herons in a swamp, trying to cause no further damage.

*Never Again* (2005) depends to a similar degree on the viewers' actions. Facing Bonvicini's large-scale construction of scaffolding hung with chains and black leather S&M love swings alone, one might suspect her approach of being little more than an accessory—a coquettish formula. But as soon as people begin to throw themselves into the leather seats, setting the chains in motion, a polytonal rattling and clanking starts up, suddenly filling the formerly lifeless ensemble with life. Visitors' legs get tangled up, creating symbolic hybrids of S&M sex and antenatal gymnastics.

In Tom Burr's installations and sculptures, the minimalisms of Modernist sculpture and architecture are robbed of their seemingly "naked" tabula rasa facticity. Mixed with allusions to gay fetish culture (Kenneth Anger films, Jim Morrison's leather trousers, porn video cabins, the mirrors and black walls of a bar), it becomes clear that the models themselves long since carried a "libidinous charge" and "only" needed recoding. In recent years, this has increasingly taken on a touch of slapstick. His objects themselves behave like stylish dandies who have drunk one too many and who are now telling vulgar jokes about the people in the room. Gordon Matta-Clark's aforementioned work *Splitting* finds itself quoted as a replica of a nineteenth-century American latrine hut which (as the splitting in this case reveals) actually has three seats side by side (*Split*, 2005). Puritanism was clearly once less puritanical than might have been thought.

# Urs Fischer, Saâdane Afif: Pirates

Swiss artist Urs Fischer's succinctly titled *Chairs* (2002) is a piece of sculptural situation comedy. In their old age, two old-fashioned kitchen chairs upholstered in fake snakeskin have tried in vain to achieve the kind of elegant stacking characteristic of more recent designer chairs. And they have become so disastrously tangled up in the process—one has its leg stuck through the seat of the other—that they appear to be having sex. When chairs become such clumsy-looking beings, the sublime is rendered visible in the utterly banal. In this light, maybe the opposite of the readymade is not Duchamp's "Rembrandt as an ironing board," but Fischer's Excalibur in a rock of cast concrete (*Untitled*, 2003). As an isolated sculpture, this much-quoted item of sacred mythical trash loses its smokescreen of pathos. Well-worn legends and curious chairs alike are released into ordinariness via transformation into art. In the process, however, both the sculptures and the myths retain a rickety robustness, a tough decrepitude. They are like a pirate with a wooden leg and an eye patch: wrecked, but seaworthy.

In one of his most remarkable works, French artist Saâdane Afif uses a rather affected shelf by star designer Ron Arad: a serpentine strip of plastic fixed to the wall with two or three screws to hold books in irregular formations. In *Pirate's Who's Who* (2000–2004), a passionate reader of swashbuckling tomes has clearly been having a field day—there are so many that not only does the shelf look close to collapsing, but the surf of the seven seas and the blood of murdered ghost ship crews comes sloshing out of their pages, running down the wall under the shelf in long purplish-green drips of paint. Interestingly, the work, which exists in an edition of six, includes not the books themselves but a contract in which the buyer pledges to acquire his or her own collection of pirate books—thus deliberately creating the potential for a contest to put together the best collection, under whose weight the shelf must then disintegrate. A nice comment on the status of sculpture midway between construction and collapse.

# Isa Genzken: Empire Vampire

In the early 1970s, Isa Genzken was already pushing at the boundaries of Minimal art by designing elongated stereometric objects with the help of computer programs. The resulting ellipsoids look like hybrids of spears and racing boats, and the hyperbolae recall tubes or pipes that have been drawn together in the middle by a vacuum. In recent years and after many productive intermediary steps, Genzken has increasingly treated the rust-bound dogmas of Modernist architecture and sculpture with the kind of humorous disrespectfulness that can only be achieved by someone who knows them inside-out. Since *Fuck the Bauhaus* (2002), she has been making scenarios and architectural models on plinths—works involving wild mixtures of materials. In *Empire Vampire* (2003), toy soldiers crawl over silver sprayed ruins made of sneakers or barricade themselves behind children's rubber boots. Most recently, Genzken has transferred this theatrical play with material collage into space: wheelchairs and walking frames are draped with various well-chosen materials (lengths of cloth, metal foil, parasols, etc.), and while this suggests a fragile glamour of drapery and decorations, the pretensions of a forever-young, fast-paced glamorousness are banished to the rehabilitation clinic. Genzken's recent works behave toward the veterans of abstract sculpture like someone who walks up to a particularly earnest character and puts a funny-looking flowery hat on their head—and suddenly everything appears in a completely different light. Don't get me wrong, though—this work is not content with its puns, retaining an elegant sense of seriousness.

# Slapstick and Its Antidote: Romantic Conceptualism. Bas Jan Ader, Kirsten Pieroth, Rodney Graham, Peter Land

In 1975, Dutch artist Bas Jan Ader, an experienced yachtsman, attempted to cross the Atlantic single-handed as part of a project entitled *In Search of The Miraculous*. But his boat was found several months later, bottom up, off the west coast of Ireland. The unresolved circumstances of his death generated the myth of Ader as a serious, tragic figure. But he was also someone with a well-developed sense of slapstick.

Chaplin and Keaton based their work again and again on the tension between tragic fate and comic misfortune. Like Marcel Broodthaers before him in the film *Voyage à Waterloo* (1969), in which the artist treads in Napoleon's footsteps wearing a clown's nose, Ader approached this tension in the idiom of Conceptualism and Performance—that is, without the sentimental, emotive, narrative elements. This allowed him to intensify the emotional impact, as naked tragicomedy emerges in isolated form. The *Fall* films (1970/71) are short silent studies on falling. In *Fall I, Los Angeles* (1970), we see the artist tumbling from the roof of his bungalow in Claremont; in *Fall II, Amsterdam* (1970) he loses control of his bicycle and plunges into a canal—just like the overambitious postman in Jacques Tati's *L'École des Facteurs* (School for Postmen, 1947).

*Broken Fall* (*Geometric*), *Westkapelle, Holland* (1972) shows Ader falling sideways onto a saw horse and into the bushes. The bushes line a path that leads to the "Westkapelle" lighthouse—visible in the background—that features in an early series of paintings by Piet Mondrian. The action is reminiscent of the classic comedy gag of leaning sideways, listing heavily like a drunk or a sailor at sea, but it refers to Mondrian's Modernist rejection of the diagonal in favor of the rectilinear that caused a quarrel between the artist and his friend Theo van Doesburg. Where Mondrian manically abstracted from physicality, Ader brought it back into play. In this way, he exorcised modern art in general and Conceptualism in particular, driving out their poses of heroic unassailability.

Historical, nineteenth-century Romanticism opposed the strictly systematic with the fragmentary and the open. The line of Romantic Conceptualism running from Ader through the 1970s and into the present—Susan Hiller, Mathilde ter Heijne, Henrik Håkansson, Jan Timme, to name just a few—works against the notion of the conceptual as a closed system controlled by intellectual heroes. Slapstick is related to this insofar as it highlights jerkiness where there is supposedly smooth running. While slapstick spoils the sublime in Romanticism, Romanticism, conversely, spoils slapstick's pleasure in fun for fun's sake. And in turn, the two together undermine the heroic narcissism of Conceptualism ("My ideas are the greatest!").

Take Kirsten Pieroth, for example: for *Twenty-seven minutes* (2004), she stole the minute hand from a clock tower and displayed the trophy to prove it (the title simply names the amount of time it took to commit the theft). In 2001, the artist (who trained as a stunt cyclist in her youth) cycled backwards to the opening of an exhibition in Copenhagen that included her work. A video documents her sitting unruffled on the handlebars, driving the wrong way down a one-way street (as if she were doing "the right thing," since she has her back to the "wrong" direction). By happy coincidence, Rodney Graham cycled backwards the same year in Berlin's Tiergarten park, in his case having taken LSD. Graham—who since the late 1970s has been a permanent fixture in Vancouver, alongside artists like Jeff Wall and Stan Douglas—turned it into an installation. The 16-millimeter film projector is set in motion as soon as someone lifts the stylus of a record player into the groove; the slapstick of this film, which shows the action in picturesque early summer, contrasts with Graham's romantically elegiac rock song in the style of early Pink Floyd. Graham's slapstick becomes more obvious in three short cinematic costume dramas. In

44     **Monica Bonvicini**, Plastered, 1998
45     **Isa Genzken**, installation view, Secession,
         Vienna, 2006
46     **Bas Jan Ader**, I'm too sad to tell you, 1970
47     **Urs Fischer**, Chairs, 2002

*Vexation Island* (1997)—shot with the glitz of a Bacardi commercial—we see a Robinson Crusoe type (Graham himself) being roused from his slumbers under a palm tree by the squawking of a parrot to find he has a head wound. He gets to his feet, looks up, shakes the tree, a coconut falls on his head, and the loop starts over from the beginning—an endless blow to the skull, trapped inside the dream of a remote island. *City-Self/Country-Self* (2000) is a costume drama set in a world of horse-drawn carriages and top hats. During a visit to town, a country bumpkin shambles unsuspectingly about, until his well-off bourgeois doppelgänger—both are played by Graham—kicks him hard in the seat of his pants with a particularly pointed shoe designed specially for cosmopolitan dandies. Or, put another way: Graham kicks himself in the ass. This episode, too, is repeated in an endless loop—as if it were goal-of-the-month in slow motion. Finally, in *A Reverie Interrupted by the Police* (2003), Cage meets Chaplin: Graham, dressed in a vintage striped prison uniform, is led by two policemen to the piano, where his hesitant improving in a disharmonious avant-garde style is determined not least by the fact that he must play in handcuffs—before he is led away again. The attention to detail with which these films are realized, then, serves the most striking development possible of one central point where all the threads come together—bang on the head, kick in the ass, playing piano in handcuffs. Every time, the artist appears imprisoned in this moment, in the latter case quite literally—as if the beautiful pictures were the jail in which he intentionally has himself locked up for the slapstick experiment.

In various video works, Danish artist Peter Land has often tumbled down flights of stairs, fallen from ladders, or, as a nightclub entertainer in a blue glittery jacket, toppled off a barstool again and again. In *The Lake* (1999), he allows himself a little more time (ten minutes) to stroll cheerfully through the woods, dressed as a hunter in a green Loden, his shotgun over his shoulder, accompanied by birdsong and Beethoven's *Pastoral Symphony*. He comes to a small lake, gets into a boat, rows out into the middle of the lake, stands up, raises his shotgun, and blasts a hole in the bottom of the boat. It sinks. He sits down again and sinks with it, until all we can see is his hat floating on the water. The romantic hero is a tragic one, but even this doesn't protect him from mockery.

48      **Rodney Graham,** City Self/Country Self (production still), 2000
49      **Rodney Graham,** A Reverie Interrupted by the Police, 2003
50a+b   **Peter Land,** The Lake, 1999

# William Pope L., Daniel Guzmán, Erik van Lieshout, Kan Xuan: Crawling, Grooving, Rapping

In the work of William Pope L., mockery takes on a significantly more aggressive tone that clothes itself in strident over-affirmation. He has copyrighted the title "Friendliest Black Artist in America." One can be dead sure that this title doesn't deliver what it promises, either in terms of "friendly" or in terms of "black." This is especially clear in his "crawl pieces"—physically demanding, absurdly comical performances during which Pope L. crawls along the ground in New York's streets. In *Tompkins Square Crawl* (1991), dressed in an immaculate business suit, he drags himself through the dust, holding a small flowerpot in his hands with great difficulty the whole time. Beside him, a (white) cameraman films the whole thing. Most passersby ignore him, until finally a black local resident comes hurrying up, who first tries to get him to stand up, which doesn't work, and who then screams at him: "I wear a suit like that to work!" before going off to call the police. His rage is understandable. After all, here is someone humiliating himself—albeit symbolically—as a representative of black homeless people and businesspeople alike in front of a white cameraman. But maybe this anger should have been directed at the message ("No, all is not yet well in relations between the 'races'"), not the messenger. Positively a relief by comparison is the artist's gigantic plan to crawl along the twenty-two miles of Broadway—bit by bit, spread over years—dressed in a Superman costume (*The Great White Way*, since 2002). At least the Superman figure has associations not only with the notion of the decent white guy and ideal hero, but also with that of the unifying American dream, however corrupt. Slapstick becomes extremely grim here, as in Spike Lee's outstanding film *Bamboozled* (2000), about a black television writer who is frustrated by the industry's subtle exclusion mechanisms and who, out of pure provocation, proposes a minstrel show with black men who paint themselves black. To his surprise and horror, the show becomes a hit.

Proof that people still dream of New York as a melting pot, even if it is in the even harsher reality of Mexico City, is supplied by Daniel Guzmán. In his short video *New York Groove* (2004), the musical and music video cliché of people suddenly starting to dance in the street becomes the subject of a kind of slapstick karaoke. Before they start, however, the protagonists—four men in badly fitting clothes—begin by kicking each other in the backside before they wobble down a shopping street in the center of Mexico City doing an impromptu formation dance, to the beat of the 1980s hit *New York Groove* by Kiss guitarist Ace Frehley. A successful demonstration of the universality of pop songs, which really is proved in the absurdly amateurish production.

Dutch artist Erik van Lieshout shot his six-minute video clip *Lariam* (2001) in Ghana. He slipped into the role of the eager student who visits the country to learn how to rap, thus reversing his actual role as naïve tourist or arrogant colonialist. Lieshout mostly shows his videos in specially designed sculptural constructions, in this case an outsize cardboard model of the packaging for the malaria drug that Lieshout had to take. Showing inside is a film collage of his experiences as a rap apprentice, culminating in a street party with a live rap battle. Lieshout tests the limits of political correctness, putting himself in situations that are potentially loaded with tension and unease. These he resolves with disarming openness and energy-laden activity, thus, as if by magic, coming through unscathed.

Amsterdam-based Chinese artist Kan Xuan makes small, short, intimate video films about oppressive feelings that call for nervous and comic relief: a spider crawling over her skin in extreme close-up (*Looking looking looking for...*, 2001); two men mercilessly tickling each other in the sun (*A Sunny Day*, 2002); or just an extremely fast cut video narrative of holes in walls (*Nothing!*, 2002). Taken together, these video vignettes constitute an ironic encyclopedia of angst management, of dealing with the extreme contradictions between individualization and mass society in the new capitalist China, which are a direct contemporary equivalent to comparable upheavals taking place at the time of early slapstick.

# Slapstick and the Frozen Grin: Maurizio Cattelan, Andreas Slominski, Olav Westphalen

We have now reached a situation where the art of the present is inconceivable without the slapstick method, including all the possibilities for uninspired adaptation and repetition in tired little jokes and unadventurous nudge-nudge/

wink-wink little artworks. For all my criticism of these effects of a patently still-robust art market that attracts imitators, clowns, and fulfillers of expectations, the real problems lie elsewhere.

Firstly, one should not deceive oneself into believing that the gains of an art that threw off the shackles of authoritarian intimidation and the haughty invocations of the sublime could not be lost again to new restorations. It could be ground down in the battle between those who detest Modernism and those who yearn for it. The former want to reclaim the splendor and glory of past eras everywhere (think faux-period McMansions in gated communities around the world, or Berlin's plans to rebuild from scratch its Hohenzollern Palace), putting them out of step with time by an average of 150 years. The latter, on the other hand, are only seventy-five years out of step and long for nothing more than dashing avant-garde gestures of radical negation of the world as it exists. All the unpredictability, the doubt, the improvisation, and the finding of surprising solutions that is expressed in slapstick has no place here.

Secondly (and perhaps this weighs heavier), the slapstick method in art is not immune to fooling itself. It needs to repeatedly ask itself what the unpredictability, the doubt, the improvisation, and the finding of surprising solutions can consist of when it inevitably forms its own order, its own "school." It must, in other words, tear down what it has built up, again and again, but without just looking like an immature child. It must preserve its playfulness and take it to a refined level, without allowing itself to be misused for superficial goals.

In the case of Maurizio Cattelan, this can be read as a movement back and forth, in terms of both scale and quality, between simple, apposite interventions and larger, less apposite moments of grandeur. Among his best works is *Stolen Bicycle*, his contribution to the 1997 Venice Biennale, which consisted of stealing bicycles (no easy task in La Serenissima, for sure) and then leaning them against existing works of art—as if someone had parked his or her bike there either by mistake, in a display of ignorant muddle-headedness, or on purpose, in the hope that some of the art's shine would rub off on the bicycle and "ennoble" it. Compared with this concise gesture, *La Nona Ora* (The Ninth Hour, 1999)—Cattelan's much-discussed lifelike wax figure of Pope John Paul II lying on the floor having been struck by a meteorite—is a big, screaming super-spectacle. Here, the brick-to-the-head logic of Krazy Kat blown up to the scale of a world religion. It may be that Catholicism has more trouble absorbing this provocation than art does in absorbing the tired joke. In any case, slapstick here

51

52

53

51    **Daniel Guzmán**, New York Groove, 2004
52    **Olav Westphalen**, Stand up, 1999
53    **Maurizio Cattelan**, The Ninth Hour, 1999

appears to be intended less as a way of demolishing religious grandeur and more as an excuse for partaking in it. Cattelan himself seems genuinely uneasy about arriving at overly simple solutions—that is, bombastic joke sculptures that also sell very well—and as a result he has of late often preferred to devote himself to other activities. Together with Ali Subotnick and Massimiliano Gioni, he ran the Wrong Gallery—a single square meter of exhibition space behind an always-closed glass door in New York's gallery district; they also curated the Berlin Biennale in 2006.

In Andreas Slominski's latest work, one can sense an attempt to escape—for example, in the form of his polystyrene paintings that reveal a love of garish, clumsily executed interiors somewhere between a Chinese takeaway and Santa's grotto—from a trap of his own making. This trap consists of nothing other than the many traps-as-sculpture that became his trademark in the 1990s: nasty contraptions to catch or kill grouse, snails, martens, and many other creatures. The artist was frozen in the gesture of a mischievous "trapper," performing a tired gag again and again, like some mediocre comedian with a regular slot in Las Vegas.

Olav Westphalen (who in another life is half of German cartoon duo Rattel-schneck) congenially skewered this danger of jokiness in art with his 1998 performance entitled *Bruhaha*. Armed with a silly wig, he performs a brief stand-up comedy routine that only gets a few laughs and that is basically a string of lame jokes about life in the suburbs. In spite of this, the comedian returns for an encore to recite the exact same routine again, but this time over a playback of the first version, including the few laughs. This happens a total of six times, each time with one recording more, until the whole thing descends into cacophonic chaos. Yes, you artists using ironic gestures and endlessly repeated one-liners, it's you he's thinking of.

The fragile balance between ridiculousness and pathos, between foolishness and the earnest, must remain truly fragile, rather than just being rhetorically posited with a frozen grin. Artists and art viewers who make themselves all too comfortable in and with the slapstick method have already betrayed its fundamentally mercurial nature. This struggle between doubtful constancy and constant doubt, however, is fought out most fiercely in the medium of painting.

# Bodiless Elegance *versus* Pungent Physicality The Painting of Decisions

## A Séance of New Ways of Seeing

Let's get one thing straight from the start: painting is not an anachronism; painting is relevant. And this relevance doesn't stem from the way painting is sometimes presented and sold like a Bentley or a Patek Philippe, with that hushed intimation of illustriousness, consensus, and admiration. As everyone knows, there's no shortage of pictures—on the Internet, on flat screens, on mega-posters, on mobile phones, and in all the countless illustrated volumes at your local bookstore. Painting must compete with this mass media image pool, whether or not it actively addresses it. At the same time, painting must compete with itself, with its own history, which in turn is part of this image pool. So can painting not just act innocent, as if it had just been discovered, as a novel way of applying colorful wet stuff to a surface and letting it dry? Sure it can. But it must then expect to be perceived as decoration, as flatly commercial, or as the work of an amateur. All these are nonetheless qualities which intelligent painting can embrace—as long as it does so deliberately.

Painting has reached a certain degree of saturation: What is there left that hasn't been seen? Maybe this is the challenge to painting, to make visible that which resists visibility: the decision-making processes, the effects of power and powerlessness that run through society and resonate in the slightest physical sensations of every individual. That, in other words, of which mass media images are symptomatic at best, but which dictates the placement and presentation of these images themselves. Might this be a worthy task for painting? To play out the micromechanics of decision-making in the realm of applying paint to canvas, even envisioning possible new decisions? Here, the acts leading to a picture's particular motif coincide directly with those concerning its material form, which shape the process of its creation—painting as a kind of solitary séance of possible, even new ways of seeing and acting.

Perhaps it makes sense to name two poles between which contemporary painting unfolds. My choice here is Gerhard Richter on the one hand and Maria Lassnig on the other. This choice is as well founded as it is arbitrary. One could also take other historical vectors extending to the present—say, Jasper Johns on the one hand, and Willem de Kooning on the other. What matters here, in any case, is to identify the creative process in the resulting pictures and to grasp this process as decisive. To understand why the classic schisms of modern painting—abstraction versus figuration, reproduction versus unique original—are just two of the possible conflicts that can be contained in a painting. To understand why it was long possible, and may still be today, to make interesting paintings that merely isolate and repeat banal, found motifs, sometimes even delegating this repetition to other painters or machines. And why it was equally possible, for a long time and maybe still today, to make interesting paintings that do *not* isolate and repeat motifs from the outside world, concentrating instead on a single "motif"—for example, the artist's own body, which is present in front of the canvas but which is so hard to grasp. How can I watch my own eye in the process of seeing, and how can I do justice to the other forms of perception by painterly means?

These, then, are the two extremes: either wresting a kind of inscrutable elegance from the banality of the objectivized world, or wresting something akin to dignity and wit from one's own obvious but ungraspable presence. One inhabits the two-dimensional world of endlessly duplicated pictures and forms, showing details and versions, simplifications, and commentaries. The other brings three- or even four-dimensionality back into play—physical presence in the here and now. Finally, both seal the long farewell to the Renaissance idea of single-point perspective, a pictorial space that can only be seen undistorted in its full harmonious beauty from one viewing position. But this idea of harmony and beauty in a strictly regulated space cannot simply be countered with claims of "everything's possible…" and its inevitable, bitter correlate: "… and nothing matters." As Sigmar Polke has been demonstrating since the 1960s, contemporary painting stays interesting when it moves between the above-mentioned poles without reconciling them.

The concrete issues, then, are as follows: What, beyond its mere market value, might be interesting about painting? What are the current developments in painting as an activity and as something I come face to face with in exhibitions? Before we can address these issues, however, we need to clear away some discursive debris that is closely connected to the market and the laws governing its ups and downs. Two persistent assertions, as big and heavy as boulders, obscure our view: first, the claim of "the end of painting," and second, when this end fails to materialize, the claim that "painting is possible again at last."

# Mock Battle at Mt. Taboo: Neo Rauch, Uwe Henneken (Douglas Crimp/Yve-Alain Bois)

Between 2003 and 2005, the "possible again at last" line was on many minds. Group shows of contemporary painting mushroomed. People who had a professional interest in art, but who had clearly not been to a gallery or fair for ten years, felt inspired to sing the praises of the paintbrush's long-awaited return to favor. And there were labels to match: "New Leipzig School," "New German Painting." Nicolaus Schafhausen, then curator at Frankfurter Kunstverein, caused a stir by smugly naming his major overview "germanpainting2003." The three elements of this title alone—nation, medium, date—gave rise to a flood of debate in German newspapers. In a similar vein, Charles Saatchi's declaration of a "Triumph of Painting" in the form of a three-part mammoth exhibition in London was greeted by musings about whether or not painting's hour had come round at last. For these debates, whether in relation to Frankfurt or London, the actual selection of works featured in these shows was of little importance. There might just as well have been a show of "Painting by Men with Big Feet" to give this other hard-done-by group its dues at long last.

The absurd thing is that since the mid-1990s, if not before, painting was far from banned. Since the collapse of the art market around 1988, painting seemed to have exhausted itself, becoming overblown and idiotic; what since the early 1980s had been produced in the name of "hunger for pictures" and "intensity" became sated and dull quicker than some might have hoped. For a short time, until around 1995, it may have appeared to the casual observer that the scene was now dominated by a hunger for analysis and talk about the conditions of the art world and society, a trend that also tarnished the aura of oil on canvas. But at the very same time, alongside this move toward Neo-Conceptualism and institutional critique, paintings continued to be made and sold at a healthy pace. The impact of video and installations notwithstanding, it was possible from around 1993 to earn not only critical acclaim with painting, but also money. Moreover, painting was increasingly relevant as a medium for reflecting both visual culture and art history.

In other words, claims are made in the name of non-existent taboos. This is especially striking in the rare cases where painting is omitted from major exhibitions—a reaction (part defensive, part aggressive) to the medium's unbroken dominance. Those who "stand up for painting" are either fighting a mock battle or perpetuating a senile border guard mentality that says true art is found only on canvases and plinths. The triumphant "painting is possible again at last" of the years 2003 to 2005, then, was an attempt to pretend there were still picture taboos that needed opposing.

Neo Rauch, too, likes to present himself in interviews as an avenger of the disinherited, assuring the rightful place of figurative painting in the face of its over-intellectual enemies. He actually has no need for such posturing; if there's one artist associated with the notion of a "New Leipzig School" whose work—whether one likes it or not—can be taken seriously as a contribution to contemporary debate on painting, then it is Neo Rauch (and also Matthias Weischer, whose hermetic, theatrically complex interiors explore different terrain). Throughout the 1990s, Rauch's pictures were populated by backdrops and marginal figures from the memory bank of the industrialized world. Interestingly, this includes both sides of the Iron Curtain. Gas stations and quayside cranes, transformer stations and shopkeepers' scales, combine harvesters and hydroelectric dams, warehouses and scaffolding, all in the drab colors of a well-regulated world that looks like it was drawn up on gray cardboard: men with severe haircuts and women with rock-hard perms go about their mysterious business, like cronies of the McCarthy and Stalin eras meeting in a David Lynch film. Welcome to Potemkin's Village—in the guise of an American industrial park. Of the barren realist academicism of his teachers Arno Rink and Bernhard Heisig, Rauch kept just what he needed for his brand of Pop Surrealism: an interest in the organization of pictorial space as a peopled, many-layered stage; a knowledge of the history of painting and painting techniques; a skill, refined over years, in linking pictorial layers and planes of color; and an awareness of the history of the portrayal of industrialization and its working environments. There is a lithography by the French illustrator Louis Charles Bombled which gives a detailed view of a huge panorama being built for the Paris World's Fair in 1900 and which bears a striking resemblance to Rauch's visual universe (apart from the beards and hats). Here too, layers of illusion and reality are wedged into one another amid scaffolds, cast-iron boilers, and set painting.

In recent years, however, while clinging stubbornly to his principles of com-position, Rauch has shifted the focus of his reservoir of ideological images and forms from the Cold War and its local repercussions back toward the nine-teenth century. It's no real surprise that Rauch has often named Ernst Jünger as a source of inspiration. There's also his 2006 collaboration (providing chalk drawings for a volume of calendar stories) with German playwright Botho Strauß, another more recent advocate of old-school heroic catharsis in lan-guage. Although Rauch lacks Strauß's ranting pathos, there is a closeness to the playwright's lighter, humoresque moments and an overall similarity between Rauch's choices of motif and Strauß's cranky mannerist allegories: finely chiseled, rattling musical boxes with a metallic sound. Correspondingly, in statements on his work, Rauch—half playful, half serious—affects a soldierly rhetoric. In an interview with German news weekly *Der Spiegel*, for example, he says he had to put on "the old trench uniform" to repel criticism from abstract painters. This is echoed in his most recent pictures: instead of agricultural equipment, there are tanks and rocket launchers; the heads are smaller in relation to the bodies, the colors bolder and more garish, and the costumes even more absurd. Taken to-gether, his statements and his pictures give the impression that, for some people, criticism feels a little too like lèse-majesté.

The pictures seem to be full of ciphers for warring discourse. In the monu-mental *Der Vorträger* (The Reciter, 2006), an apprentice reads aloud from a book, alone on a stage with his hand in his trouser pocket, surrounded by empty speech-bubble graffiti. Directly opposite him stands a tank draped with garlands, on top of which a man festooned with grenades is just helping his scarlet-clad female comrade out of the hatch. At the edge of the stage, a haranguing blue-yellow demon in an orange cardigan accusingly holds out a strip of zigzag-folded paper toward the speaker. Is this monster a critic, and the folded paper his ideal of Conceptual art? On this we can only speculate; Rauch plays his tarot cards close to his chest.

Admittedly, compared with other proponents of new romantic flights of fancy, Neo Rauch appears distinctly un-mysterious, a veritable stickler for clarity. Again and again, Romanticism is vaguely evoked in works that have nothing to offer but a revival of romantic motifs. Caspar David Friedrich as the uber-daddy of a world populated by lonely young and middle-aged people, in the forest or at the lakeside. The not-so-great galleries are full of this stuff. As a movement in the early nineteenth century, Romanticism actually embodied a critique of instrumental reason and its false certainties: Novalis and Friedrich Schlegel, fragment and open form, the progressive and the retrograde, the ambivalent and the effusive, nature and inwardness. But in the method of these works, little of all this remains. In the paintings of Scottish artist Christopher Orr—fogeyish gems in model railway format—human figures stand around forlornly in ravines of fog. Uwe Henneken is a counterexample. Romantic motifs do appear in his work (churning storm clouds, a burnt-out oak tree), but he heightens their colors and doesn't merely draw on them as a reservoir of the weird and wonderful. Potential associations with Biedermeier romanticist Carl Spitzweg are countered by the requisite stiff dose of humor. One of Henneken's pictures, *Fliegenfänger* (Flycatcher, 2006), even seems to be a direct quote, but here, the characteristic hunched bourgeois gent of Spitzweg's small genre idylls appears only as a shadow which seems to have detached itself from its owner like in a bad dream, but which is being pestered by a very realistically portrayed blowfly.

Henneken works with the tradition, but he doesn't settle down in it. The apologists of a school of painting whose only legitimization is found in regressive defiance, on the other hand, give their "end of painting" argument a positive spin in terms of "possible again at last." At some point, they claim—maybe as early as Kazimir Malevich's *Black Square* (1914/15)—the limit of a "last possible picture" was reached; this was the ultimate in abstraction; there's nothing left to say. According to this view, there's nothing left in painting but variations on what has already been accomplished. Whereas the logical conclusion would be to say that painting is obsolete, the revisionists simply turn this around and say: now that the last picture has been painted, we can paint without a care in the world.

The assumption that painting was a medium with an expiration date has always had a strongly polemic function within the debate surrounding art's role in society. In the early 1980s, with his essays "The End of Painting" and "The

Photographic Activity of Postmodernism," the influential critic Douglas Crimp was writing above all against an understanding of painting as an expressive trace. At the time, this view was once more doing the rounds of the galleries in the form of so-called Neo-Expressionism. For Crimp, only Ad Reinhardt's black pictures, Daniel Buren's stripe pictures, and Robert Ryman's white pictures— all painterly negations of this notion of an expressive painterly gesture—were acceptable as worthy end points. This attack was sparked off by the (much delayed) impact of Walter Benjamin's essay "The Work of Art in the Age of Mechanical Reproduction" (1935/36). Today, even the title of this text has been reproduced to death, but in the early 1980s, it contained fresh ideas regarding the increasingly everyday presence of color reproductions of pictures.

Reinterpreting Benjamin's theory that technical duplication robs the artwork of its authentic here and now, and thus of its "aura," Crimp recast the "withering away of the aura" as a liberation from the "idiotic" pretensions of the hand-made, arguing that the "aura" is in fact resurrected precisely by the absence of a graspable original in the artistic appropriations of photographers like Richard Prince, who photographed found advertising photographs, or Cindy Sherman, who posed as female role models for stills from movies that were never made. The ghostly apparition of all the culturally cemented stereotypes and poses of women and men, yuppies and plebs, is encountered in isolation, severed from an ostensibly authentic origin.

A slightly different tack was taken by art historian Yve-Alain Bois in his text "Painting: The Task of Mourning" (1986). He, too, considers Robert Ryman exemplary, and the avant-garde painter is portrayed as the Last Mohican of resistance to the capitalist colonization of all realms of life that has reduced art, too, to a mere commodity fetish—as if solitary heroics, of all things, could offer salvation from the profanation of art. But this in fact reproduces one possible strategy of capitalism, namely the niche market in highly sophisticated luxury and contrived scarcity. Painters like Peter Halley, who in the 1980s simulated and subverted modernist abstraction with an ironic undertone, are accused by Bois of merely cannibalizing the sublimity of the classics. Borrowing a term from the philosopher Jean Baudrillard, he calls them "manic mourners." The true task of contemporary painting, he says, can only be to continue working through the legacy of painting as an act of mourning.

Whether manic or not, mourning, understood as the ability to remember, is always preferable to obliviousness. Painters who load their figurative pictures with mass media markers of banality or glamour or both—weapons, rock stars, teenage sex, trout pouts—to boost their impact would do well to consider that compared with purely mechanical reproduction of an existing image, a faithful copy in paint of the same image often asserts just one thing: "Look, I've taken the trouble to paint this, so it must be ennobled as an observation and as a picture." But in many cases, the observation has long since been made, which only leaves the ennobling. The idea of taking the art context into consideration, frowned on for being too much like homework, is replaced by the diligence of a teacher's pet. Warhol's painting-by-numbers pictures from 1962 were an early, intelligent statement on precisely this. And the point of John Baldessari's commissioned works from 1969 (executed by amateur painters) and Martin Kippenberger's series *Lieber Maler, male mir* (Dear painter, paint me, produced by a professional poster artist) was not to reenact the painterly mimesis of banal or glamorous motifs, but to demonstratively delegate routine tasks.

With its wild gestures and surreal motifs, "primitive" painting of the kind that has in recent years once more been heroically resisting this paradigm of the good, hard-working, photo-realist brush-worker, is sadly often just as oblivious to history. As if punk had never happened, and as if Pollock had never happened, metaphorical or actual testicles are dragged through the paint again as the wild man leaves his mark. Whether insolently slapdash or meticulously tidy, what's missing in both this primitivism and the various gradations of photo-realism is a certain interesting unruliness of the material, the sometimes laborious quality of the old-fashioned game of paint on surface.

Now, as always, interesting painting means those new pictures that could only have come about in painting and not in any other way. The "new" doesn't exist as a sparkling clean something out of nothing, but as the dirt that gets stuck in the spirals of history (the spiral as a model of development that is neither linear nor cyclical; dirt as that which at first just seems to be left over but which then takes on meaning after all). Of course, the Modernist dreams of a tabula rasa, universal validity, and radical newness are passé—but, one should not continue to expect painting to content itself with well-behaved skillfulness or sleepy convention.

Today, be it in New York or Berlin or elsewhere, anyone perusing the many galleries and art fairs will find themselves facing quite a glut of bad "pictures in the style of," which—obviously with some success—attach themselves like hungry ghosts to the souls of aspiring young collectors who don't know what

54  Neo Rauch, The Reciter, 2006
55  Uwe Henneken, Flycatcher, 2006
56  Tomma Abts, Ewo, 2006
57  Tomma Abts, Meko, 2006
58  Tomma Abts, Ehme, 2002

they're doing. Be it industrious copycats in the slipstream of the Leipzig School or other gems (cute high-gloss porn and neo-romantic retro remain popular), these pictures will probably be bought like ill-fitting clothes by someone who feels awkward leaving a store empty-handed after trying things on for two hours. If there's one characteristic of the avant-garde that is worth salvaging, it's the intransigent rattling at the bars of things long established. This is something which neither tautological reflection on the world of painting itself nor mere recourse to photographed and filmed reality can even begin to replace.

# Reproduction versus Uniqueness I: Gerhard Richter, Glenn Brown (Feat. Tomma Abts)

Despite being in huge demand, there *are* paintings that still have a spark of self-doubt in them, as if asking: Am I really needed? But let's assume for the moment that painting doesn't have any such problems of legitimization. Regarding a conscious approach both to competition from technically reproduced pictures and to the history of painting itself, there's no need to worry about either Gerhard Richter or Glenn Brown. But regarding the productive aspect of self-doubt in their work, a different question poses itself: What is the relationship between the actions and decisions that shape a painting and our own actions and decisions as physical and social beings? I'm not concerned here with a direct, linear link between a painter's biography and psychology and the way he or she paints. Nor am I talking about the idea that has existed since Impressionism, if not before, of a "literal translation" of the finest nuances of perception into painterly marks.

The abstract painting of Tomma Abts is a good place to begin outlining this issue in more detail. As critic Jan Verwoert has pointed out in an essay on her work, the question of the decision-making process in painting cannot be satisfactorily answered by pointing to either the rational intention or the irrational intuition of the painter, as both falsely imply a congruence between starting point, realization, and end result. It is, as Verwoert says, rather the case that painting, "on the basis of its irreducible inner differentiatedness," produces "its own form of rationalism." This sounds less abstract when you actually look at a painting by Abts; you immediately see in concrete terms how it appears to be governed by rules of its own, a sequence of freedoms of choice. She always starts with the same size canvas, a classical portrait format, vertical, forty-eight by thirty-eight centimeters. What emerge are clearly defined forms, more complexly fractal than strictly and simply geometrical. But what at first looks like two-dimensional origami or psychedelic wallpaper turns out on closer inspection to be more like polygonal volumes flattened and pressed into the surface, as if a cosmic steamroller had run over constellations of wildly orbiting planets (Abts paints on a table, the canvas horizontal). These constellations are not planned, however. Abts begins without a model or a sketch, without any fixed idea of the result. In the course of a process of overpainting, she raises forms out of the surface or lays them bare in areas she has masked. At a given moment in this often lengthy procedure, the picture comes to life, taking on a creature-like vibrancy, the shapes forming a kind of binding congruency. Identifying this moment is the final decision involved in the making of each individual picture (followed by other decisions, including how it should be exhibited). It is a play with inherent dynamism, with the unruliness of the process as compared with total permeation by the artist's will. So there is something supra-subjective at play here, something that owes a debt on one hand to the autonomy of the painterly process—and, on the other, to everything that is not painting.

There are behavioral analogies between the solitary decisions of painting and decisions made in the social world. Painterly acts can be read as the ritual mimesis of possible social acts: you get the same systematic, logical, self-confident, even stubborn pressing ahead; but you also get the same tactical obfuscation by modifying, reworking, or blotting out acts once performed and decisions once arrived at, followed in turn by recall and retrieval. Seen this way, the canvas becomes a kind of two-dimensional voodoo doll that "magically" interferes with the weave of decisions made in the social environment, and with the reactions to them—a voodoo doll, however, that also instantly rejects this proxy function and, like the artist-individual, insists on having its own way.

With his paintings made after photographic originals, Richter developed a "manual-mechanical" working method which—once the choice of motif and coloration has been made—at least rigorously holds in check, if not entirely prevents, any impulsive interference in the painting process. Unlike Dada, his appropriation of existing source images is not based on montage/collage, but simply on copying, as in Pop art. The liberating thing about this approach, developed in the mid-1960s, was the way it made the painter-as-subject disappear in the individual paintings (the artist no longer expresses himself via interventions in the source), while emphasizing it all the more in the context of his series and procedures (as an arranger, seer, exemplary-professional viewer of pictures). The crisis-ridden nature of the process of painting is "regulated," from the initial choice of motif to the final smudging techniques, the painterly equivalent of photographic blurring or camera wobble perfected by Richter. The details and the composition of the chosen motif are fixed in advance and accepted as such by the artist through his selection, although he may use cropping and subtle changes in perspective to accentuate and influence the picture's impact in decisive ways. For example, in his "RAF Cycle," the series of works on the Baader-Meinhof terrorists, he cropped the original image of the dead Andreas Baader in two ways, once showing a hand on the end of a thin arm (*Man Shot Down 1*, 1988), and once not showing it, reinforcing the impression that the dead body is floating (*Man Shot Down 2*, 1988). On the path from starting point to end result there are no mannerisms, no moods—just stoic realization.

In spite of this, there is scope for the unexpected within these strict rules. Writing in 1985 about his abstract pictures, Gerhard Richter noted that painting is a "blind, desperate effort, like that of a person abandoned, helpless, in totally incomprehensible surroundings." He neither knows in advance what the picture should look like, he writes, nor does he know where he is aiming as he paints. Richter also plays down the difference between his non-figurative pictures and those painted from photographs, adding in brackets that in "other cases"—that is, non-abstract pictures—"the problem is very much the same." But that is the question here: Are the "surroundings" really so "incomprehensible" for the "abandoned person" if that person is working from photographs?

Even in the exceptional cases where impulsiveness does seem to occur (functioning as a kind of commentary), it is subsumed under the program, as in the early picture *Party* (1962) and in the much later cycle from 1995 in which Richter portrayed his third wife Sabine Moritz and their newly born son Moritz. In *Party*—painted one year after Richter's relocation from East to West Germany—four dressed-up women in party mood sit side by side, legs crossed, a tuxedoed man in their midst, like them cheerily lifting a punch glass for the black-and-white snapshot. But there is blood flowing from the man's mouth into his glass, and the women are covered in cuts—made in the canvas with a knife, and crudely stitched up like wounds with blood-red thread. The original on which the picture is based is included in Richter's *Atlas*, the compendium of image material begun in 1962, to which he is still adding and which consists of over four thousand cuttings, photographs, and sketches, arranged into over six hundred full-page plates. The man in the picture turns out to be Vico Torriani, a Swiss-German popular singer who came to epitomize the singing Mr. Nice Guy with hits whose titles translate as "Pineapple From Caracas" and "Calcutta Lies On The Ganges." He was a star in the West Germany of the 1950s and early 1960s, a society that enthusiastically plunged itself into travel and partying in its efforts to forget. Richter's intent is obvious: the crude quotation of canvas slicing à la Lucio Fontana is meant to literally lacerate the skin of this jolly party atmosphere. The strategy is far too simple, as if it were possible to highlight repression or hypocrisy just by tearing through a "surface." Richter quickly recognized this himself, henceforth avoiding such demonstrative gestures.

In 1995, Richter painted eight pictures entitled *S. with Child*. This series stands out not so much because even the original photograph taken by Richter himself refers bluntly to the familiar iconography of the Madonna and child, or because it could be read as violating his own principle of not allowing his pictures to be reduced to an underlying biographical truth. Instead, it stands out because the "concessions" to a conservative model—firm roots in art history, revealing the private as a heroic artistic act, and portrayal of a woman in a traditionally "female" role—are demonstratively counteracted in six of the eight pictures by a concession to modern distancing from all of this in the form of Richter's positively brutal use of a palette knife or spatula, scraping across the entire picture surface like soiled rollers inside a photographic developing machine. In contrast to the gentler blurring that not only creates a technically uniform surface, but also an aura of light and memory, these scrapes suggest gnawingly impulsive doubt that expresses itself as a vandalistic attack on the freshly completed picture.

But this balancing of conservative self-presentation and iconoclastic doubt feels contrived and as such not doubting at all. The primary subject here is the persona of the mature painter himself, who, following his divorce from Isa Genzken, whom he married in 1982 when she was already a well-known sculptress in her own right, now paints a picture of the young mother, a former student in his painting class, holding his firstborn son, with himself, as the father, in the role of the absent authority who is very much present, directing everything—the perspectives, the framing, the distribution of roles, the suggestions of closeness and distance. With the knife scrapes, Richter demonstrates to a broad art audience that he knows he cannot paint a straight Madonna without rendering his project absurd. At the same time, however, he signals to a "narrower" art scene,

59

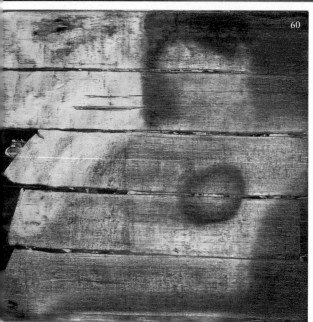

60

61

**Gerhard Richter**

59     Man Shot Down 2, 1988
60     S. with Child, 1995
61     Self-Portrait, 1996

with its rumors about the relationship between the paintings and his private life, that he reserves the right to interpret and present that life. But Richter may have sensed that this role of Joseph playing God (for who else can this father be, who portrays mother and child like Mary and Jesus?) was a dead end. In 1996, he made two self-portraits, the only "photo-realistic" ones in his oeuvre (an earlier picture, *Untitled (self-portrait)*, from 1971, is a blurry abstract). One shows Richter lit harshly from the front against a dark shadow, staring out past the camera, in a blue shirt and scarf, looking vulnerable and tired; the second picture, this time with thicker, blacker frames on his glasses and wearing a tie, Yves Saint Laurent-style, shows him looking down at the ground as if in concentration, the portrait blurred as if behind opaque glass, unapproachable.

But—to emphasize this once again—we are not interested here in speculations about which private motivations lie "behind" the choice and subsequent treatment of photographic images. For Richter's work (and not least his abstract paintings) shows the importance of painterly method to any understanding of the way the painter relates to his own actions. In the case of one group of his purely abstract compositions, including pictures made in 1995 immediately before and after the mother and child series, Richter leaves the making of the picture as far as possible to a particularly extreme manual-mechanical painting technique: In one movement, he draws a large spatula over the picture support. Both techniques (blurring the image and using a spatula) are analogous not so much to "biomorphic" movement as to industrial and technical processes—to the imprecision of a photographic image on one hand and the spreading of ink in screen printing on the other. These final steps in the painting process, then, involve either micro-movements (a soft swishing brush) or macro-movements (the large spatula) that are not typical for the human body. There are also abstract compositions, like the *Inpaintings* of the 1970s, where Richter was evidently aiming for gestural processuality. It's as if he is deliberately pushing richly gestural approaches from Informel to Abstract Expressionism into entropy. Instead of creating compositional spaces or a dynamic allover (a texture of marks covering the entire surface of the canvas), he skillfully "muddles" the picture ground in the way he spreads the paint, as though the gestural had become a robotically self-executing advance into the void.

At first sight, then, one might think that Richter skeptically and specifically rejects decision-making once the painterly process has been set in motion. That, in other words, "decision" is only to be found—as in many examples from

Conceptual art—in the original idea and in the result once presented, while between these two points a kind of automatic process takes place. This is one of the main reasons why his name is often linked with Conceptualism. And indeed he does shift the focus of artistic decision-making onto the structural level of the organization of an inventory-based pictorial system, the *Atlas*, or onto a systematically deployed inventory of techniques of painterly abstraction. However—and this is crucial here—he does so without denying himself the manual realization of his paintings (with one known exception, in the early 1970s, when he sometimes used assistants to help produce his *Color Charts*). This particular aspect sets him clearly apart from Conceptualism.

Why, unlike Baldessari and Kippenberger, did Richter never have his paintings executed by well-trained commercial artists? Stock answers include: because he deploys a specific manual technique which only he has really fully mastered, and because he invests the pictorial motif with a specifically affective charge, calling for quasi-ritual engagement with the act of painting. Neither of these suggestions is wrong, of course, but both fail to address the question of the decision and the actions determined by that decision. The painter sets up a game, the point of which is that he submits to the execution of self-imposed tasks, whatever the consequences.

Richter's eureka-like discovery, in the mid-1960s, that a banal photograph from real life can lead to a painting opened up a radical freedom in decisions for or against possible motifs: stags, airplanes, kings, secretaries. But this radical freedom only makes sense if it goes hand-in-hand with a radical suppression of his own persona as the executor of the work. He's his own master when the choice of motif and detail is being made, but his own minion when this decision is being enacted and transferred to the canvas. Social power struggles are transposed into the painter's relationship with himself: The total freedom of a choice based on taste, and the equally total submission to the consequences of this choice as the "executing assistant" once the decision has been made.

The English painter Glenn Brown always works from existing paintings (in the form of reproductions in books). In the pantheon of painters he takes as his points of reference, there's a wide span between the two ends of a spectrum of possible relationships between painterly and social acts. One end is very clearly defined by Gerhard Richter, who has been crucial to Brown's artistic approach, although he has not, to my knowledge, ever directly provided the source material for any of Brown's paintings. The other end is marked by Frank Auerbach, whose working methods are diametrically opposed to Brown's, but who has served all the more frequently as a source. Oscillating between these two poles in Brown's visual world is a scintillating palette of overexcited surrealisms and undermined expressionisms.

In the case of Frank Auerbach and the working method which he has pursued as steadfastly as Richter for over half a century, the relationship of master and minion is very different, as is the nature of the decisions involved. As a portrait artist, his characteristic focus on live sitters recalls the relationship of analyst and analysand. Once a week, at a fixed time, the story told by the patient is overwritten (over-painted) afresh. Where Richter controls the crisis by structural means, Auerbach emphatically unleashes it. During the genesis of a painting, the question as to who, in this relationship of painter and sitter, is master and who is minion is poised precariously (to use the terminology of psychoanalysis) between transference and countertransference. And, as in the relationship of analysand and analyst, there must also be an element (at least potentially) of sexual attraction. This in itself is problematic, since Auerbach's characteristic impasto style inevitably suggests a direct parallel between the depth of the paint applied and the depth of a sensual touch.

So when Glenn Brown refers to his own working method—especially with respect to his portraits—as "voyeuristic," he is not just being ironic. The voyeur, by definition, does not intervene in the action. However, the depth of the "sensual touch" he feels is—as an imagined action—located in the infinite realm of the imagination. On one hand, this relates to the fact that Brown only works from paintings (Richter only does this on rare occasions, as when he recreates details from his own abstract compositions, or when he copied and "blurred" Titian's *Annunciation*). On the other hand, it also relates to the act of painting itself. In Brown's work, not unlike Richter's paintings from photographs, the main effort goes into executing micro-motoric movements, movements that are "bodiless" in the sense that they, like writing, require everything apart from the hand to be at rest.

Like Richter, then, Brown is his own master when it comes to decisions concerning motif, framing, and dimensions (although, unlike Richter, it's not unusual for him to combine a number of source images, which in fact takes him closer to what Richter would no doubt regard as the vulgarly manipulative working methods of Salvador Dalí). But, again like Richter, he is also his own minion when such decisions are being transferred to the canvas. Frank Auerbach offered

Brown the eureka of a liberating escape route from the endgame that this working method seemed to entail. In his series based on Auerbach portraits (made between 1998 and 2000), Brown rendered their gestural application of paint as a high-gloss print, thus completely robbing them of their corporealness, their physical fullness. He did the same with Georg Baselitz's feet: Brown turns the crude portraits of the German artist's feet (made since 1963 with the toes pointing upward in anticipation of his later upside-down pictures) into a surface that possesses a delicately rotten shimmer but that is totally smooth and immaculate, as smooth and immaculate as *The Osmond Family*, the 1970s pop group after whom Brown's picture from 2003 is named.

But Brown's "flattening" is not merely ironic. It is a statement on physicality itself and its relationship to the world. To describe this with a comment by critic and curator Robert Storr on Richter, which to a certain extent also applies to Brown, he "removed the body as the agency of the psyche or spirit." Yet this is also the point where Brown fundamentally differs from Richter. The latter's removal of the body from his subject matter has, over the decades, increasingly been directed toward achieving a form of the sublime (usually secular but sometimes openly religious) that wavers between cruel and merciful, whereas in Glenn Brown's case the "poison" of contamination with the body is in evidence (that is, embarrassment). Even where Richter rhetorically allows doubt and failure to feature in his work, he has increasingly banned unpredictability from the actual results (which may also explain the growing lack of humor in his pictures). "To some extent each painting is a controlled failure," Brown once said, pointing the way to an understating of the function of embarrassment in his work. After all, embarrassment is nothing other than failed sublimity. The squashed Baselitz feet and Auerbach heads, flattened like something run over by Bugs Bunny's bulldozer, are an almost banal cipher for this.

The idea of action and decision as it appears in Brown's pictures vacillates between the absurdly exaggerated pathos of the ultimate solitary act—suicide—and the sobering, realistic embarrassment of erotic undertakings, such as a failed sexual approach. This spectrum is illustrated by two exemplary works: *Exercise One (For Ian Curtis) After Chris Foss* (1995), a picture from the series of paintings based on originals by the science-fiction painter Chris Foss and dedicated to Ian Curtis; and *Three Wise Virgins* (2004), one of Brown's oil-paint sculptures. Ian Curtis, legendary singer of the nihilist-romantic punk band Joy Division, hanged himself and his cat in 1980. In order to paint the series, Brown "detached

**Glenn Brown**

62     Exercise One (For Ian Curtis) After Chris Foss (copied from the illustration "Asteroid Hunters" 1979), 1995

63     The Osmond Family, 2003

64     Three Wise Virgins, 2004

[himself] … from the world," as he has said, describing the feeling of long, late hours in the studio. *Exercise One*, the painting of a rock floating lost in space, resonates with the hopelessly sad ridiculousness which is attached to the act of suicide and of which Curtis was well aware (he is said to have been listening to Iggy Pop's album *The Idiot* that night). Here the pop surrealism of space stations in cosmic mist that dominates other paintings in this series is altogether absent: an ice-bound rock, like the Matterhorn flung into outer space by some monstrous power, is caught in the orbit of a large, cold planet.

*Three Wise Virgins* is a sculptural object made using oil paint that stands there as a polymorphous lump in the White Cube, the standardized, neutralized exhibition space. Compared with Brown's imagined visual worlds, it embodies the sobering reality of the downward pull of gravity for which sculpture has often been derided ever since Baudelaire's day. The title points to the biblical parable (very popular in the Middle Ages) about the wise virgins who, unlike their foolish counterparts, took extra oil for their lamps when they went to attend a wedding ceremony, so as not to miss out on the honor of a nocturnal encounter with the bridegroom. So the parable is about foresight, about actions where oil gives control over future events. But Brown's three wise virgins are actually fools: Three red balls protrude like clowns' noses from this turmoil of disordered, not exactly virginal-looking corporeality. Forward planning—be it administration of society or the control of the artistic process—becomes slapstick: the collapse of grace as the last great act.

# Reproduction versus Uniqueness II: Maria Lassnig, Dana Schutz

Whereas Richter decided to restrict his subject matter to existing photographic motifs or pure abstraction, from the 1950s on Maria Lassnig did the exact opposite, focusing exclusively on conscious perception of her own body, minus (insofar as this is even possible) what she could see in mirrors and photographs. But it was not about the unconscious, at least not in the Surrealist sense. Lassnig— who was born in 1919, grew up in Carinthia, Austria, and studied during the war in Vienna—did experience the tail end of Surrealism in early-1950s Paris, meeting André Breton through Paul Celan and persuading Benjamin Péret to write a prose text for her portfolio of drawings (which did display a residual Surrealist influence). But the Surrealist technique of automatic writing interested her not so much as a method of giving "unmediated" expression to the psyche in words or drawings, but rather as the starting point for a method of more conscious transfer from the sphere of bodily experience. In other words, in the era of French phenomenology à la Maurice Merleau-Ponty, she is (without having actually studied him) much closer to his concept of corporeality than to the Freudian school. Merleau-Ponty speaks of the experience of ambiguity when a person's own two hands touch each other (the inseparable overlapping of the sensation of "outside" and "inside"). For a moment, subject and object are one. The painterly equivalent to this is unagitated, alert rather than tense. There's none of Jackson Pollock's paint-dripping dance over the canvas, that speaks less of an introspection of physical sensation than of its ecstatic relinquishing. And there's certainly none of the theatrical speed-painting of someone like Georges Mathieu, who translated Pollock's dance into an indulgent crowd-pleaser: In 1956, Mathieu performed at a Paris theater for an audience of two thousand, finishing a huge picture with hundreds of tubes of paint in half an hour; thanks to Mathieu's calligraphic bent, the results were always surprisingly decorative.

At this time, everyone, especially the men, still had the experience of fighting World War II in their bodies, followed by the austere order of the early Cold War. It is this which, in the less accomplished moments of Tachisme or Informel (the European answers to Abstract Expressionism), seems to come out as a kind of flailing about in front of the canvas, a gestural displacement activity resulting from numbed physicality. In Lassnig's work, however, motor functions do not constitute the emphatic, demonstrative element. Instead of all the grand theatrical gestures of the men, she made pictures called "static meditations," which trace the border between the body and the surrounding space like a series of accurately thrown lassos, as clear dark lines on a white ground. These lines soon increase in density, becoming what Lassnig calls "dumplings," a term which, with inimitable concision, anticipates the disrespect that's sure to be directed at painting that dismisses grand gestures. The dumpling sits on the plate—a round object with steam rising from it. The same is true of the painting of body awareness: it is tersely everyday, provocatively undramatic—but not to be underestimated!

The painterly idea of the body awareness pictures comes across not as mawkishly spiritual, but with an unyielding alertness and presence. In Lassnig's journal, there is an entry from 1980 in which she gives a precise description of the process of introspective body awareness that gives rise to most of her pictures:

"I draw and paint a picture in a particular body position, for example sitting down, resting on one arm you feel the shoulder blade, of the arm itself only the upper part, the palms of the hands like the grips on a crutch. I feel the points where my backside presses into the divan, my stomach because it's filled like a sack, my head is sunken into the cardboard box of the shoulder blades, the skull is open at the back, in my face I feel the nasal opening, as big as a pig's, and around it I feel the skin burning. I'll paint it red."

The comparisons with prostheses, simple containers (sack, cardboard box), and the earthbound, mud-loving pig are linguistic substitutes for that which becomes evident in the pictures, right up to Lassnig's current work, as in the picture titled *Drei Arten zu sein* (Three Ways of Being, 2004). An unraveled self-portrait of the eighty-five-year-old as someone affectively tracking herself down in three different ways of being—the exact opposite of the three monkeys who hear, see, and say nothing. On the left: squatting, back arched, in piglet pink and pistachio green, with the occasional heated transition to lavender-livid red, reduced to a torso, with a towering cyclopean physiognomy, the back of the head spread out to make a second face or a helmet. In the middle: a slouching scarlet figure with pig's snout and devil's tail. On the right, finally: the quiet echo of the left-hand self-image, but more laid-back, more relaxed, a pensive face with jutting cheekbones, resting on a hand; with a few strokes (orange and yellow are added), the white primed canvas becomes the body's color. All of this surrounded by bright yellow, slapped on with a relative lack of interest. "Background creates mood and atmosphere, and I don't need that," says Lassnig, still painting at her advanced age with the confidence of experience and with little patience or understanding for the mumbo-jumbo of diligently rendered Romantic or Surrealist mental landscapes. What remains is the sheer presence of the body, understood not as an emphatic presence but as something that is hard to grasp—as something far from identical with the already objectified image in the mirror or in the camera, and as something that seeks to communicate itself via the painterly imagination as a visual approximation in a succession of new variations. But it is nonetheless the same gravitational heaviness of the body that painting so long wished to see banished to sculpture, if not removed from art entirely.

The first possible misunderstanding, then, would be to see a kind of post-Surrealist expression of the psyche at work in Lassnig's oeuvre. The second misunderstanding, more serious than the first, would be to believe that Lassnig's

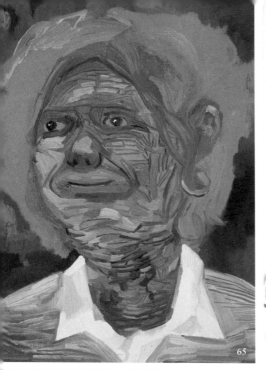

65      **Dana Schutz**, Self-Portrait as a Pachyderm, 2005
66      **Maria Lassnig**, Untitled (diagonal on two crutches), 2005
67      **Maria Lassnig**, Untitled, 2002
68      **Maria Lassnig**, Static Meditations, 1951–52

body awareness pictures are merely caricatures or grotesques. In spite of this, in pictures like the one just described, humor and distortion do play a part. It's the kind of humor that does without getting excited, preferring to work with the stoic principle of the deadpan—like when you suddenly have to burst out laughing because someone has simply stated the truth about a certain situation, a truth that's latently obvious to all present. It's not portrayal of the body as if in a funhouse mirror for amusement, but an attempt to visualize precisely that which a mirror cannot capture. This alone determines the "distortion" here—if only one knew what was being distorted and in what direction.

When Lassnig went to New York at the end of the 1970s (the time of the Apollo missions), she painted *Selbstporträt als Astronautin* (Self-Portrait as an Astronaut, 1968/69): Seen from above, she floats free, her head like the opening flap of a large yellow backpack that is also her torso, as if she has mutated into a cyborg, becoming one with the apparatus that makes life in airless space possible. Canadian theorist Marshall McLuhan, who understood media and machines as extensions of the human body, would have understood the picture immediately. But Lassnig's "body awareness paintings," as she herself calls them in English, met with little understanding in the United States. People thought they were looking at grotesque if not pathological fantasies. Her plight was not unlike that of Philip Guston, who around the same time abandoned Abstract Expressionism in favor of "impure" painting of figurative cartoon scenes that earned him mockery and hate. People accused Lassnig of not being able to paint, at least not like the American artists associated at the time with a resurgence of figurative realism. Like Alice Neel, for example, who in 1970 painted her famous portrait of Andy Warhol, eyes shut and naked from the waist up, the scars from his operation after the attempt on his life still visible. Or like Philip Pearlstein and his male and female nudes, painted in meticulous detail, often life-size and signaling bohemian liberal-mindedness, but in cramped, bourgeois-domestic settings. In terms of the possibility or impossibility of visualization, Lassnig's exploration of her own body is actually closer to what artists like Vito Acconci, Bruce Nauman, or Dan Graham were doing in performance and video.

But Lassnig is a painter, and so she turned for a time to a "realistic" mode of painting, orienting herself more strongly toward what the eye sees than what the body feels. *Selbstporträt mit Gurkenglas* (Self-Portrait with Gherkin Jar, 1971) is a garish green exercise from this period, showing the artist naked, holding the gherkin jar in front of her belly, her gaze going out past the viewer with an air of defiant reverie. At this time, Lassnig discovered the philosopher and physicist Ernst Mach, in particular the famous drawing he used to preface his *Beiträge zur Analyse der Empfindungen* (Contributions to the Analysis of the Sensations, 1886). We see the view out of his left eye as he lies on a chaise longue—the view out over his moustache. In 1972, Lassnig made a drawing that recalls this slightly, called *Die Verankerung* (Anchoring). The lower part of the body is reclining, seen from the point of view of the head, but with the upper body rolled up and away as if with the key from a sardine tin.

So if Lassnig decided at the beginning of her artistic career not to base her portrayals of the "figure" on anything she had seen, was her temporary turn to so-called "realism" a rotten compromise? Or just a coming to terms with the ineluctable nature of photographed reality? For, one might object, to ignore photography, to exclude what has been seen from perception, even if only for the moment, is not possible in any case; visual media have long since become part of the way we experience our own bodies every day, most obviously in postures and ways of walking: catwalk poses seen in *Vogue*, dance movements seen on television. How, then, can "body awareness" be separated from all "external" visualizations? But Lassnig is aware of this problem, and instead of simply asserting such a separation as an artistic fait accompli, she presents it as a horizon. "I really can achieve it, and I really want to," she says, even today: "But of course, it cannot be achieved totally. I admit that. It cannot be achieved totally."

Making something visible that cannot actually be seen or portrayed, at least not by making a reproduction, doesn't necessarily produce smoothness. At present, many painters are far too content to cleverly mix up a few more or less cleverly chosen visual sources. Lassnig's pungent approach is the antidote to all this empty elegance.

The work of young New York painter Dana Schutz opens up the possibility of carrying Lassnig's approach into a present where any attempt to separate body and media awareness has become impossible once and for all—but without the contradictions having simply resolved themselves. Like Lassnig, Schutz certainly doesn't always paint from existing sources. Many of her paintings show things that are hard even to imagine. Like someone eating his own face, eyes suspended like marbles in the hollow grotto of a mouth full of teeth and a phallic tongue, and no nose (*Face-Eater*, 2004). When she first came up with the idea of painting people eating themselves, around 2003, she was thinking of abstraction as something that needed to be kept in mind when making "figurative" work. As tired as the opposition between abstraction and figuration may be, Schutz's figures obviously bear on it. They create an allegory of the self-consuming history of painting, the teleology of an increasingly sophisticated emancipation from the representation of religious and then secular reality (in more recent paintings of 2007/2008, the "self-eaters" have been replaced by protagonists who are "singed" as if by the sudden onslaught of a nuclear explosion). We see a man lying on the ground, bending his leg to eat his foot (his mouth open toward the sky like one of Picasso's Guernica victims), forming an absurd rectangle that echoes the rectangle of the canvas, like a sick joke about self-referentiality (*Self-Eater 2*, 2003). At the same time, he becomes an allegory of painting as a system that depends on this history of sophistication and variation to legitimize itself as a competitor in contemporary visual production, in a digitized visual culture that consumes itself by producing an explosion of versions and copies of anything you can imagine—but not so much of things you can't.

To do interesting painting today means to challenge the historical amnesia and visual entropy of the digital image pool. Even if their stuff sells, painters are not privileged in this respect; instant success on the art market can easily turn into a long-term fate of critical disdain. Within the wider field of culture, painting remains quixotic. And so it's up to a painter like Dana Schutz to approach the matter with both self-assurance and skepticism. Her canvases are "too big," the way showy gold chains are too big, but also skeptical and at times bad-tempered, the way intelligent teenagers are in their loathing of the bland aestheticism and brash sexuality of pop-modernity. Schutz's pictures favor a carefully chosen palette of vomit and mold and rot, between pink and purple, turquoise and olive, ocher and crap. They gallop straight into the hitherto largely male-dominated field of painting that is self-consciously unfitting, an impure negation of solemnity and of political opportunism. The usual term for painting of this kind would be "grotesque," but in this case the word smacks too much of clownery and misses the subtler tones of the unfitting. Skin is a favorite theme for Schutz, not just in terms of coloration, but also as sculptural texture, perhaps most obviously and vividly in her *Self-Portrait as a Pachyderm* (2005). The artist, with a Prozac smile and druggy eyes whose whites are not white but lilac, gazes dreamily into the distance, her head surrounded by a glowing orange halo of hair, her rhino-thick skin protruding from the picture surface like tumors. It's as if Schutz is picturing herself, amid the hype surrounding her young career (she was born in 1976, started painting at age fifteen, and had her first solo show in 2002), as a female Yoda, as a painter who uses The Force to stabilize her ostensibly frail self.

Similarly ambivalent is the portrait of a bleached-blonde beach babe in Florida (*Daytona*, 2005). Her eyes are silly green marbles, her smile looks brain-drained, her skin like that of a grilled chicken. And yet there is a deep empathy for her that undermines the ridiculousness one might easily ascribe to an aging bimbo trying to forget her own physical decay, as she inhabits her specific landscape with the smug self-satisfaction of a Mona Lisa. Confidence and skepticism, empathy and parody don't cancel each other out or harmonize, but produce interesting paintings by a process of friction.

If one were to express the constellation described here using the examples of Richter and Brown, and Lassnig and Schutz, in pairs of opposites, then the classical Modernist question of abstraction versus figuration is combined with Benjamin's theme of reproduction versus original. Richter approaches abstraction/figuration in terms of reproduction, while Lassnig does the same in terms of the original ("original" understood here as a moment of the unique in the relationship between painter and painting). Not that Richter's works are not "originals," but his pictures result from the structuring of reproduced photographs, and even the purely abstract pictures exorcize the "original" by the anonymizing use of manual-mechanical techniques. He exercises a radical freedom in his choice of motifs that only makes sense within his system if it is followed by an equally radical submission to the painterly requirements of transforming the motif into a painting. His goal remains elegance. In Lassnig's case, the exact opposite is true: she submits radically to self-limitation by basing her work solely on her own body awareness. But she is relatively free in the execution of the resulting works, not needing to bother with "diligent" coloring in and copying. Her main aim remains pungency.

In Brown's work, one can observe the way he traces the opposition between these two poles, taking Richter as his starting point (with Auerbach in the role of Lassnig). He takes "diligent coloring in" to absurd lengths and then uses contrasts between motif and title as a humoristic way out of the prison of a brand of painting that makes itself unassailable with an armor of faithfully reproduced virtuosities. Bodily awkwardness and presence, that seemed to have been done away with, make an unexpected and very deliberate comeback.

Dana Schutz, who in terms of technique has little in common with Brown, approaches the same position from the opposite position, from Lassnig's direction. In her work, the body is no longer the last remaining site of authentic affect that eventually overrides embarrassment; instead, it is the site where the visual models, the ideals of beauty and power, the role models and patterns of desire by which it is shaped and permeated are acted out. Whereas Brown translates Auerbach's impasto technique into a flat illusion, Schutz's self-portrait and the Daytona Beach lady pile the paint on thickly, suggesting not gestural spontaneity but a kind of leathery, pachydermic hardening.

Presented with the choice between abstraction and figuration (as demanded by painting's prophets of doom), or the choice between reproduction and original (as invoked by the advocates of art photography), the more interesting contemporary painters say: I choose to dispense with these choices. Both pairs of options share a clear preference for their first term, in the service of "progress" and "emancipation," thus all too deliberately provoking the outrage of those they reject as outmoded. Both also dismiss a particular approach as superfluous, in the first case making hand-painted imitations of reality (or surreality) and in the second the idea of painting by hand at all.

The ironic thing is that the strategy of declaring an entire cultural technique obsolete inevitably acts as a challenge to that technique's potential for self-assertion. The two sides entrench themselves in institutions, allowing them to live off of each other perfectly happily in the long term. The one side suspects painting's handcrafted aspect of serving an esoteric mythology of the painter's supernaturally inspired body. The other side calls this critique pathological, a puritanical repression of the corporeal. Ignoring the existence of these battlefronts is not enough; after all, there are lessons to be learned from such dogmatic exaggerations. Ultimately, however, this isn't going to get us anywhere. So what will? Not in the futurist sense of moving beyond, but in the sense of developing that which is already there, which has a genealogy, however submerged it might be?

One path, hinted at in the twin constellation of Richter/Brown and Lassnig/Schutz, would be to ask whether I might view painting by hand not only as something that asserts a suspect gestural presence and should therefore be replaced by reproductive techniques like photography (the line taken by Douglas Crimp), but also as something that represents acting and choosing in exemplary form, between self-imposed tasks and their execution, making it just as immune to obsolescence as action and choice themselves. An unresolved contradiction in

Crimp's position is that the specific conditions and myths of a medium appear as either decisive or not decisive at all. On the one hand, the visual idea is no longer dependent on the medium of painting; on the other, it's supposed to owe its continued existence exclusively to the medium of photography. Duchamp was more far-sighted. Otherwise, on abandoning painting he would simply have turned to photography instead, which is precisely what he did not do.

# Sigmar Polke: Handicap as a Lever

*The Life and Opinions of Tristram Shandy, Gentleman* (1759–1767), a book by English country priest Laurence Sterne that was a bestseller 250 years ago, opens with the following sentence: "I wish either my father or my mother, or indeed both of them, as they were in duty both equally bound to it, had minded what they were about when they begot me; had they duly considered how much depended upon what they were then doing…" Just as a priest who speaks of mum and dad having sex in the first sentence of his book is revealed as a free-thinker, so there is a good measure of courage at play when painter Sigmar Polke begins a biographical essay (published in 1976 in the catalogue of the major exhibition in Tübingen, Düsseldorf, and Eindhoven) by admitting: "The fact of my birth would be of no further relevance to my artistic career were it not for the fact that I was born with weak vision." His most painful childhood memories, he continues, include a picture of his family in the postwar period bending over a freshly printed copy of *Bäckerblume*, a free magazine distributed at bakeries, delighting in the pictures of tasty breads and pastries, while young Sigmar's attempts to get close enough to see anything at all resulted in "lots of little dead dots" dancing in front of his eyes. The point of mentioning this is to suggest that this handicap alone, not insignificant for a budding painter, was at the root of the technique, used by Polke from the early 1960s, of transferring the Benday dots from mechanical printing to canvas by hand.

The ironic evocation of this handicap is the lever used by Polke to subvert the entrenched debate between reproducibility and originality that still dominates the discussion many years later. Polke was not the first artist influenced by Pop art to work with Benday dots. Roy Lichtenstein showed the way, applying the technique meticulously. In Polke's work, on the other hand, the dots are freely placed, sometimes cheekily spreading into nasty blobs, as if the ink kept getting out of control. *Berliner* (Doughnuts, 1965) shows the popular cakes in the foreground, the laughing baker in the background stolen directly from the *Bäckerblume* logo. But this clean work is flecked with the blots of a slovenly copyist, with little black specks like fly droppings. Anyone who reads this as just an implied critique of the petit-bourgeois idyll of gluttony falls victim to their own educated middle- or upper-class projections. In fact, over the decades Polke has always displayed an affection for kitsch, the decorative urge, and dubious taste. His astute humor is directed instead against the attempts of fellow artists and critics, even in their quotations from popular culture, to uphold the iron rules of a heroic artistic doctrine that considers itself above the lowly sphere of the banal. In other words, we find ourselves deep inside the territory of the slapstick method, to which Polke has contributed in many forms. But this of course does not rule out a narrower interpretation in the context of discussions of painting and what they might mean for the so-called real world—when slapstick deals with repudiating hollow claims of authority, the question of artistic choice and action is implicit, a question posed in especially exemplary form in painting.

Polke's *Vitrinenstück* (Vitrine Piece, 1966) is a key moment in this respect. The installation consists of three free-standing partitions of the kind used in administrative offices and non-art exhibitions. They are positioned around a vitrine. On the right-hand panel, in the kind of stick-on white capitals often used for signs and announcements, there is the following text: "I was standing in front of the canvas, about to paint a bunch of flowers, when I received an order from higher powers: Not a bunch of flowers! Paint flamingos! I was going to carry on painting: But then I realized they really meant it." The middle panel displays the result: two line drawings in white on black, in the style of typical living room decor of the period, a direct quotation of decorative kitsch. Above this is repeated: "The picture that was painted by order of higher powers." And on the left-hand panel, confused, typewritten notes about the higher commands dictated to the artist by extraterrestrials who drew attention to themselves in his room as, among other things, flying peas. "They will control us all, we will be their slaves. They want to spread their culture, their religion and language … they want to help us … to show us the right path … we must do what they tell us, otherwise we would destroy ourselves," writes the artist, next to a photograph that shows him solemnly holding to his ears the saucers through which the higher powers communicated with him. The vitrine itself contains the actual objects involved in the episode (the saucers, the peas) as well as evidence of further orders (matches with the tips removed, a fragment of a dot painting destroyed on higher orders); but most importantly, it also contains a copy of the catalogue from the 1955 Documenta, open at a page with a photograph of a jury meeting from the Künstlerbund exhibition in Cologne in 1952, including such renowned artists as *Brücke* members Karl Schmidt-Rottluff and Erich Heckel, earnest-looking veterans of Expressionism and Informel, approaches to art still dominant in Germany until well into the 1960s. It now becomes clear that the piece humorously undermines two key concerns in painting: first, the ossification of cultural bureaucracies and juries that quickly turn artistic currents into doctrines, and second, the notion of painting which, according to an old tradition, views the artist as a medium of immanent creative inspiration. In 1966, the year this piece was made, the Franco-German co-produced television series "Raumpatrouille Orion" (Space Patrol Orion) began broadcasting. And 1961 had seen the launch of the German sci-fi series "Perry Rhodan"—the pulp magazines still being published today, arguably the longest continuous story ever told—about the space hero's conflict of decisions (Polke and his then close friend Gerhard Richter quoted it in a text collage, turning it into an allegory about similar conflicts in painting. As science fiction became an established everyday presence in German life, Polke humorously coupled space mythology with art world power structures. Painting becomes the battlefield of a master and servant drama that can only be coped with by means of silliness. The restriction of choice by rusty dogmas is contrasted with the endless expanse of space as the endless expanse of artistic possibilities.

This is especially evident in three pictures made in 1968: The same year as Maria Lassnig made the above-mentioned portrait of herself in a space suit, Polke painted *Polke als Astronaut* (Polke as an Astronaut), a gray balloon with a smiley face, painted straight onto topical fabric printed with a pattern of space-walking astronauts. *Moderne Kunst* (Modern Art) is a caricature which, so to speak, self-destructs after being read. On a black ground, various quotations of Modernist painting styles—Constructivist intersections, Mondrian corners, Pollock spatters, Kandinsky arcs—are arranged like space junk, and underneath them in italics appear the words "Modern Art," like a caption in a tabloid newspaper. *Akt mit Geige* (Nude with Violin) also contains the title on the white lower band as an element of the picture; above it on a black ground there is no trace of a nude or a violin, but cogs, an eye, hairy cartoon feet pointing skywards (an allusion to Baselitz?), a jumbled assemblage in a void of meaning. As in the graphic convention familiar from comics, it's as if various protagonists are caught up in a wild fight and all we can make out in the confusion is a foot here, an eye there. By citing all manner of clichés from Modernist composition and abstraction, Polke plays on two levels at the same time, just like Duchamp in the case of the Cubists and their popular detractors. He parodies both narrow-minded hostility to this formal idiom ("My kid paints like that!") and the conservative tendency within art that clings to it. This program of parody liberates the artist from constellations that have long since become codependent (haters of classical Modernism versus classical Modernists).

But rather than simply bidding farewell to "serious" debate on painting with a few amusing tricks, Polke seriously addresses its central contradictions. First, he addresses the conflict between reproducibility and originality which—after Pop art, if not before—is no longer identical with the conflict between banalization and refinement; and second, as a direct consequence, he addresses the conflict between surface and depth, between the two-dimensional flat world of the picture plane and the multi-dimensionality of the space in which painting moves both literally (as an object in space) and figuratively (as a play of light and color). The cartoon paintings from 1968 begin to consider this in the form of two-dimensional, pictogram-like elements whizzing around in an endless black space as if in the fifth dimension. In Polke's work of the 1970s and 1980s, this developed into a diversified visual language. He experimented with chemical reactions in materials (silver oxide, humidity-sensitive paints) and with surface properties (shiny varnish, matte finish, transparent resins, etc.). He pushed the non-reproducibility of painting to great lengths—the range of different levels can only be seen by looking at the work directly, not in illustrations. But at the same time, he didn't abandon the two-dimensional, the flat fabric patterns and cartoon-like allusions. Traditional perspective is often squashed down to cartoon-like two-dimensionality—or jazzed up to spiritist fifth and sixth dimensions.

In a large picture from 1994, Polke brings together all these aspects again as a sphinx-like statement on his own method: *Die drei Lügen der Malerei* (The Three Lies of Painting) is one of the pictures for which he used a semi-transparent polyester fabric on a stretcher that shows through as part of the picture. But this polyester support is interrupted by a vertical strip of yellow fabric printed with a pattern of colored handprints. To the right, in the hatched style of the engravings in old encyclopedias, are a tree and a mountain, linked by a barren, desert-like plain; by letting the paint run, Polke makes it unmistakably

69     **Sigmar Polke,** The Three Lies of Painting, 1994
70     **Albert Oehlen,** Self-Portrait with Shit-Stained Underpants and Mauritius Blue Penny, 1984
71     **Sigmar Polke,** Doughnuts, 1965
72     **Sigmar Polke,** Modern Art, 1968

clear that we are looking not at a printed graphic but at a freehand painting. The leafless tree is broken down like a biological illustration into roots, trunk, crown, branches, and twigs. The peak of the mountain is severed, beheaded like a boiled egg, and the dividing line coincides exactly with the visible horizontal bar of the stretcher. So the three lies are nicely gathered together. The first lie, that of illusionistic three-dimensional perspective, is nailed by the blatantly visible horizontal bar running right through the middle of the picture. The second lie is that of composition: the Golden Section and the balanced distribution of landscape elements (mountain, tree, plain with horizon) are forced into the background by the strip of fabric, only to be squeezed from behind by the visible stretcher, in turn further divided into a grid pattern by three vertical bars. The third lie concerns faithfulness to materials and methods. The hands look painted but are printed; the landscape looks printed but is painted. But not even the idea of "three lies" is the truth, as the biggest lie is the fourth—that of total transparency, of decoding the "three lies," of a genuine insight into the mechanisms of the painter's method, hinted at in the joke of a mountain that is "analytically" broken down like the tree, as if we might learn anything more about the mountain if its peak is chopped off, or about painting if it reveals its ingredients. (In fact the mountain is also a coded allusion to alchemy, another pet subject playfully explored by Polke.) "The Three Lies of Painting" leaves the kind of tedious interpretative routines that seek to favor either picture or object, idea or material, surface or depth, reproduction or original, puffed-up earnest or hollow joke helplessly behind. Welcome to the habitual reality of art-making: the joy of ceaseless experimentation.

# Albert Oehlen, Charline von Heyl, Daniel Richter: Wresting Beauty From the Impure

For more than a quarter century now, Albert Oehlen, who studied under Sigmar Polke in Hamburg in the late 1970s, has been carrying on in this direction and beyond, with decisive steps evident in the resulting oeuvre from decade to decade. His beginnings in the early 1980s were shared with his friend Martin Kippenberger, with Werner Büttner, and with his brother Markus Oehlen: profaning the art of painting as a punk gesture, doing away with false perfection by means of the right punchline. And to make sure no one got the wrong idea, the painter himself was the primary object of ridicule when it came to juxtaposing the valuable and the devalued. How else is one to understand a picture like the eloquently titled *Selbstporträt mit verschissener Unterhose und blauer Mauritius* (Self-Portrait with Shit-Stained Underpants and Mauritius Blue Penny, 1984). The painting's subject stands there with a smart haircut, his back to the viewer, holding up the priceless stamp with tweezers, but his connoisseurship is compromised by a very obvious mishap.

More than other painters in his milieu, Oehlen immerses himself in the laws of painting, and submits to self-imposed tasks that he stubbornly plays through to the end. For example, an entire series of dinosaurs, the pitiable creatures of a bygone age—an age to which painting, too, is supposed to belong; or pictures with mirrors stuck to them, the deliberately simple-minded signal for the viewer identifying him/herself in the picture. Oehlen purposefully seeks out what has been firmly discarded and presses it back into service, managing to amaze himself and others in the process. This depends on a willingness, in cases of doubt, to always prefer a "messy" artistic necessity over the anemic stylistic exercises of aesthetic refinement. Around 1989, it was this that made Oehlen depart from the by-then-routine rapid-fire approach of 1980s painting. Instead, he began to mercilessly overload his pictures with the degrees of abstraction of a succession of layers of paint, overstretching both himself and the picture during the creative process, sometimes for days or weeks, until, as if by chance or magic, the picture reached a state with which it and the artist were happy—hard-won beauty. As writer Jörg-Uwe Albig aptly put it, Oehlen "now force feeds painting not with unfitting content but with painting itself." And Oehlen was ready with a silly name for his new approach: "post-non-figurative painting." With this step from figuration to abstraction, Oehlen said in an interview in 2004, he by no means considered himself to be breaking new ground; rather, he "recreated a development of Modernism," but under new conditions. Although this "recreating" is both a reconstruction and a parody, it is not a method which, once devised, calls simply for dogged implementation. On the contrary, each picture remains a walk into unknown territory, with the risk that color and form will slip into an undifferentiated swamp.

But even this freely abstracting approach, Oehlen discovered, can become a routine that believes itself above the vagaries of content going awry. The *how* of painting can only be tested out on the *what*. Or in other words: in the long run, you can't forego clear references to the world without getting lost in stylistic exercises. In the mid-1990s, figuration erupted back into Oehlen's by now totally

overstuffed arsenal of abstraction, this time as a messed up flood of image combinations under digital conditions. The computer collage posters he has been
making since this time are put together with standard desktop software and the
kind of "clipart" elements used, for example, by snack bar owners to design
their menus. The results are chaotic combinations of shadowed fonts and 3D
graphics, a kind of desktop Surrealism with a fondness for aesthetic head-on
collisions. Along the top of one picture, "Saxophon Eyes" appears in pistachio
green techno letters, and along the bottom "it's a fantasy!" in purple script; in
between is a new-wave mannequin with hair piled high, surrounded by a pink
graffiti line, behind her a Hieronymus Bosch scene, and behind that a sketchy
drawing of a wild animal spouting water. What remains constant is the element
of "too much." Surrealism with its amassing of dream details is not a random
reference here; Oehlen admires Dalí's impudent manipulation of illusionary pictorial space, as he does the obscure works of American artist John Graham—active in the 1920s and 1930s as an impresario for famous artist friends in New
York and allegedly the first to discover Jackson Pollock—whose canvases stood
out above all because the people in them were always portrayed with a squint.

The overstraining which Oehlen imposes on his pictures and on the history
of painting remains quite unheroic. It shows an awareness of the opposite problem of "unabashed" figurative copying of banal or glamorous motifs. While the
latter descends into feeble-minded carelessness, the former increasingly risks
freezing up in self-imposed doubts and distancing maneuvers. The continual
evocation and erasure of historical and contemporary references, the "recre-
ation" of the shift from abstraction to figuration in Modernism—all this leads
to long-term cramp. Such is the descent into the hell of references. In painterly
terms, one-time Kippenberger assistant Michael Krebber is the most eloquent
representative of this school of self-obstruction; he manages to derive dignity
from it, not least as a good teacher at the Städelschule in Frankfurt. To return to
the theory of a correspondence between action in painting and in society: painting as a hell of references maps to the social confinement and mutual control
experienced in the art milieu. Charline von Heyl and Daniel Richter, both coming from a position influenced by Oehlen, each show a different way out of this
dead-end situation in the development of their work.

Von Heyl's pictures from the early 1990s, like Oehlen's abstractions of the same
period, are filled with conscious quotations and skillfully deployed techniques
(batik-like smudging and densely worked oil), an incessant oscillation between

foreground and background, and between abstract plasticity and figurative hints (if necessary with ironic allusions to rolling pins and ovaries, coats of arms and pretzels). Recognizably created in many steps and layers, they have a brooding, vehement quality to them, as if waiting to subdivide into countless further levels. Since the late 1990s, her pictures have been becoming steadily clearer and fresher, but without forfeiting their painterly eloquence in the slightest. In retrospect, it's as if—to choose a comparison with language and philosophy—someone began by learnedly discussing and quoting complex theorems, and then at some point began to philosophize herself in a way that keeps all the theories in mind without having to constantly parrot them. The place of "statement," however sublimated or coded, is taken by a void which, in the best cases, activates what von Heyl has called "stunned attention" in the viewer, to whom responsibility for making "statements" on this perceptive experience is passed. The fact that this development coincided with Charline von Heyl's move from Düsseldorf to New York is perhaps no coincidence; the new work reveals a detachment from earlier constraints, a sigh of relief in new terrain. *Boogey* (2004) signals this with a plain choice of color. A central red cloud— part blurred like flames, part running out in knotted lines and shot through with thin black shadows—glows against a cadmium-yellow background which in other places actually turns out to be painted in the foreground; like the colors themselves, the beginning and the end of the painting process push against and through each other; the image flickers like a loose connection between positive and negative. Other recent pictures, too, look like someone has translated the early-1960s poster-tearing of French Nouveau Realisme into a polyphonous painting technique (often executed with a sponge or other utensils, not a brush), but without depending on figurative eye-catchers. A title like *Big Joy* (2004) takes this casual unrest to positively programmatic lengths at the same time as subduing it, since the picture does without gaudy color contrasts and the interplay of many levels. On a two meter square format, a brownish gray mist rises, seeming to have spread over two thirds of the otherwise pale canvas in just a few seconds; it's shot through with finely chiseled black lines and patches that betray the meticulous working method. As a result, the picture seems to be filled with an unreal glow, a "big joy" of release. Von Heyl's abstract work has long since ceased to be demonstrative; it allows itself gaps and simplicity and is nonetheless worked through all over. Many of her pictures breathe a libertarian pleasure that manages to do without emphatic sex mania—unlike, for example,

73  **Albert Oehlen,** Look Just Look, 1980
74  **Charline von Heyl,** Big Joy, 2004
75  **Albert Oehlen,** Untitled, 1999

the New York-based English painter Cecily Brown, whose pictures often suggest that they are nothing other than a heightened Abstract Expressionist trace of bodies intertwining and dissolving.

Daniel Richter's initial situation was similar to that of Charline von Heyl. As a latecomer to painting and sometime assistant to Albert Oehlen, he began, in the early 1990s, to make medium-format pictures that compressed the range of painterly gestures to the point of implosion. It was if someone had locked a bunch of Abstract Expressionists in a studio and forced them to paint over each other's marks on the same canvas. The result was a visual equivalent of electro-acoustic feedback, making every smudge and splash resonate with the history of abstract painting. The problem with this was an almost literal heavy-handedness, the deliberate ugliness of shapes and colors gripping each other in a headlock. Accordingly, critics often sought refuge in the accompanying biographical details—Richter's past as an eloquent character from Hamburg's anarcho-punk scene. Then, around 1999—three years after polemically stating that he painted abstractions because art had "produced so many pathetic, idiotic pseudo-protests it makes you sick"—he began painting monumental scenes of social struggle, a kind of post-socialist, late-capitalist history painting, but with little reduction in the density and variety of painting styles. With considerable confidence, he juggled opposing painterly approaches: the conflict-ridden, dissonant urgency of early Baselitz; Gerhard Richter's cool mimesis of visual culture; Jörg Immendorff's canvas theater of political rhetoric. Not forgetting a good portion of craziness, a clownish take on Edvard Munch. Finally, a formative influence was undoubtedly exerted on Richter by the dense, cinematic landscapes painted in the mid to late 1990s by his English friend and colleague Peter Doig with their often singular protagonists and eloquently chosen quotations from art history transformed into motifs of desire.

Social reality is thus portrayed above all as a nightmare, but one whose absurdity is real. And though it may not make the viewer physically sick, it is at least dizzying and eerie. Hideous, demonic figures with glowing button eyes like lemurs people pedestrian precincts and nocturnal scenes. In *Das Recht* (The Law, 2001), grinning men swing clubs over a Guernica horse amid empty box files in a forest. In another work, figures crowd into an inflatable boat on a black sea, their bodies broken down into color spectrums like a computer tomography image, around them the thunder of a white-flecked spray of paint. In the heads of the art historians, this may trigger a dramatic slide show of all the rafts and shipwrecks in painting, but the picture's title, *Tarifa* (2001)—the name of the southernmost border crossing point in Spain—points to the present. These are the people who search the strait between Africa and Europe for a hole in the net of the Schengen Agreement—in vain, as the eye of technology is already on them. In *Gedion* (2002), a group of people stare up at something outside the frame, at some unnamed horror that has turned their faces into ghostly masks. They are standing in front of a Modernist grid facade similar to that of the German department store chain Horten. It's possible to make out the shop's logo, but it has been altered into a fragment of the demand "Hört auf" ("Stop")—a nod to Immendorff's influential painting *Hört auf zu Malen* (Stop Painting, 1966). At the time, Immendorff intended it not as an insider's contribution to the debate on the death of painting, but as a call for painting to cease unless it was motivated by political commitment. In Richter's picture, a naked man with a Napoleon hat floats next to the fragmented slogan, and among the petrified people with white faces stands a little girl in a little red dress—both direct quotations from works by Vasily Surikov, the nineteenth-century Russian painter who tried to mix genre and history painting in a bid to be understood by "simple folk." Immendorff's call for political painting thus appears as a demand that is still valid, but which has begun to crumble, relativized by paranoia and paralysis.

Hubert Fichte, a writer Daniel Richter has repeatedly referenced in his work, once remarked that the task of art is to "transform the murderous into grace." Faced with such a near-impossible task, the game of reference and deliberate resonance gets into trouble, as the solution it represents remains illusory. In this light, the dynamic of master and minion that casts painting as a terrain of self-imposed tasks and their execution (or non-execution) appears quite directly as the question of how to behave politically as a voiced and embodied subject. In some cases, Daniel Richter's pictures can be like a skilled debater who has actually already convinced us, but who then goes too far in wanting to anticipate all objections in a loud, hectoring voice. That is one side. The other is that at their best moments, Richter's pictures reveal all the messiness of potential entanglements, the conflict between formal abstraction and social concreteness, the vacillation between withdrawal and exhibitionism. Posing as a "politically engaged" painter would in itself be somehow foolishly presumptuous, but retiring to safe cultural production is also not an option. All that remains, then, is to live with the insanity and embarrassment of contradictions: *Das erstaunliche*

*Comeback des Dr. Freud* (The Astonishing Comeback of Dr. Freud, 2004) shows us the father of psychoanalysis as a grinning cardboard mask, worn by a naked blonde in red high heels, like something out of Woody Allen's nightmares, in the midst of a hopelessly tangled jungle scene.

# Superflat and Iconic Abstraction: Takashi Murakami, Rafał Bujnowski, Wilhelm Sasnal

From Polke's ground-breaking work between silly humor and deadly earnest, various lines can be drawn, one of which leads to the above-mentioned Albert Oehlen, Charline von Heyl, and Daniel Richter, who pick up on his masterly use of constant overstretching of pictorial levels and painting techniques. But there is another line—that of deliberate under-challenging, of acting stupid, of two-dimensionality. As a highly influential critic in the 1950s and 1960s, Clement Greenberg identified a successive focus in painting on what set it apart from other media—its essential quality (quality in the double sense of precious and distinct) being its genuine two-dimensionality, its flatness. To back up this argument, he traced a line from Manet via Cézanne to Pollock, artists he claimed had charted the historical path out of a pictorial space based on illusionary perspective toward two-dimensional compactness, an abstract arrangement of fields of solid color, which he termed color field painting. Philip Guston did not belong to the small group of painters in the 1960s favored by Greenberg under this label, but at this time he too had long been experimenting with an idea of pure abstraction, even if hints of figuration were already beginning to creep back in, a few clusters of color like eyes and mouth or windows. Under the impression of the civil rights movement and the Vietnam War, however, Guston could not go on sitting in his studio "matching a blue with a red," as he put it. Instead, he wished to make his painting productive for the political matters that occupied him on a daily basis by adopting cartoon strategies of simplification—because the cartoon refuted the clear-cut division between two-dimensionality and figuration.

His painting *Flatlands* (1971) is a high point in this development. It portrays the depravity of America's power elite as a steamrollered landscape of Ku-Klux-Klan hoods and severed body parts. The title hints at many things: the "flatlands" are the wide open, savanna-like plains of the Midwest, where the cold heart of reactionary white America beats. But it is also the "flatlands" of the big cities, the urban zones of desolation by slum formation. Finally, it may also be a reference to the ideological stultification which in Edwin A. Abbott's Victorian satire *Flatland* (1884) prevents the inhabitants of a two-dimensional world from perceiving three-dimensionality and thus their own pigheadedness.

The contemporary manifesto on unconditional cartoonesque two-dimensionality was written by Japanese artist Takashi Murakami. It shimmers in the colors and contradictions of a comic culture that insists on global distribution and, at the same time, on its rootedness in artistic tradition. Murakami has little in common with Polke or Guston—apart from the pleasure taken in forearming himself with echoes of comic and cartoon culture against the claims to seriousness of purist modernist painting. Murakami's manifesto, published in 2000, bears the programmatic title *Superflat*. Murakami understands the superflat as a specifically Japanese visual language whose roots he traces on the one hand to manga and anime, the Japanese comic and animated cartoon culture, and on the other to the Japanese mannerism of the Edo period in the eighteenth century. Anime emerged from imitations of the Disney cartoon tradition, but soon developed its own visual idiom of iconic abstraction. Above all, it heightened the American comic technique of reducing the figure and face of the "hero" to simple lines and the backgrounds against which they move to flat fields of color. This reduction was decentred in the style of the legendary anime pioneer Yoshinori Kanada, whose science fiction animations for Japanese television in the late 1970s focused on intergalactic battle scenes and explosions that fragmented and distorted notions of space and time like a piece of chewing gum. "Instead of creating a balance toward the center of the picture," Murakami writes, the "eccentric" anime artists in the tradition of Kanada work with a "minimal balance maintained toward the four corners of the square." Murakami identifies this as a key link to the artists of the Edo period, whose works he examined as a student of classical Japanese art. These artists worked with an almost two-dimensional pictorial space, an effect achieved by not using linear perspective and the corresponding differences in size, but also via increased detailing of all pictorial elements and via their decentered distribution. The parallels to decorative art forms (embroidery, carpets, decorative rugs) are obvious and not unwelcome, especially since the works to which Murakami is referring were painted mostly on structuring elements of Japanese interior decor (sliding doors, screens). The decisive aspect, however, is the "eccentric" diffusion of elements—blossoms, stones, animals, etc.—that causes the viewer's eye to glide restlessly back and forth. It is this which clearly distinguishes them from pictograms, which depend crucially on being centered within the picture on account of the urgent need for swift recognition.

In his comic book *Understanding Comics: The Invisible Art* (1993), Scott Mc-Cloud explains, among other things, his theory of iconic abstraction. Why are a few dots and lines enough to make something the reader can identify with? Why is it enough to draw two small black circles sitting on a larger black circle to be instantly reminded of Mickey Mouse? McCloud describes the underlying psychology of perception as follows: when two people interact socially, each of them does so out of a self-image that is both more sketchy and more idealized than the image they have of the other person. So while one's mental image of oneself is an iconic abstraction (whether with a positive or negative connotation), other people are experienced in full "realistic" detail. In comics, this separation between perception of self and others has been used to allow reader identification, what McCloud calls the "mask effect." The characters are iconically abstracted, while the backgrounds through which they move are often rendered realistically (particularly striking in Hergé's *Tintin*). "This combination," explains McCloud, "allows readers to 'mask' themselves in a character and safely enter a sensually stimulating world." In other words, realism objectivizes, while iconic abstraction subjectivizes. In manga, the principle characters are often highly simplified, whereas other characters—especially opponents—are drawn more realistically, "emphasizing their 'otherness' from the reader." Iconic abstraction marks the rift between perceived image and meaning, between form and idea. When the reader identifies with a protagonist, it means nothing less than a temporary closure of this rift. In the aesthetic of superflat, on the other hand, the rift is closed long before we even get involved; the "objectivized" (that is, realistic) elements have been completely banished, leaving nothing but a sphere of subjectivized fantasy per se that is both compressed and exploded. In this sense, they are not fetish objects, but "fetish subjects" in their own right—not so much an object to which fantasies cling as an embodiment of this process itself. And because these pictures also completely refuse realism, without becoming entirely abstract, they set themselves apart all the more starkly from the surrounding reality.

In the case of Gerhard Richter and Glenn Brown, even the most controlled painting gesture resonates with the insistence of wishing to execute this movement oneself at all costs, even if only as a symbolic act (the same as you don't let other people shake hands for you, even if in purely practical terms it might be feasible). In Murakami's case, by contrast, this act is either delegated—he works like an anime office with two dozen assistants—or, in the sense of executing details himself, pointedly pragmatic like product control or a seal of quality (the final touch by the director of a small business). Although a residue of action is preserved as part of the production procedure, from the viewer's point of view it has shifted completely into the realm of the imaginary: There is no identifiable trace of individual artistic activity.

The physicality of those who produce the picture disappears behind the production process; the physicality of the comic characters is flattened, free of shadows, without brushstrokes. Bodily fluids do feature, as intergalactic protuberances in the style of Yoshinori Kanada: a Japanese cousin of Mickey Mouse named DOB, sporting a red bowtie and huge teeth and designed by Murakami, is shot into an immaculately red sphere by a milky white jet, with even the drips of paint rendered as meticulously circular spots, like something frozen by a high-speed camera (*Zuzazazazaza*, 1994). DOB has no idea what is happening to him because, according to his creator, "DOB is cute, but he has no meaning and hasn't a clue about life, sex, or reality." In this way, Murakami embraces the culture of the otaku, the fans obsessed with technology and pop culture who emphatically take the eccentric view of fantasy as their reality. With *Kawaii! Vacances d'été* (2002), Murakami seems to have devoted a monumental history painting to them, three meters tall and nine meters long: Stylized flowers with laughing mouths and button eyes grow straight up into a bright blue sky, cushioned by fluffy comic clouds, and stalkless blossoms fly around like butterflies, eccentrically stirred up by an invisible breeze. Not all the flowers are laughing, some only smile, and a few even shed little tears. This is the final summer vacation before the dark cloud of adolescence, the unreal beauty of a camaraderie which is relatively carefree despite all the minor scrapping and which only appears so unsullied in retrospect, in the knowledge of what came next (you don't need to have attended a Japanese school to understand that).

Murakami's nose for apt iconic abstraction does not diminish his business sense. Based on the Bill Gates model, he asks his staff to submit daily email work reports. Frankly provocative, he says he is more interested in "the production and sale of wares than in exhibitions." Murakami's ideological short-circuiting of art factory and entertainment production company seemingly reflects Japanese pop culture, where the role of the contemporary artist is effortlessly absorbed in the production of abstract imaginary pictures, avatars, and comic heroes for television, cinema, comics, video games, and the Internet. Super-flat is an attempt to give all this a name and a program of specifically artistic objectives. But Murakami takes dehierarchization to absurd lengths when he not only produces plastic toys for three dollars a piece, but also Louis Vuitton bags for five thousand dollars, designed with the Japanese sweetness of cherry blossoms. At this point, superflat becomes simply supervapid; the libidinous charging of surfaces, which in Murakami's objects and pictures is still tied to the iconic abstraction of the happy dreams of childhood and the wet dreams of ado-lescence, enters the yawning void of I-have-something-you-don't-have, a fact orchestrated to an apt climax in the fully operational Louis Vuitton boutique one had to pass through at the end of Murakami's 2007 retrospective at MOCA in Los Angeles. All of this with the ironic postscript that countless cheap imita-tions of the handbags re-inject a healthy dose of super-silly bargain hunting into the sphere of the supposedly super-exclusive.

In the discussion of "reproducibility" in art, the purely technical-mechani-cal side of the manufacturing process is overemphasized. Once the production of pictures has been delegated, by Murakami or any other artist, the fact of whether or not they are produced by purely technical or by "manual-techni-cal" means—whether they are (photographic) prints or painting—is relatively unimportant for their further duplication and reproduction. In the past, this du-plication remained relatively "stupid," doing no more than stoically multiplying and distributing the results. But in the digitized culture of image exchange and organization on the Internet—from Google Image Search to YouTube's video funfair, made possible by millions of contributors—things are changing. Today, the way pictures are searched for, found, and displayed is in itself latently "in-telligent," at least in terms of structural networking and refinement of the way they automatically circulate and are able at any time to form new orders and groupings to which specific interests are attached. Material that was believed to be long lost suddenly becomes accessible again, and the important and unim-portant trade places in a flash. Iconic abstraction—rigorously two-dimensional, eccentric rather than centered—becomes an emblematic visualization of this development.

In the case of Polish painter Wilhelm Sasnal, one might think that iconi-cally abstracted motifs inevitably become centered by his use of relatively small formats. In other words, the works seem to be primarily painted pictograms, executed with quick but precise strokes. But this is not quite the case. In 1996,

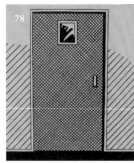

76 **Daniel Richter,** The Astonishing Comeback of
  Dr. Freud, 2004
77 **Daniel Richter,** Gedion, 2002
78 **Wilhelm Sasnal,** Maus 1, 2001
79 **Wilhelm Sasnal,** Maus 4, 2001

together with four other students at the Krakow art academy—Rafał Bujnowski, Marcin Maciejowski, Marek Firek, and Józef Tomczyk—he founded Grupa Ladnie ("ladnie" means "pretty" or "nice"), with group shows taking place under this name until 2000. "Pretty" and "nice" was of course a sarcastic anticipation of the accusations of harmlessness that were bound to be leveled against painting that devoted itself in small format and reduced style to the "lesser" things of Poland's newly capitalist everyday life, from apartment blocks to cell phones to vinyl records. But this unobtrusive miniature Pop art is fundamentally linked with the idea of the pictures being perceived in rows, as a "salon hanging," or even in piles. In this sense, then, they are decentered, eccentric, eliciting a searching, restless gaze like Murakami—but here the basic view is more one of laconic irreverence toward the development of society, scanning its banal surface for markings and standards.

Rafał Bujnowski has taken this approach a step further. For *Obrazy do mieszkania* (Pictures for the Apartment, 2002), he went so far as to paint five different motifs as many as fifty times on small canvases. In the exhibition, they were leaned against the wall on the floor beneath a picture of the standardized floor plan of a small apartment, on which the various motifs are assigned to specific rooms to make sure future buyers make no mistakes: the wedding couple in the bedroom; a glass of juice and the picture with the four lemons in the kitchen; a construction worker in underpants for the hallway; a child in a sandpit in the living room. In post-socialist Poland, a fairly ruthless strain of capitalism enters into a strange union with bigoted Catholicism—as a result, the multiplication of the pictogram pictures comes across as a description of this flat world of large-scale dirty business and small-scale home sweet home.

Even more clearly than Bujnowski, Sasnal's work reveals an ongoing exploration of the possibility of filtering the painterly qualities out of things observed (be the motifs found or his own), of finding out what exactly makes them pictures that are worth remembering, more than "just" pictograms. These pictures include a silver arrow racing car seen from above, protruding into the frame like the mouth of a shark (*1939*, 2002), and the knee of artist legend Robert Smithson (1938–1973) hanging over the armrest of a sofa (*Untitled (Smithson)*, 2002).

On account of a clear parallel in their initial methods, Sasnal (born in 1972) has been compared on various occasions with Belgian artist Luc Tuymans (born in 1958). Like Gerhard Richter before him, Tuymans can certainly be credited with influencing many young painters. He paints in a fast, reductive style from photographs, with a feel for the right detail. His palette ranges from mothball gray to urine-stain yellow and stagnant-water green (balanced by the occasional refreshing flight into lemon, apricot, and lavender). Whether he is painting a portrait of Heinrich Himmler (*Himmler*, 1998), as a faceless figure remaining in shadow, or Condoleezza Rice, starkly cropped to just her eyes and mouth (*The Secretary of State*, 2005), the picture remains caught between exorcizing and evoking historical weightiness—with the painter in the middle as a hero of doubt and of shock.

For all the parallels in method and approach, nothing could be further from Sasnal's attitude. He, too, works with iconic abstraction from photographic originals as a kind of process of sedimentation. But he doesn't speculate on a lurking darkness to lend him meaning, explosiveness, and pathos. As if to underline this, Sasnal makes a very subtle reference to the impossibility of representing the Holocaust in painting. Tuymans defied this provocatively with his empty *Gaskammer* (Gas Chamber, 1986), a sketchy, small-format painting. By contrast, Sasnal turns to one of the few works—if not the only work—of narrative graphic art that finds the right tone in the face of the horror: Art Spiegelman's *Maus* (1989-1991). Spiegelman combines the comic-book mask effect of iconic abstraction with the classical form of the animal fable: the Nazis as cats, the Jews as mice, the Polish helpers as pigs. In this way, he opens up the possibility of narrative empathy without glossing over the distance and thus allowing a false sentimental identification with the victims.

Sasnal's *Maus* (2001), a medium-format oil painting, goes one step further back, removing the narrative element completely and referring to it only in the title and the quotation of the black and white graphic style of the comic. It depicts crudely made bunk beds, above them a grid pattern denoting the shadow that falls over the scene, and that's all. In the comic there's a corresponding sequence of frames in which a Polish overseer uses a baton to search the empty beds for a young woman whose husband has just thrown her a parcel of food over the fence of the camp. Following Sasnal's reference, then, we are confronted with a portrayal of Polish collaboration and the touching picture of a love that manifests itself in the midst of the killing as a desperate attempt to help someone survive. Showing without showing; in Sasnal's picture, the spatial perspective suggested by the beds is almost totally flattened by the overlaid grid pattern; there is no way out. The picture says: Spiegelman's *Maus* says it all, I can only point to it, and anything more would be presumptuous—iconic abstraction and two-dimensionality as a way out of the exhaustion of painting between esoteric abstraction and pathos-ridden historical figuration.

# Painting as a Modular System in Space: Daniel Buren/Robert Barry, Kai Althoff, Lukas Duwenhögger, Jessica Stockholder, Thomas Scheibitz, Tal R, Laura Owens, Gillian Carnegie

In 1967, a few years before he came to prominence as a bona fide Conceptualist, Robert Barry painted four small canvases in monochrome red, each roughly the size of a vinyl single. Painting at its lowest point: Who on earth is supposed to be interested in this? Living room decor? False modesty? That's how easy it is to miss the point when someone does something really astonishing—even revolutionary. For these four small canvases are not hung above the sofa or over the mantelpiece, but at a measured distance from one another in the four corners of a regularly proportioned exhibition wall free of other works. All of a sudden, the small objects have become markers of the large white surface between them; four small pictures become four small objects—but also one big picture of which they are the corners. We see the wall itself as a picture. This effect of reversal is further emphasized by rounding off one corner of each canvas, the four outermost edges of the larger rectangle, so that one automatically thinks of a huge screen (that also usually has rounded corners).

The same year, four characters caused a huge stir at the Salon de la Jeune Peinture in Paris. "Buren, Mosset, Parmentier, Toroni" stood in large letters over the corner of the exhibition assigned to them. Each of the four prepared a signature work and executed it at the venue. Daniel Buren covered a stretcher with commercially available fabric with vertical stripes, of the kind commonly used in France for marquees, and modulated this predefined striped pattern with white acrylic paint. Olivier Mosset painted a simple black circle on a white background. Michel Parmentier tried broad gray and white horizontal stripes And Niele Toroni covered the canvas with square brush marks at regular intervals. That was all. But not quite. At the end of the day, they withdrew their pictures, leaving behind only a note stating that they were no longer exhibiting. Plus a pamphlet. Because painting is a game; because painting is the application of the rules of composition; because it freezes movement; because it is the representation of objects; because it is a "springboard for the imagination"; because it is spiritual illustration; because it is justification; because it serves an end, because it gives aesthetic value to "flowers, women, eroticism, the everyday environment, art, dadaism, psychoanalysis, and the war in Vietnam"—for all these reasons, wrote the four painters, "We are not painters." The iconoclastic gesture was perfect. But the dramatic spectacle obscured what was really interesting about the action—the fact that painting still took place. As a way of marking a specific place—in this case the painting salon—it was executed in this place and then removed from it. Another striking thing: contrary to the statement, the whole affair retained a certain playfulness. And it served a purpose—even if that purpose was the establishment of new aesthetic standards.

Of the four, Buren was the most successful in developing this game of give and take. He was loyal to his marquee motif over a long period, varying it cleverly as a marking not only of the borders of the exhibition space, but also of museums and major galleries in general, moving out into public space (lengthways stripes as banners across the street, on advertising boards, etc.). Over the years, criticism of the conditions under which art is shown in institutions has sadly become a hollow formula that is warmly welcomed by precisely these institutions. What once seemed to breathe the pathos of criticism has long since become nothing more than a kind of art equivalent to the Adidas stripes—as at the 2006 Venice Architecture Biennale, where Buren embellished the French pavilion with big tires stretched with striped material that were hung between the columns of the portico. But this does not detract from his earlier achievements. For like Barry, Buren opened people's eyes to the fact that painting not only takes place inside the picture frame, but that it can also take the surrounding space into consideration.

But hold on a moment: Has painting not always done this? Does not every portrayal of the fourteen Stations of the Cross, not to mention the introduction of single-point perspective in the Renaissance, already take the space into consideration? What about the panoramas of the nineteenth century, 360-degree paintings on a monumental scale that imitated entire scenes from nature, townscapes, and battles? What about the Mexican muralists of the 1920s with their large-scale outdoor wall paintings? And then the Constructivists—wasn't El Lissitzky's

*Prounenraum* (Proun Space, 1923) already a kind of walk-in three-dimensional version of his visual idiom? And what about De Stijl, what about Mondrian's design for a *Salon de Madam B.* (1926) that was almost a direct translation of his pictorial aesthetic into architecture? And what, finally, about Brazilian artist Hélio Oiticica, who began around 1960 to construct freely hanging objects out of wooden boards painted a single color? All valid objections. Painting that remains within the limits of flat rectangular panels is essentially a historical—if highly successful—exception: a mobile, flexible format, easy to work on, to store, to transport, to exhibit, and of course to sell. But one should not always try to see in the new only what went before. When Buren and Barry once again step outside the borders of this exception, what is interesting is that they do not simply abandon the rectangular limits of the picture. They do not relinquish the banal condition of a painted rectangular surface in favor of some kind of three-dimensional applied painting. Instead, they take this rectangular painted surface itself as the basis of a modular system. Their pictures become a variable demarcation of space. They are arranged according to conceptual criteria, related to each other and to the space, thus only becoming visible as art once the viewer has seen them, thought about them, and identified them as such.

For Barry and Buren in the mid-1960s, spatially organized painting was still explicitly linked to the rejection of painterly forms of expression other than this sparse monochrome or striped marking of a surface and the surrounding space. Anything else would have been a distraction. It would have been too easy to miss the spatial dimension if more "content" had gotten in the way. This was only conceivable in the aftermath of the endgame of Minimalist painting (Ad Reinhardt, for example). This is no longer the case. Today, there are many painters who understand their work in terms of an interplay with spatial-installational approaches, but without the need to be any less multi-faceted. Some examples follow.

Kai Althoff's figurative paintings radiate a melancholic obstinacy, as if they have a patina consisting of the history of the artistic, bohemian milieus of Modernism and the tensions between love and ambition, and friendship and competition, that drove them: but also the history of 1950s and 1960s illustration and major figures like Tomi Ungerer and *Yellow Submarine* illustrator Heinz Edelmann—as if harmless-seeming children's book characters were leading an intellectual afterlife in Althoff's pictures. Again and again, Althoff manages to convincingly transfer all this into installational environments where the pictures are leaned along the wall like records or scattered over the floor in a domestic situation like fashion magazines. By redefining the function of pictures in this way, the ultimate fetish of the art market is shown as an ordinary everyday object, although one that retains a charge of desire and hedonism.

Lukas Duwenhögger's paintings often feature scenes of coded allusion, of looks and signals exchanged between gay men. They are painted in a historicist style of dandyish sophistication that also deliberately oversteps the conventions of taste, as in the choice of sickly sweet color combinations. The pictures become part of installations where they are shown in arrangements with elements of interior design (curtains or items of furniture). In this way, painting becomes the fulcrum in a flickering movement between public art spaces and private interiors, and between the constraints of public morals and the pleasure privately derived from codes.

Jessica Stockholder paints abstract color fields in three dimensions, whereby the "abstract" aspect is relativized by her use of both classical application of paint and colored found objects (often bright plastic household items). The resulting installations are carefully conceived three-dimensional works. Unlike Stockholder, Thomas Scheibitz keeps painting and sculpture apart, but only in physical terms; in the same way that he constructs his paintings by interlocking craggy fields and lines (including hints of letters, ducklings, or matchstick men), he also makes painted sculptures that tumble out of the painting as if humoristic scene-shifters had been at work.

*House of Prince* (2004) by Danish artist Tal R consists of two hundred pictures all based on a similar compositional model: a broad strip along the lower edge of the picture, a thin strip along the top, and the surface in between held in at each corner by what look like outsize photo mounting corners. This leaves an octagonal field in the center, in which Tal R lets loose all manner of color and material combinations, from suggestions of simple pictograms through to actual champagne bottle corks and irregular patterns of shining colored light bulbs. They are emblems and haptic objects at the same time; and like a board game, a pack of cards or a handful of dice, they occupy and vary the exhibition space.

Younger artists like Laura Owens from the United States and Gillian Carnegie from England paint pictures that are part abstract, part figurative, and accessible to even the most rudimentary taste in "beautiful art." But ultimately, such an approach risks missing the point entirely. For both Owens and Carnegie work in the tradition if not of Buren then certainly of Barry, in terms of the way they relate their own pictures to each other conceptually in exhibition spaces. In the work of both artists, this seems to be not just something that takes place after the picture has been made, but rather as part of the actual painting process. Instead of negating tradition and the museum, they present a casual critique of the way they deal with history: Why do certain painters disappear in the depot while others are placed on a pedestal? According to which criteria are pictures related to each other, or not?

Laura Owens plays around not exclusively but very often with tired signals of cuteness and harmlessness—birds fluttering their wings in a cage, bees buzzing around the hive, bunny rabbits, butterflies, flowers. She is equally eclecticist in her appropriation of painting styles with a reputation for being purely decorative: softer, more eccentric brands of color field painting and Abstract Expressionism; traditional Asian styles; folk art and amateur painting; carpets; embroidery; and textile decoration for sofas and wallpapers. But she wraps all this up in an eloquent examination of painterly techniques of application and composition: impasto, almost like relief or mosaic, then smooth and sleek; strong spatial effects and then two-dimensional; refined and virtuoso, as if by accident, and then deliberately clumsy like folk art. With embedded breaches of the rules and with a loose, casual feel, Owens de-heroicizes the underlying earnestness of her own work as a painter. In doing so, she follows the ideal of one of her Californian teachers, the Conceptualist John Baldessari: that art should play simultaneously on various levels of reception, welcoming both a "superficial" reading based on the picture's obvious content, and a more profound one that observes the methods and structural interventions. There is an untitled picture from 1998 (all of Owens's pictures are untitled) in which thin lines and splashes of color in a range of lavenders and pinks are spread across the canvas in the highly unspectacular style of a fabric design for bathrooms. With a little imagination, the amoeba-like shapes and fanciful lines can be read as references to works by Juan Miró or Arshile Gorky. But then comes an absurd turn: the monumental vertical canvas is signed "L. Owens"—upside down in the top left corner. This is how it starts, then: I'm left in the dark as to whether a curator has maybe made a mistake and hung the picture the wrong way up (no, this is not the case). So I'm standing in front of the picture, craning my neck to decipher this writing that is well above eye level.

In the mid-1990s, Owens painted pictures of exhibition spaces hung with paintings—her paintings. This self-mirroring gave a taste of what she was to do in the following years—that is, conquer the space that surrounds the canvas. On the first of a pair of large-format pictures from 1999, numbers are applied to the canvas straight from the tube, like a lesson in elementary math; the second picture shows the same numbers in the same position, but reversed. With the two canvases hung directly opposite each other, a strange effect is achieved: one has the impression of standing between two comedians telling each other puns, with one of them reciting the other's punch lines backwards. In another two-part work from the same year, first shown at Sadie Coles gallery in London, a spider monkey sits on a branch in the lower third of the left-hand canvas, while in the upper third of the right-hand canvas another spider monkey dangles from a branch and squints across at its fellow creature. The two exchange their glances across the bare wall, and the distance between them is as wide as the two canvases put together. In addition, the pictures are fitted exactly to the gallery, covering the wall from floor to ceiling, as if they were a decorative element. As a visitor, I stand between them and get the feeling that Robert Barry's idea of positioning canvases to make the bare wall part of the picture has taken on a new meaning: first, because the monkey's gaze jumps across the gap, and second, because I'm the one disturbing a rendezvous and darkening the free space of possibilities (that is, the bare wall) with my shadow. The Conceptual doctrine of questioning the relationship between artwork and space is overstretched with the ludicrousness of a meeting between primates.

In Owens's work, the amusingly pretty functions as conceptual camouflage for the ceaseless advancement of painterly intelligence. In the case of Gillian Carnegie, this function is performed by an apparently conservative painting style that goes as far as a fondness for an Old Masterly palette—and by an ongoing series of small-format portraits of her own posterior. "Before you can accuse the artist of, quite literally, selling her arse," writes English critic Polly Staple, "she pre-empts the possibility, controlling the viewer's position and bringing the erotics of commodity fetishism to the fore." Here, the traditional relationship between male painter and female model, that runs, with a strong subtext of sexual exploitation, through countless nudes in the history of painting, is cancelled out by radiant buttocks. Of course, one might accuse Carnegie of merely speculating on the voyeuristic effect of "Look, the artist's sexy ass!" But why, then, should she keep on painting variations on this one motif, including one series that is far from erotic? Moreover, Carnegie uses repetition and variation not only to empty out and recharge the traditional genre of the nude; she takes a similarly systematic approach (in this sense following in the footsteps

80

81

80    **Laura Owens,** Untitled, 1999
81    **Gillian Carnegie,** Turner Prize 2005,
       installation view Tate Britain, London

of Gerhard Richter) to other traditional genres of painting, making series of still lifes, landscapes, monochromes.

The impact she is capable of achieving with such a seemingly banal approach was brilliantly demonstrated by Carnegie with her exhibit at the 2005 Turner Prize show in London. In an elongated room with a freestanding partition wall in the middle, a number of motifs appear in several variations. The leaves and branches of an autumnal tree are rendered in sharp, chaotic strokes, aggressive at close quarters but coming together peacefully again as one takes a few steps back. So far, this is a modernist convention that has been played out thousands of times. But the same motif is to be seen again on the opposite wall in a smaller format—and once again, the smears of paint that look so chaotic are executed in almost the same way, with the same two fat vertical strokes in the center that denote neither branch nor leaf but simply "stroke." The difference between copy and variation is blurred, almost literally. The two buttock pictures in the show, on the other hand, form a nice contrast. One is fairly aggressive, in red with stark shadows, and the other, directly opposite but far away at the other end of the gallery, visible in the passage past the freestanding partition wall, is a softly lit version. Then, there are two large-format black monochromes. The title *Black Square* is already a reference to Malevich's work of the same name. At first glance, it really is nothing more than a black square. But like Ad Reinhardt's black paintings, the light falling on the surface reveals nuances, created in this case by thickly applied paint, worked like a relief so that the black square becomes a nocturnal forest scene with huge tree stumps and leaves on the ground. The conceptual thinking that goes into these pictures cannot be separated from the way the material is handled. Not that the buttock pictures and the black-in-black pictures don't stand up on their own, but the intelligence evident in the way they are positioned in the space, the switching between contrast and copy in midstream, is what brings out the best in them. Out of the routine reproduction of long-established traditions of painting emerges a modular system that deploys itself eloquently in the space. Carnegie's achievement lies perhaps not so much in blurring the line between figuration and abstraction—many others have done this (even if *Black Square* is an exemplary work in this respect). It is also not just a matter of her blurring the line between reproduction and originality (even if she does paint from photographs and make copies of her own works). The crucial thing is not even her blurring of the line between conceptuality and materiality (even if in each of her pictures, conceptual meaning and material substance are in a constant state of tension). All this has a part to play, but what makes me believe that Gillian Carnegie's work is destined to endure is the way she positively demands moving, physically present viewers capable of thinking for themselves. This extends to her elegant, evasive approach to the feature made by the UK's Channel 4 television on each of the four artists nominated for the Turner Prize, and shown in the exhibition. Usually, the features include a few minutes in the studio, a few words from the artist's mouth, and some footage of works with explanatory comments from a voiceover. Instead of this, Carnegie insisted that she would remain out of sight and that instead of speaking about her work she would provide the voiceover, reading passages from the assiduously art-historical catalogue text, recited in a droning tone and accompanied by the low-key but ominously nervy sound of the band Throbbing Gristle. In other words, she took the soft aesthetic of television features and the avuncular tone of museum educational materials and, with the precision of a stuntman, made them collide.

Watching Gillian Carnegie and Laura Owens developing and communicating their work is a feast for both the eyes and the intellect. But one should not underestimate the seriousness with which they both treat a simple but regularly ignored dimension of showing painting: How do I as a physically present viewer move between and past pictures, and what happens to me as I do this? Do I feel like a king pacing about the rooms of his palace? Like a pilgrim strolling from one station of the cross to the next? Like a pathologist inspecting specimens? Or like a speleologist, torch in hand, probing the surreal darkness, hoping not to step on the tail of a saber-toothed tiger? Or am I just an ordinary member of society, ideally having entered the exhibition free of charge, wandering around in a leisurely manner, eyes open, hopefully in a halfway alert frame of mind? Whatever the answer, it's not just a question of how I move, but also of how the art anticipates and grasps this, while strictly avoiding schoolmasterly condescension and intimidating grand gestures. It's a matter, in other words, of assuming as a matter of principle that every viewer has the potential to gain their own understanding of the work (provided the work in question allows this at all). Including the ability to tell the difference between bluff and genuine brilliance.

More than ever before, painting has learned to practice what might be termed "syntactic hanging," using pictures to form sentences in a space. In a sense, of course, this is a return to the origins of painting, but—and this is the point—not quite. For although there is an increased emphasis on spaces, they are neither new caves nor new chapels of painting. Art as an esoteric "back to the roots" or as a religion would be grotesque in view of its conflicting role within society: Status symbol for the powerful on the one hand, medium reflecting the profane visual world on the other. We are dealing, then, not with a harmonious whole but with a syncopated, fragmented rhythm that remains variable—a property we will return to in more detail regarding video and film installations in the next chapter.

Good painting stretches and contracts between two- and four-dimensionality in order to escape, at least for moments, from its fate as a JPEG file circulated to stimulate the wet dreams of speculative collectors. We have looked at approaches where painters submit mechanically to their methodical decisions during the painting process, and at other approaches where it is in this very process itself that the important decisions arise. But in the exhibition display—in front of me as the viewer—these pictures gather to make new, tacit agreements, obstinacies, moments of stunned hesitation. The painting of decisions doesn't do the work for me.

# Illusion *versus* Anti-Illusion Film/Video in Exhibition Architectures

## Fairytales and Factualities

The increasing availability of video projectors, flat screens, and digital playback devices has facilitated the creation of elaborate video spaces and multiple projections, allowing large-scale exhibitions to be walked through as modular, temporary architectures. Instead of following the linear sequence of a film projected on a screen, viewers move through a choreography of projections. A similar experience was already possible in so-called "immersive" art spaces that sucked viewers in, inundating and confronting many or all of their senses with coordinated or contradictory impressions: the frescoes of Pompeii, the light effects of medieval stained glass windows, Baroque painted ceilings, the magic lantern, the panoramas and dioramas of the nineteenth century. Crucially, however, the experience of video installations is due not just to simple "immersion," but to a new kind of three-dimensional montage. The images and sounds are related to each other in the space as a syncopated sequence by means of algorithmic coordination, most often with the help of computers.

What happens to the audience in such film and video installations? Is it suggestively seduced or, on the contrary, critically activated? Or is this the wrong question? What do I perceive when I enter these projection spaces? What's special about this experience compared to the experience of cinema, television, or the Internet? Or, to put it in more basic terms: Who moves through what kind of visual media space, and how?

Reading the specialist literature on the subject, a standard answer emerges: *viewers* are transformed into *flaneurs* strolling through *black boxes* flooded with a *spectacle* that manipulates their senses (or, provided it's a critical deconstruction of such a spectacle, triggers their critical reflection). But this description is off the mark on four points: the viewer, the flaneur, the black box, and the spectacle. Isn't it time that we discard the idea of the entertainment industry's media spectacle as a grand fairytale that lures us—aimlessly strolling consumers—into the darkness, whereas true art is engaged in a heroic project of enlightenment, ruthlessly decoding and laying bare all the myths and machinations that control the entire hocus-pocus? Wouldn't it be better to acknowledge that it's actually the tension between the affective "contamination" of the mythical and the laying bare of mechanisms that fuels both entertainment *and* art? This is the hypothesis I will be exploring in this chapter.

# Ways Out of the Cave: Phantasmagoria, Cinéorama, Dziga Vertov, Charles and Ray Eames

Many stories about indoor projections begin with Plato's image of the cave. Captivated viewers stare at a wall, watching the dancing shadows of something taking place behind them. They are convinced that what they see is the only reality. But only by stepping outside the cave into the light of day can the truth be recognized.

This idea of enlightenment as liberation from the bonds of illusion appeared to have won a decisive triumph with the French Revolution of 1789. But the revolutionary Paris of 1793 saw the appearance of the Phantasmagoria, a new form of entertainment which used the magic lantern and other tricks to stage a show of illusions in the dark—at the precise moment when the triumph of political and scientific reason over superstition and subservience took a turn toward terror. A few years later, in 1799, Etienne-Gaspard Robertson used the deserted Convent of the Capuchins in Paris as the location for his show. As film historian Tom Gunning vividly describes, the audience arrived as night fell, making its way past crumbling walls and down a long corridor which Robertson had decorated with fantastic paintings, before entering the Salon de Physique, where the sparks of electricity (a new discovery at the time) flew, and where other technical playthings could be admired. Only then, to the sounds of the glass harmonica (an array of glass vessels played by rubbing wet fingers around their rims), did the audience enter the dimly lit hall where Robertson promised the apparition of phantoms and the dead (or, more precisely, the illusion of their apparition). The audience sat down, the light was extinguished, and after an initial silence, sound effects imitating rain, thunder, and church bells were heard. Then, the magic lantern came into play, the projector concealed and the figures appearing as if from nowhere on blackened sheets of glass. Prominent figures who had died in the years of the Revolution (Danton, Marat, and Robespierre, but also King Louis XVI) appeared as specters come back to plague the present.

According to Gunning, "the Phantasmagoria literally took place on the threshold between science and superstition, between Enlightenment and Terror," between scientific presentation and necromancy. And this tension was emphasized as the actual attraction: "Although some viewers of the Phantasmagoria may have been simply fooled and led to believe in the existence of the illusions they saw, most spectators clearly understood and enjoyed the show as what it was repeatedly announced to be—a trick, a game of fooling the senses." The aim was not to generate an unconditional belief in the existence of the supernatural, an aim at odds with the presentation of scientific experiments. Instead, it was about combining entertainment with a challenge to the recently established faith in the dictates of reason—a test of its stability. In other words, it was not just illusions and trickery in the crude sense.

In the late nineteenth century, the first films were often shown as simultaneous projections in funfair tents, allowing visitors to stroll around between the various images. The Cinéorama at the 1900 World's Fair in Paris combined this experience of simultaneity with the 360-degree illusionism of an earlier form: the large-scale painted panorama. Ten projectors pointed in all directions, their images simulating a ride in a hot air balloon, since the film had been shot with ten synchronized cameras from a balloon lifting off from the Tuileries Gardens. Those watching the film were themselves positioned in a balloon basket above the projectors, causing them, as newspapers at the time reported, to fall prey to the illusion of rising up into the air. But the Cinéorama was not a success. After three days, the show was stopped due to the fire risk posed by overheated projectors and flammable film stock. The technique was never used again.

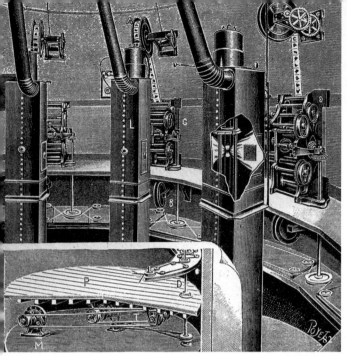

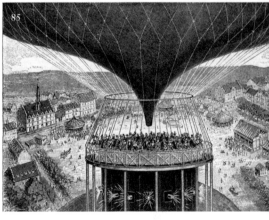

82-85    Cinéorama, World's Fair in Paris, 1900

In the twentieth century, movie theaters adopted the conventions of the theater, keeping the audience in its seats in front of a fixed projection. With a few avant-garde exceptions, camera equipment was banished from the images, appearing only by accident, as when microphone booms protruded into a scene. By the 1960s, from the point of view of critical film theory and experimental approaches to film, the entire conventional apparatus of cinema was suspected of being analogous to a hierarchic model of society that tended to treat the individual like a child—the products of the dream factory being dreamed by a passively receptive audience. Structural Film reacted to this with the idea of not just using this apparatus (camera, film stock, editing, story, etc.), but also making it an explicit subject of filmmaking.

The legendary Russian director Dziga Vertov was a key precursor in this field. His documentary *Man With A Movie Camera* (1929) portrays a day in the life of the metropolis of Moscow. Whereas the Cinéorama deployed elaborate means to create the illusion of flying as an unbroken panorama, Vertov used the shock tactics of rapid movement and quick cuts, contrasting hectic passages with still images. His roaming camera seeks out unconventional angles and perspectives. And although he didn't work with synchronized cameras or multiple projections, he did use multiple exposure.

Vertov makes film equipment itself the subject of his film. We see the cameraman on top of the car driving alongside the carriage before we see the images taken by the camera of the carriage and its passengers. We see the editor at work, followed by the piece of film she was working on. We see the crowds on a Moscow boulevard, followed immediately by a close-up of the face of an old farmer's wife, then a strip of film with perforations with three pictures of a little girl. The result is an experimental stream of consciousness that sets film art sharply apart from the fictionalizations of literature and theater, achieved by the continual showing of film technology itself. The camera has an aggressive presence, Vertov emphasizes the possibility of surveillance. The economic policy initiated by Lenin after 1921 tolerated elements of private enterprise to boost the economy, but Stalin's takeover of power in 1928 finally spelled the end for bourgeois elements like the people in the carriage.

Vertov hoped to establish his experimental film language as the dominant style in the new Soviet state, but under Stalin this was not to be. His film anticipated by decades what in the late 1950s were still considered daring, unconventional techniques: the roaming camera, the quick cuts, the fragmented, multi-perspective view. In 1959, designers Ray and Charles Eames realized a film that gave this approach a remarkable new form, taking the ambition of the Cinéorama to a new level: orchestrated, kaleidoscopic multi-projection.

The same year, U.S. Vice President Richard Nixon made a state visit to Moscow. This was a time of attempts at diplomatic rapprochement. Nixon gave Khrushchev a tour of the American National Exhibition, an extensive presentation designed to express the wealth of technological and cultural production in the U.S.. With unusual openness, and in a strange tone of friendly rivalry, the two men discussed the different ideological concepts of the two superpowers— but they also talked about the washing machines and color televisions that the Americans had proudly brought with them to Moscow. The show's eye-catcher was a geodesic dome designed by Buckminster Fuller, a modular structure that landed in the Soviet capital like some alien craft. It was the venue for screenings of the Eameses' film, commissioned by the U.S. government, which bore the title *Glimpses of the USA*.

Seven screens the size of half a football pitch, their corners rounded like those of a TV screen, floated high above thousands of standing viewers. The film lasts just twelve minutes, but contains over 2,200 shots, shown simultaneously as a multiple projection. The music is by Elmer Bernstein, composer of dramatic soundtracks for *The Man with the Golden Arm* (1955) and *The Ten Commandments* (1957), and a paternal voice guides the audience through a week in the life of the U.S.. The film starts with a starry sky which, the voice explains, the Americans share with the Russians. There are nature scenes from the Midwest, then a bird's-eye view of an American suburb, where the film zooms in on the average American family gathered around the breakfast table before Daddy goes to work and Mummy sees the children off to school. Bright shiny automobiles, city scenes in the subway and on the street, parks, research centers, shopping malls, and factories with huge parking lots where (as the voiceover doesn't fail to mention) the workers park their cars. Steel works, huge lines of combine harvesters, cowboys. The pictures are orchestrated in a restless rhythm of still and moving images, macro- and micro-perspectives. Evening comes, jazz, night-life, we see the same person seven times, it's Marilyn Monroe singing (a scene from Billy Wilder's *Some Like it Hot*, also made in 1959). Then the weekend, a picnic in the park, people swimming, fathers flying kites with their sons, contemplation at the art museum, worship in church, but also a Native American ritual, the end of the week. The American way of life.

In a lecture given in fall 2006 at a symposium on the "Beyond Cinema" exhibition at Hamburger Bahnhof museum in Berlin, architectural historian Beatriz Colomina spoke in detail about the Eameses' multiple projections. The audience in Moscow reportedly had tears in their eyes. Why the tears? Were they envious of such a convenient, well-organized world of smart cars and large family houses? Or was it just the shock of sensory overload, making them cry like a stiff facing wind? Black-and-white photos show the captivated audience staring upwards, as if witnessing the landing of a spaceship. And in a certain sense they were. The coup consisted of telling the country that had won the race to put a satellite into space: "You've got a tin can in orbit? We've got visions of a better life, painted on an artificial firmament with the technology of advanced cinematic projections, color television, and computers!" (A gigantic IBM computer was part of the American self-presentation.)

But taking into account the wider political climate of the Cold War, the propaganda battle was more complex still. The space race was merely the friendly side of the nuclear arms race. 1959 was the year Herman Kahn wrote and delivered the lectures published in expanded form as *On Thermonuclear War* (1960), the book in which he tried to show that such a war could be fought and won. The same year, the first American submarines capable of launching ballistic missiles came into service, guaranteeing second-strike capability in the case of an attack by the USSR. A Moscow audience moved to tears by a stylized film about a week in the everyday life of the U.S.? It must have had something to do with this showdown, for which the question of who did or did not have the automobiles and the refrigerators was merely a cover. The film does play on such effects of impressing and bragging (shiny bodywork, automated kitchen utensils), but its impact depends at least as much on empathy. Don't Russian families, too, have breakfast together on Monday mornings, or go for a picnic by the lake on Saturdays? In times of imminent global destruction, Charles and Ray Eames invoked global community, based on their airy, Modernist notion of domesticity and the everyday. The banal quotidian similarities flash up as atomized fragments.

Like Vertov before them, the Eameses were ideologically invested and involved in their time. In 1929, Vertov's celebration of a day in the life of the revolutionary proletariat was a stylization that glossed over the real hardships of the workers under Stalin. And the Eameses glossed over the hardship and discrimination of African Americans, although they are visible in the film, not as servants—that

86

87

86    **Dziga Vertov**, Man with a Movie
      Camera, 1929
87    **Charles & Ray Eames**, Glimpses of
      USA, 1959

would have been a strategic mistake with regard to a Soviet audience—but as city dwellers, as schoolchildren, as jazz bohemians (in the years before the Civil Rights movement, such inclusion was not a matter of course). At the same time, they also left out the nuclear threat that formed the backdrop to their vision. As they showed seven highway intersections from above, they should also have shown seven mushroom clouds. Without wishing to ignore the differences between the beginning of Stalinism and the end of the McCarthy era, the main parallel between the Eameses and Vertov is the link between political ideology and aesthetic innovation. Both made films commissioned by the state and, at historical moments of political crisis and ideological conflict, both sought to break down narrative logic and the technological conventions of media—and both did so as a way of salvaging the promise once held by the ideology in question.

Fragmentation of perception is often interpreted as an expression of trauma. The need to block out memory makes the image splinter, like that well-worn motif of psycho-kitsch, the broken mirror. But if this splintering is used and orchestrated deliberately, if it gets intuitively or mechanically worked through, then trauma becomes vision, and blocked-out past becomes possible future. For Vertov, the working class *is* in possession of the means of production, thus also possessing the possibilities that machines and media can open up. And for the Eameses, the U.S. *is* the land of boundless possibilities. What moved the Muscovites to tears was not a longing for refrigerators and automobiles, but a vision emerging from the multiplication of images, banishing the trauma of atomic confrontation—a vision of reconciliation between man and machine, and between ordinary human beings.

# Ways Out of the Black Box: Nam June Paik, Robert Whitman, Andy Warhol, Dan Graham, Joan Jonas, Valie Export, Anthony McCall, Michael Snow, Jeff Wall, Thomas Demand, Wolfgang Tillmans, Steve McQueen, Monica Bonvicini

In the 1960s, and certainly under the impression of the Vietnam War and the crushing of the Prague Spring, few were inclined to believe in visions that were part of state-sanctioned cultural programs. Expanded Cinema and psychedelic light shows were the decade's answers to Vertov and the Eameses. Instead of their push toward the center of political power, there emerged subcultures and countercultures. Here, too, multiple images and lights were used, either by two-dimensional layering or by three-dimensional fragmenting. But the approach was more improvised, and less strongly orchestrated and rhythmicized. With multiple projections, light effects, and performances, conventional cinema's limitation of projection to a single screen was abandoned once again.

The exhibitions "Into the Light" at New York's Whitney Museum (2001) and "X-Screen" at Vienna's MUMOK (2004) reconstructed this history. In 1964, Nam June Paik realized *Zen for Film*, a piece consisting of nothing but a strip of transparent film stock running through the projector in a loop; Paik stood in the light, casting his shadow onto the screen, and performed simple actions—he was the film. Robert Whitman's "film sculpture" *Shower* (1964) is a film of a naked woman that is projected onto the curtain of a shower cubicle with an actual shower running inside.

While Whitman's piece is marked by a rather superficial emphasis on the surprise effect of merging projected illusion and real presence, Andy Warhol's experiments with multiple projections took things a step further. *Outer and Inner Space* (1965) consists of two sixteen-millimeter films projected side by side, each lasting thirty-three minutes. They show Edie Sedgwick—Warhol's then-favorite personification of feminine glamour—talking to a picture of herself on a video monitor (Warhol was among the very first artists to use video), but also to a person outside the frame. Due to the double projection, we see Sedgwick four times; sometimes one of her speaks, and sometimes all four speak. Just as Warhol's "Marilyns" are duplicated by screen printing, the effect is achieved here by coupling video and film in projected and real space. At the same time, the self or "inner space" of the film's star is also duplicated, kaleidoscopic, un-graspable. The next step was Warhol's *Exploding Plastic Inevitable* (1966), the phantasmagoria of a nightclub full of projections, performers, dancers, and live rock music (by the Velvet Underground). Sensual overload. Depending on mood and attitude and drug intake, this challenge to the senses could be experienced as pleasurable or painful.

In the mid-1960s, Dan Graham made conceptual works, mostly in the form of advertisements or articles in magazines. In 1965, he published an uncommented strip of cash register receipt in the advertisement section of *Harper's Bazaar*,

88    **Andy Warhol,** Outer and Inner Space, 1965
89    **Dan Graham,** Roll (installation view), 1970

90     **Dan Graham**, Body Press, 1970–72
91     **Valie Export**, Conjoined Dislocation II, 1973

coincidentally sandwiched between ads for Tampax and Warner's brand brassieres. In 1966, he documented the new boom in tract housing in the form of an article for *Arts Magazine*, linking the seriality and uniformity of these mass-produced homes to Minimal art. He also wrote articles of cultural criticism on Eisenhower, the Kinks, and Dean Martin's drunken television appearances, which he related to Bertolt Brecht and Andy Warhol. All of this was before 1970, when Graham realized a piece entitled *Roll*. One camera, placed on the ground, filmed him filming with a second camera in the direction of the first, while rolling across the ground from left to right. The two resulting films are projected onto opposite walls of the gallery space. The same year, he made another film, *Body Press*, now considered a pioneering work of artistic film installation: Two naked people, a man and a woman, stand with their backs to one another inside a reflective metal cylinder; both hold Super-8 cameras in front of their stomachs with the lens pointing toward the mirror, and begin to move the cameras in rising and descending spirals over the surface of their own bodies, including their backs; still filming, they then swap cameras behind their backs and repeat the process. The exhibition piece consists of both films projected as large images onto opposite walls of a gallery space. As one circles the two projectors in the exhibition situation, disorientation inevitably sets in; but with time, the helical scanning of two bodies that repeatedly crosses over establishes a strange rhythm. The reflective metal skin and the camera pressed to the skin become an analogy—a kind of transgender yet asexual ballet of seeing bodies under the conditions of film technology. In this performative approach to the medium itself, it is the body's own movements that dictate the pace of the images. In the work of Joan Jonas, a similar thing happens when live performance, live video feed, and projection multiply overlap. Or in Valie Export's piece *Adjungierte Dislokation* (Conjoined Dislocation, 1973), which is something like a fusion of Graham's pieces *Roll* and *Body Press*. With two eight-millimeter cameras strapped to her chest and back, the artist moved through the city filming in both directions, while a third sixteen-millimeter camera filmed her as she went; in exhibitions, the three films are projected simultaneously side by side.

After 1973, Graham abandoned the medium of film, not least because the production costs were too high. Beginning in 1974, he built modular video spaces (some mirrored, some not) where monitors show the movements of visitors who enter the room, with a time lag of several seconds. As a result, those present watch themselves and others being watched; art throws the viewer's gaze back and entangles it in a feedback loop. (Other artists, including Bruce Nauman, Joan Jonas, Peter Campus, and Peter Weibel have also worked with live video in this way.) Stimulus response patterns are deployed to create an ambivalent mood between discomfort and amusement.

In 1978, Graham devised *Video Projection Outside Home*. The idea was to install a large television projector (then a brand new product from the Advent brand) on the lawn in front of every house in a typical American suburb, showing the channel being watched at any given time in each house. Sadly, this project was never realized. But the idea of a cinematic gaze also plays a part in Graham's architectural-sculptural glass pavilions, made from the late 1970s on, mostly for outdoor locations—in the reflections in glass and mirrors, and in the framing of what one sees in or through them.

A high point in the first period of film projections in art spaces is Anthony McCall's *Line Describing A Cone* (1973). Here the viewers are involved to an even greater degree as active participants in a scenario. I enter a dark, empty room where all I see is the film projection of a single white dot. While I'm expecting a conceptual lesson in geometry and my eyes are still adjusting to the darkness, smoke rises from a dry ice machine so that the line of the beam that makes the point on the projection surface becomes visible in the space. Slowly, as the dot widens into a circle, the line becomes a cone whose outline vibrates with the irregular clouds of smoke. The cinematographic fixation on projector and screen is replaced by an interest in the virtual sculpture that hovers between them in the space. At first I stand outside the cone, slightly reluctant to break through its surprisingly dense surface, but when I step into its center and look back toward the projector, I see a dramatic fantasy scenario. As the conical beam cuts through the billowing smoke, the clouds look like rotating galaxies. I test the cone's borders with my body and my eyes by plunging in and moving out again. It's like Darth Vader could emerge from the darkness at any moment—or Michael Jackson, who (as critic Mark Godfrey has observed) danced in front of a similar cone of light in the "Rock With You" video in the late 1970s. But the main emphasis is on the participatory aspect, when a playful moment emerges from the lesson in geometry as if from the proverbial mist; interaction not as a prescribed program but as a game that is both simple and ungraspable.

In 1974, Michael Snow made film and film collide. *Two Sides to Every Story* is projected onto both sides of an aluminum sheet hanging in the space. Both loops show a female character performing a series of movements between two

92 **Dan Graham,** Video Projection
Outside Home, 1978
93 **Anthony McCall,** Line Describing a
Cone, 1973 (installation view,
New York 2002)

cameras on tripods (each camera is visible in the footage shot by the other). At one point, she sprays a green circle onto a sheet of glass so that the view of the cameras to either side is obscured again—optical illusion and multiplication of perspectives grate against one another, while the audience can never see both projections at the same time, having to constantly circle them.

Jeff Wall once commented that museums have yet to add a dusky "lunar department" to their sunlit exhibition spaces. His carefully orchestrated scenes presented as large backlit color transparencies have never wanted to give the impression of portraying a "found" reality. Since his early works of the 1970s, he has challenged established notions of documentary photography with a staged, painterly iconography that brings the means of film to bear. This is already suggested by the medium of the lightbox: an everyday item in advertising, fleetingly glimpsed in the urban environment, but also in science, as in its use for viewing X-ray images.

In his two-part work *Eviction Struggle* (1988–1989), Wall breaks down the relationship between a passing and a focused gaze. The work consists of a large-format transparency showing a residential area from an elevated viewpoint, using the classic Hollywood device of a crane shot. This camera angle alone underlines the shot's staged character. We see policemen wrestling with a bearded man in a T-shirt in the front garden, his wife coming to his aid, passersby gawping. In the exhibition situation, the second part of the work is installed on the other side of the wall on which the lightbox is hung; nine video screens showing loops of the individual protagonists in close-up and in slow motion are positioned exactly where the person in question is seen in the large image. This repetition in moving images turns the poses—fist to chin, puzzled look—into slapstick routines. The eviction order which (according to the title) has led to this tragicomic struggle is accepted with the same indifference and coolness by passersby as by the camera itself. At the same time, however, Wall's method turns this supposed indifference into a form of participation; his pictures are alive with a tension between the cold-blooded control of their execution and a fascination with the loss of emotional control.

*Eviction Struggle* is Wall's only video piece to date. Moreover, in 2004, he reissued the picture in a digitally reworked version under the title *An Eviction*, slightly altering the constellation of protagonists (some of the passersby have disappeared, others have been added). In a certain sense, then, the video version is now "orphaned." Wall uses video merely as a test medium to prepare his

94a+b  **Jeff Wall**, An Eviction, 1988/2004

large-scale scenes with multiple characters. With the *Eviction Struggle* installation, shown as part of an exhibition on the connection between still photography and film (Centre Pompidou, Paris, 1990), he revealed the "source code" of his working method just this once. While the color transparency has a film-like character, the video loops make it clear that moving images in gallery spaces are not just a transposition of the Phantasmagoria or of cinema into the mode of the art exhibition. His pictures may take on a phantasmagorical, surreal character, but the way they are shown emphasizes an analytical approach structured according to the principles of a carefully coordinated hanging of paintings.

A similar situation is found in the work of Thomas Demand. His precise paper reconstructions of environments and "crime scenes," made as close as possible to life size, are shown to the viewer only in the form of high-resolution photographs. In this way, the painstaking work that went into creating the illusion remains hidden, but so does the media story on which the picture is based. Be it one of the offices in Florida where the 2000 U.S. presidential election was decided by a recount (*Poll*, 2001), the rubbish-strewn kitchen in the hideout used by Saddam Hussein (*Küche/Kitchen*, 2004), or the interiors of Niger's embassy in Rome, from which the documents (forged, as it later turned out) used by the Bush administration to "prove" that Iraq had bought yellowcake uranium were purportedly stolen (*Yellowcake*, 2007): in exhibitions, the pictures are shown with no explicit textual reference to their historical source (though information may be given in the press release). In Demand's short film *Recorder* (2002), we see a tape recorder turning slowly and tirelessly, accompanied by an electronically modified, hypnotic version of a short instrumental by the Beach Boys. What we are looking at is a faithful paper reconstruction of a machine used by the group to make their legendary lost album *Smile*. With the characteristic jerkiness of stop-motion animation, the short loop further heightens what is already present in the photographs. Our uncertainty concerning the narrative background of what we are looking at—is this an ordinary or a "special" tape recorder, kitchen utensil, etc.?—creates the dreamlike, ghostly gap through which the exhibition viewer enters the sequence of images in the installation, relating them to one another instead of simply registering them—with an "Oh, I see!"—as *trompe l'oeil* images based on a media story.

Besides photography conceived as part of installations with a background in painterly or sculptural approaches, there are also artists influenced by print media, something that is especially evident in the case of Wolfgang Tillmans.

His photographic practice is rooted in his work for music and style magazines from the late 1980s, involving participatory photographic observation of the gay and youth culture scenes. But over the course of the 1990s, his repertoire of subject matter and techniques evolved far beyond this, from private moments to everyday and far-from-everyday scenes, through to abstract compositions: pomegranates on a windowsill, a picture of Isa Genzken, a picture of Tony Blair, a penis pointed at an in-flight meal, a solar eclipse, a Concorde taking off, red swirls from the developer tray as a photogram straight onto the picture. Still life, portrait, landscape, abstraction. Because of this broad spectrum seemingly rooted in the classical genres of painting, one can easily overlook (as in the work of painters Laura Owens and Gillian Carnegie) how the resulting system of images is actually played out. The exhibition wall is treated as a two-page magazine spread on which pictures—both photographic and inkjet prints—are arranged in various sizes and positions; but at the same time, there are also often vitrines in which pieces of printed matter are combined with Tillmans's pictures. Such arrangements would be unthinkable without the everyday experience of printed images in books and magazines. Like the people featured in his work, Tillmans's pictures are defined primarily in terms of their relation to one another.

These links between fine art photography and the hanging of paintings or hanging-as-layout would seem to suggest a much less dominant role for the black boxes of cinema and the Phantasmagoria as models for recent film and video projection spaces. In spite of this, the black box remained a paradigm for video installation art until well into the 1990s. There were various reasons for this. First, there was the need for a certain degree of darkening in order to achieve acceptable image quality. Second, there was a desire to conceal the image-generating technology, the wires, and the shortcomings of the space in order to facilitate the creation of a virtual "dream world." Third, there was a deliberate referencing of the long tradition of showing films in the dark. And fourth, there were allusions to other meanings of "black box": a technical device with which one interacts without knowing its inner workings, a data recorder, a closed cybernetic system, etc.

Firstly, however, video projectors and flat screens are now of such high quality and so affordable that darkening is more a question of staging than of pure necessity. Secondly, most attempts to create forms of computer-assisted interaction in the dark have proved unsatisfactory, due to their tendency to treat the viewer as a guinea pig, or simply because their conceptual structure is weak, mired in the demonstration of technological feasibility but often lacking ideas or artistic merit. Total darkness is used as if it already went halfway toward dispensing with the body entirely in a virtual space (the black box as a kind of pressure chamber before entering the holodeck onboard USS Enterprise). Thirdly, not least thanks to Structural Film, projection technology has often enough become part of the artwork. Film installations by Tacita Dean, Rodney Graham, Matthew Buckingham, Marijke van Warmerdam, Henrik Håkansson, Manon de Boer, and Simon Starling, to name just a few, explicitly include the projection technology (projector, loop device, etc.). And fourthly, the single black space has in many cases long since been replaced by a modular sequence of situations.

As a result, the more interesting contemporary works no longer send us into the dark out of technological necessity or methodological habit, but only when it makes sense in conceptual terms. A good example of this is Steve McQueen's *Carib's Leap/Western Deep* (2002). For this film, the audience was seated in a pitch-dark auditorium (a purpose-built space at the 2002 Documenta in Kassel, and an underground former cinema in London the same year). All doors are shut tight, there is no light whatsoever, and the film begins. We hear the mechanical creaking and rattling of a lift in a mine shaft, with just the occasional glimmer, a faint reflection from a helmet or a piece of metal, a face. The idea that the film illusorily cancels out my own being-in-the-dark is contradicted—I am reminded of my strange situation as one of many people sharing the present moment in a pitch-dark room. The footage is shot on Super-8, necessarily operating at the absolute limit of what can be captured with a lens and photochemical processes, which in itself is a metaphor for the exhaustion of the South African miners in the gold mine who are the subject of the film. In this piece, the idea of an imagination-stimulating black box is taken seriously one last time only in order to let it collapse.

As we resurface from this catharsis that is not cathartic at all, the black box proves to be no longer the rule but the exception. In the long term, architecture, sculpture, and installation cannot reasonably be ignored. Monica Bonvicini's *Destroy She Said* (1998) consists of numerous scenes from the 1950s, 1960s, and 1970s, featuring women throwing themselves against walls, staggering down eerie corridors, or, dressed in a negligee, staring at cracks in the plaster. What is revealed here is a convention among male directors, from *cinéma d'auteur* right through to B movies: Woman as the desiring and desired body caught in the

95a+b   **Monica Bonvicini**, Destroy She Said, 1998
(top: installation view, Pasadena 2006)

96      **Steve McQueen**, (still from) Carib's Leap/Western
Deep, 2002

97 a+b **Philippe Parreno**, El sueño de una cosa, 2001–02 (bottom: exhibition view, Portikus, Frankfurt 2002)

artificial isolation of modernity. The idea of collecting and sequencing typical genre scenes according to a particular criteria as a way of unmasking narrative strategies, their ideology, and their unconscious, has been used by other artists (Matthias Müller and Christoph Girardet, Martin Arnold, Christian Marclay, and Harun Farocki, to mention just a few). But in Bonvicini's work, this is just the first step. The film excerpts are projected onto two slanted, free-standing screens and the room is strewn with pieces of wood of the kind used to make these screens. It's as if the images of collapse have entered the space and as if, conversely, the space has revealed how these images are constructed, quickly cobbled together out of stubborn, old stereotypes that happened to be lying around.

In this way, the exhibition architecture itself genuinely becomes part of the showing of film images, and few artists have developed this aspect further than Philippe Parreno. In his exhibitions, he uses different colored carpets to suggest a particular path to walk, phosphorescent posters that can only be seen in the dark, blinds and lights operated automatically in sync with projections, and wall labels with the titles of the works realized as small lightboxes. At Portikus in Frankfurt in 2002, he showed a one-minute thirty-five-millimeter film of peculiar nature scenes from the Scandinavian tundra. The film was originally conceived as a comic interlude for blocks of cinema advertising in Sweden; in one scene that parodies the speeded-up scenes in nature films, a cactus-like object is inflated like a balloon by a hidden mechanism. In Frankfurt, Parreno projected this film onto a replica of Robert Rauschenberg's *White Painting* (1951) that is made up of five vertical-format sections. As soon as the one-minute film was over, the light came on for four minutes and thirty-three seconds, before the room was returned to darkness for a second screening of the film—the pause as a reference to John Cage's silent composition of the same length that was inspired, among others, by Rauschenberg's painting. Besides this assiduous self-positioning with regard to heroes of modern art, then, this piece was about being content with neither white cube nor black box, conceiving the exhibition instead as a "musical score," as Parreno himself put it—an organized interplay within a precisely measured timeframe that runs through quite different spatial experiences but in the same location. Organized interplay, precisely measured, controlled by hidden mechanisms. Isn't this beginning to sound like some grand spectacle?

# The Spectacle: Guy Debord's Nightmare Bill Viola (With Pier Paolo Pasolini), Matthew Barney, Douglas Gordon and Philippe Parreno (With Hellmuth Costard), Olafur Eliasson

Faced with complex film/video installations, many professional art observers instinctively reach for the concept of "The Spectacle." This does not refer to a spectacle in the usual sense of a large-scale event full of attractions, either ceremonial or for entertainment, though this association is always there. Instead, it refers to the concept developed by Guy Debord, whose book *The Society of the Spectacle*, published in France in 1967, describes the visual world of the media as an ideological manifestation of a consumer culture that alienates people from themselves and from each other.

Guy Debord was not the first to make the connection between commodity fetishism and alienation. In *The German Ideology* (1845), Karl Marx used the *camera obscura* as a metaphor to criticize the philosophy of German idealism since Hegel. Like this device where light enters a box through a small opening so that the outside world appears upside down, idealism, too, inverts the material basis of lived experience. The Phantasmagoria is also used by Marx as a metaphor—for the fetish character of commodities. In *Capital*, he writes: "In the act of seeing, there is at all events really a passage of light from one thing to another, from the external object to the eye. There is a physical relation between physical things. But it is different with commodities. There, the existence of the things as commodities and the value relation between the products of labor which stamps them as commodities have absolutely nothing to do with their physical nature and the physical relations that originate from this physicality. There it is a definite social relation between men, that assumes, in their eyes, the phantasmagorical form of a relation between things." As Tom Gunning emphasizes, "phantasmagorical" is by no means to be understood merely as an equivalent of "fantastical," referring instead to what in the nineteenth century would have been the far more immediate association of the word "phantasmagoria." Just as the Phantasmagoria conceals the devices that make the pictures appear in the space as if by supernatural means, the work that went into a commodity is also concealed—so that the commodity, too, appears as if created by a phantom hand.

In Debord's theory, these two aspects are merged. Instead of using images and those looking at them as a metaphor for commodities and their consumers, as Marx did, the two aspects taken together constitute "the spectacle." This spectacle is "a social relationship between people that is mediated by pictures," but in the sense that this relationship is usually an alienated one. This is Debord's position not only as a theorist, but also as a filmmaker. His famous but rarely watched film *Hurlements en faveur de Sade* (Howlings in Favor of De Sade, 1952) is an early absolute anti-film. While lengths of transparent leader strip run through the projector, we hear different voices uttering vowels in a guttural tone like Kurt Schwitters', or reciting aphorisms like "Love is valid only in a prerevolutionary period," answered by "Those girls don't *all* love you, you liar!" Between such passages, there are minutes of total silence and blackness (for these, Debord used perforated magnetic tape to avoid the crackling sound always generated by actual film stock). One last brief sentence: "We live like lost children, our adventures unfinished." Then a final fifteen minutes of blackness.

Avant-garde art, Debord writes, can only be "an art of change and a pure expression of the impossibility of change. The more grandiose its demands, the further from its grasp is true self-realization. This is an art that is necessarily avant-garde; and it is an art that does not exist. Its vanguard is its own disappearance." The diagnosis is clear: Art that becomes part of the spectacle has ceased to be art. If it does not become part of the spectacle, it is still art, but it disappears from the consciousness of the masses. At best, artists can disturb this procedure with a handful of guerilla tactics—such as Dada-inspired *détournement*, the stealing and recombination of cultural components. Debord also refers to the spectacle as a "permanent opium war." He sees himself as a partisan in the cultural struggle. He admires and quotes the theorists of war Sun Tzu (*The Art of War*) and Clausewitz (*On War*). Ultimately, however, this is a war in which artists have no chance, Debord claims, as co-optation must inevitably set in. Even Jean-Luc Godard was considered by the Situationists as an imitator flogging Situationist ideas to the spectacle. All of this bespeaks a kind of radical, poetic nostalgia for a time before the widespread accessibility of images, before television and mass production—a nostalgia that is structured like a childhood trauma.

Common usage of Debord's concept of the spectacle has long since distanced itself from such poetic terrain. In highbrow journalism and art criticism it always turns up when writers wish to strip something of artistic relevance, along the lines of: the more elaborate the event and the higher the paparazzi factor, the greater must be the alienation and emptiness in real life or real art that is being covered up and drowned out. The good guys are sorted from the bad. On the one hand, those who cultivate an unambiguous refusal of the "machinery of illusion" by unmasking its mechanisms and sending out avant-garde signals of negation; on the other, those like the movie and television industries who are engaged in a huge campaign of putting people to sleep, flooding art institutions with images and other media disasters. But this diagnosis is given either without actually addressing its cultural manifestations, not to mention those it allegedly blinds and corrupts; or by becoming a heightened consumer who inevitably becomes libidinally involved and who is caught in the act of enjoying—but who rhetorically explains this away to him/herself and others as a kind of morbid fascination and who claims to remain above its object and see through its evil charm.

The concept of the spectacle emerged at a time when there were two or three national television channels but no Internet, when there were cinemas but no video rental shops or DVDs. In purely quantitative terms, then, the spectacle has become more powerful, more extensive, more of an inundation. Nothing is immune to advertising, no degree of trendy, radical, or critical acumen can protect you from being co-opted for profit. But in qualitative terms, the spectacle has become something which none of the three attributes proposed by Debord— concentrated, diffuse, or integrated spectacle—can adequately describe. The economy of attention has become far less predictable, a highly fragmented, individualized, and digitally differentiated domain. In the eyes of the paranoid (and Debord would doubtless have agreed) this is the ultimate triumph of totalitarianism: Microsoft and Google, in league with the secret services, as the true dictators. But such apocalyptic visions are only good for putting an end to all further discussion; they completely ignore all counter-tendencies or describe them as always already misappropriated; culture appears as one big deception. The concept of the spectacle flattens distinctions with polemic intent: It covers everything from a neo-Nazi parade, to advertisements with naked women, to a children's party at a shopping mall. From this point of view, any discussion of film/video installations in art is a total non-starter.

In the art world, increasing use is being made of strategies to generate hysteria by magically asserting art-historical importance in terms of statistics (record prices at auction and visitor numbers) or names (linking with curators, fellow artists, institutions), instead of constructively establishing this importance by showing and discussing the art itself. The question is thus not whether or not a given work involves elaborate production and lots of fuss, but how this is done, by what means, and to what effect. If we look at the work of Bill Viola and Matthew Barney, or at Douglas Gordon and Philippe Parreno's joint film project on the soccer star Zinédine Zidane, we see that even if one grants that artworks may take on the dimensions of Culture Industry products without being automatically disqualified, there is still more than enough left to criticize.

Bill Viola is among the world's most successful video artists, if not the most successful. His works are collected and shown by the most prestigious museums, where they draw big crowds. His productions are elaborate, but ironically, these large-scale works manifest a rejection of today's media spectacle—using state-of-the-art technology. Viola tirelessly evokes art-historical, religious, and spiritual aura. In *Stations* (1994), for example, the title alludes to the much portrayed Stations of the Cross. What the viewer sees are five larger-than-life video projections of naked figures, of different ages and genders, who plunge into dark water and then drift upside-down, brightly lit; these pictures are reflected in polished slabs of black granite that lie flat on the floor (showing the figures again horizontally). All of this is accompanied by loud underwater gurgling in top hi-fi quality. The audience, itself drifting in this suggestion of a huge water tank, is thrown into a flux of associations ranging from the womb to a shipwreck in icy seas.

More explicit references to art historical sources are found in Viola's video piece *The Greeting* (1995), a detailed reconstruction of Jacopo da Pontormo's mannerist painting *The Visitation* (1528–1529): Mary meets the considerably older Elisabeth, two saints sharing a deep, intimate gaze, both pregnant, in the presence of two witnesses. Viola reduces the number of characters to three, but retains the Renaissance architectural backdrop and the range of colors. Painterly rendering of folds is replaced by bourgeois bohemian "naturalness." As in the original, the three women are clothed in flowing, brightly colored garments, and although no longer barefoot, they wear ancient-looking sandals. Two women converse, before a gust of wind that stirs the hems of their skirts announces the arrival of the third, the youngest, who enters the picture from the left. She knows the older of the two and they greet each other as intimately as Maria and Elisabeth before them. Only once the new arrival has whispered something in the older woman's ear is the other woman included again. All this is shown in extreme slow motion, stretching the single, static shot from forty-five seconds to ten minutes.

The extreme slow motion and the similarly stretched-sounding soundtrack of wind noises and scraps of conversation heralds something important like a Roman fanfare. As a result, every gesture—the older woman signaling happy surprise, the second woman looking indignant at not being the center of attention—is highly emphasized and thus laden with a significance which the film then fails to deliver. The scene is just a slapped cheek or a tangling of robes away from being slapstick; comedy appears only in the guise of the unintended joke. When she arrives, I can see that the youngest woman is pregnant; in the case of the other two, I can only speculate as to whether they are or have been mothers, or whether this is even relevant—but the didactically highlighted gestures and mimicry are intended to evoke just this kind of speculation. On the surface, the religiosity of the original is undermined by modern-day banality; compared with the holy rapture of being pregnant with future saviors, the accent here is more on the ceremonial moment of the greeting, including possible frustrations and rivalries. The single static shot and the extreme slow motion demonstratively shift the video image in the direction of painting: I am supposed to take the slowness of the slow motion as a model for my readiness to take a contemplative pause and follow what's happening. But something feels wrong about this implicit appeal, as it serves to bring back the solemnity of the original. Even the most monumental picture of a saint has the modesty not to prescribe a minimum time spent contemplating it, as this is defined by religious ritual or the extent of the praying viewer's need for worship. But this video suggests that I might miss an important detail if I don't attentively watch the whole ten minutes, better still study the sequence two, three, or four times. Viola's projection prides itself, so to speak, on embodying the aspect of time, making it superior to the painting, which can suggest sequences of events but not present them directly. It wishes to partake of the cultural value of the painting, at the same time outshining it with its own media value. The everyday scene is to be charged not only with significance, but also with a biblical dimension, in accordance with the spiritual truism that eternal truths are revealed in everyday moments.

The message for the contemporary viewer, familiar with the type of woman portrayed or even embodying this type, is that everyday life contains magic moments of timeless significance, moments made visible by the artist Bill Viola and turned into the object of our longing for inspiration. Here lies the key difference between Viola and Pier Paolo Pasolini, whose films also refer to biblical and art-historical source material, but who discovers in it contemporary class distinctions, contemporary misery, contemporary social exploitation. Instead of staging a synthetic pseudo-reconciliation, he mixes the two levels—the historical/spiritual and the contemporary/material—in an anarchic act. When he refers to Piero della Francesca in *The Gospel According to Matthew* (1964), or to Giotto in *The Decameron* (1971), his aim is not to evoke their art historical aura or reconstruct their pictorial spaces, but to appropriate their methodology of reduction to the essentials.

For the professed atheist Pasolini, religion is a traditional power within society displaying both liberating and repressive tendencies, but it is not a guarantor of spirituality that transcends social differences; on the contrary, they are even more starkly highlighted. In Viola's work, the differences between people pale to insignificance beside birth and death, beside the great questions of living and dying. But in its mode of presentation—the monumentality of the projection and the sound, the polished granite, the way the space is supposed to become one big place of quasi-religious contemplation, a great cave of the pre-conscious, lit only by the projections—this allegorical claim is tainted by the sort of unironic blend of pathos and sentimentality that can so easily turn to bigotry. Hey, so there is a difference after all between the great artist who recognizes and wisely shows us all the spiritual dimensions, and the simple-minded, wide-eyed little viewers who should put their trust in him! That is Viola's strategy: always to present birth and death, living and dying, as biblically monumental determinants, instead of permitting the thought that their true severity and mystery lies in the fact that there is also something small, banal, and piteous about them. He sees a clear link between himself and Michelangelo, each video installation a Sistine Chapel, instead of taking a look at the washed-out canvases of someone like Edvard Munch (which might have been an antidote).

Viola and his followers believe they are opposing the media circus of secular capitalist reality—The Spectacle—by posing the real existential and spiritual questions, in epic monumentality, slowness, and contemplation. His video spaces are staged as chapels and cloisters that offer spiritual refuge from the banalities of media-soaked everyday life. As a critic, it's not enough to point out that Viola is himself part of this spectacle. For the problem is not the monumentality and elaborateness in itself, but the notion that synthetic realism of this kind might be capable of generating profound insights into the spiritual dimension of life simply by generating one-to-one images of moments like birth, death, or dreams and then blowing them up to a large format.

In the case of Matthew Barney, the situation is far more interesting from the outset. His ingredients are more diverse and more adventurous. Instead of Viola's biblical gesture, he favors a sect-like sense of the mysterious. The obscure appears world-shaping, the world-shaping obscure. His works are always based on biological metaphors derived from a sporting understanding of his own body (at college, Barney was a football player). In his series *Drawing Restraint* (since 1987, ongoing), it is the idea of developing muscles by opposing force (elastic bands, walls, weights, etc.); in *Cremaster*, his five-part cycle of films and installations, it is the muscle of that name which regulates the distance of the testicles from the body by reacting to sensations of heat, cold, arousal, or fear. This results in a system developed over long years which is as elaborate and epic as it is absurd—and which must, as a consequence, be carried through all the more unerringly. Art as a master plan for mythmaking.

One only has to read the official synopsis accompanying Barney's film to grasp this approach. *Cremaster 3* (2002), for example, revolves around the creation of the Chrysler Building in New York, whose architect is a master freemason (played by sculptor Richard Serra). An Apprentice (played by Barney) offers the Architect his services, with unexpected consequences: "After a prologue steeped in Celtic mythology, the narrative begins under the foundation of the partially constructed Chrysler Building. A female corpse digging her way out of a grave is the undead Gary Gilmore, protagonist of *Cremaster 2*. Carried out of her tomb by five boys, she is transported to the Chrysler Building's lobby and deposited in the back seat of a Chrysler Imperial New Yorker. During this scene, the camera cross-cuts to the Apprentice troweling cement over carved fuel-tank caps of five 1967 Chrysler Crown Imperials, each bearing the insignia of a different *Cremaster* episode." It is amusing to imagine Barney trying to explain to an ordinary film producer why he needs five cars of this precise model in order to fill them with cement and destroy them in crash scenes set in a reconstruction of the Chrysler Building's lobby; or why he should please procure such-and-such a number of tons of Vaseline. Barney's budgets may be extraordinarily high by art standards, but they still fall far short of what is spent on an average Hollywood comedy. In an art context, however, they may be a risk in financial terms,

98      **Matthew Barney**, Drawing Restraint 1 (documentation still), 1987
99      **Matthew Barney**, Cremaster 3, 2002
100     **Matthew Barney**, Cremaster 5, 1997
101     **Matthew Barney**, Drawing Restraint 9, 2005
102     **Bill Viola**, The Greeting, 1995

but they do not have to justify themselves. Vaseline is for Barney what grease and felt were for Beuys. Such repeated use of materials, then, is an established convention and a well-known recipe for success. However many death metal musicians, flight attendants, satyrs, glaciers, salt lakes, Mormons, and two-step dancing cowboys put in an appearance, Vaseline and related substances are always involved.

In the film *Drawing Restraint 9*, Barney and his partner Björk (the experimental pop musician) appear as the only Western guests on a Japanese whaling ship. The climax is a scene that was obviously inspired to no small degree by Nagisa Oshima's erotic classic *In The Realm Of The Senses* (1976). But instead of Oshima's blunt portrayal of eroticism and sexual violence—the female lead strangles her lover and then cuts off his genitals—it works with allegory: in the course of an intimate embrace, during which they slice off each other's extremities with long knives, the couple, surrounded by tons of petroleum jelly, begin to metamorphose into whales.

Barney pulls out all the stops, firing off signals of encoded mystery, polymorphous perversity, and extremely refined surrealistic fetish. This was not necessarily foreseeable at the beginning of the *Drawing Restraint* series in the early 1980s, when he used bare walls, his bare body, and a few props to turn Bruce Nauman's existential notes on the art of performance in empty spaces into a kind of sport. Succinctly formulated, it was about using the body or simple tools to leave marks as a drawing—both as a graphic mark and in the physical sense of traction. Since then, however, these succinct markings have developed into full-size artifacts that are often highly complex to produce. Barney is smart enough not just to transfer his film props straight to the gallery; instead, his sculptures are usually hybrid constructions combining several props or motifs from the film. But this doesn't really solve the problem. The *Cloud Club* (2002)—to name one example that falls out of *Cremaster 3* like a windfall from a fruit tree—is a concert grand piano; it is "tuned up" with various mysterious metal objects based on Masonic motifs, and its insides are filled with concrete. Moreover, the keyboard is obstructed by a large rectangular metal plate which in turn rests on a pile of potatoes so that the piano too is tilted. The steel plate alludes to Minimalist sculptures à la Richard Serra; the concert grand and the potatoes refer to Joseph Beuys, who once covered such a piano in felt and who explained that even peeling a potato is art provided it is a conscious act (at one point in the film, we see a woman stamping Masonic symbols into potatoes with her stiletto heel).

There is one important difference, however, between Barney and the intellectual forefathers he evokes. Serra tests his vision of sculpture in public spaces, and the years of heated discussion occasioned by his *Tilted Arc* (1981) is an eloquent testament to this (Serra's huge black metal slab that cut across New York's Federal Plaza caused annoyance above all to the office workers in the immediate vicinity and was removed by court order in 1989). And Beuys not only invented the concept of "social sculpture," but also defined his artistic work strongly in terms of his teaching and political activities. There is little trace of this in Barney's work. He offers a fantasy of polymorphously perverse outwitting of gender and power, but with Serra and Beuys he leaves the male genealogical line completely intact. The fantasy is bodied forth in extreme detail and on a monumental scale, but as a gallery or cinema show it remains ungrounded. Ungrounded in the sense that, unlike Serra and Beuys, it avoids any excursion into reality outside the film and the gallery, so that it can only refer back again and again to its own allegorical narrative and to the history of art. Which is why Barney's sculptures emerge from his films like a soufflé from the oven: once it's out, it's tasty, but it soon collapses in on itself (some of the best show precisely this collapse, like the stylized leftovers of the action with the Chryslers).

Curator Nancy Spector makes an honest attempt to defend this practice by saying that the sculptures and installations "are not cinematic relics or props but hybrid three-dimensional incarnations [... that] represent key architectural moments in the narrative." But this is precisely the problem. Why must there be a spatial representation at all, apart from the obvious need to sell art objects? The indecisiveness of this approach is given away by the fact that scenes from the films are screened in the installations containing the sculptures (at least in the presentations of the *Cremaster* cycle in Cologne, Paris, and New York). This only makes it clearer still that the films are structured like epic, eye-pleasing computer games over whose course one has no control and whose motive—apart from a demonstrative reference to power, hubris, and gender—remains firmly in the realm of rumbling mysticism. The soundtracks are full of brilliant slurping, squelching, and gurgling noises, like a great digestive tract eating itself: the shriveling meaning in Matthew Barney's work lit up by his allegorical pyrotechnics. Barney is like a bird of paradise that has built itself a particularly beautifully decorated golden cage from which there now appears to be no escape. All his audience can do is look in through the bars. There's a parallel here with the second Star Wars trilogy, released beginning in 1999: The anarchic craziness of the first three films from the 1970s and 1980s, whose off-beat roster of strange characters and techno effects were ultimately more important than the underlying science fiction fairytale plot, is crushed by the need to tell an epic story to the end, come what may, and to do so with digital perfection. Either way, Star Wars was the triumph of movie merchandising. But this is not the only reason why the unruly creative firework display finally gave way to rigorously executed hard work. What we have in Viola, Barney, and George Lucas are Wagnerians without a Bayreuth; they lift off with dazzling overtures, only to become burdened down with epic drudgery. Eventually, the tendency to the *Gesamtkunstwerk* becomes a compulsion.

Which brings us back to the concept of the spectacle. Debord's achievement was to shift the emphasis away from the critique of the conditions of production to which many Marxists limited themselves and toward a critique of the result—of commodities and their media circulation, and of consumer culture. Incidentally, this also allowed him to anticipate the rise of the service sector. But at the same time, his description of the spectacle resembles the apocalyptic visions of science fiction writers. "Imprisoned in a flat universe bounded on all sides by the spectacle's screen, the consciousness of the spectator has only figmentary interlocutors that subject it to a one-way discourse on their commodities and the politics of those commodities." It's quite clear that the historical background here is the triumphal progress of television, even if in 1964 "only" forty percent of French households owned a television set, and color TV would not become widespread until the 1970s. Things were to get much worse, then—but better, too. For the question is whether the spectators really are automatically prisoners. They appear imprisoned only to the extent that they had no opportunity to develop sufficient media competency—education and cognitive experience of usage. There's no need to join those within Anglo-American cultural studies who enthusiastically stylize the consumer as a critical guerilla tactician using consumer decisions (to buy or not to buy) as a way of outsmarting the culture industry. But in the art context, at least, it's fair to assume that most art viewers bring with them basic media competency, as well as a healthy dose of media skepticism. In spite of this, the idea of the viewer as a prisoner appears again and again in discussions of video and film installations: A few heroic gestures of disruption standing against this great inescapable immersion, the inundation of our senses that robs us of our critical distance. We are surrounded by flickering projections, the automated hypnotists of the spectacle.

But if I speak of the spectacle in blanket terms, if only a "dead" spectacle is a good spectacle, then the criticism doesn't stick. I may have "realized" that large-scale visual media ensembles somehow plague me, but I believe I only have the choice between refusal and submission. As the work of Viola and Barney illustrates, however, the extent of this supposed lulling effect depends on my consent as a viewer. Does all of this even speak to me? I don't mean the pseudo-autonomy of those who distance themselves ironically, or the self-discipline that puritanically rejects enjoyment. On the contrary, maybe I want to enjoy myself—including the possibility of opening up to new impressions and stimuli—but I can't. This is due not to the "spectacle" as such, but to the concepts of image, space, individual, idea, or imagination by which it is governed in any given case. Only when I don't see the problem in the very existence of "spectacular" film/video installations am I capable of real criticism. This precisely expresses the attitude of the disappointed pop culture fan. Here, rather than appearing as separate from "undistanced" enjoyment, fierce criticism may arise directly from a basic attitude of empathy. But—and this is the real point here—even enthusiastic, obsessive viewers don't always just submit totally to sensual stimuli. Their enthusiasm is often derived precisely from an enjoyment of recognizing the structures, from identification not just with characters but also with the director. This is a development which in Debord's day could only be observed among dedicated cinephiles, not among television viewers. The makers of early television arrogantly assumed their viewers to be naïve—a view which, ironically, they shared with their sharpest critics.

But the media competency of a generation that grew up with video recorders, video games, and video cameras is not so easily fobbed off. Even in purely cognitive terms, the ability to comprehend editing, camerawork, scenarios, and narrative structures has grown exponentially. In his book *Everything Bad is Good For You* (2006), Steven Johnson illustrates this development by comparing popular television series from various decades. In *Starsky & Hutch* from the 1970s, there is a humorous frame narrative that sits at either end of a linear whodunit in which the two policemen solve the case, including a showdown. The complexity of the plot of any episode of American "quality" television series like *The Sopranos* or *The Wire* is far higher. Here, four, five, or more narrative strands run alongside each other, their plots complex in terms of both psychology and action, sometimes unfolding not over one or two episodes but over entire series. The way situations and actions are structured is thus far more complex, based on the assumption that viewers will be prepared to buy the DVD box if necessary to understand all these clever connections during repeated viewings. Of course, the cognitive intelligence this requires doesn't necessarily translate into social and political competency. But it doesn't get in the way of such a development. In any case, a noticeable emancipation has taken place from passive consumer toward active producer. "Web 2.0"—using the Internet as a forum for DIY content-makers to publish and exchange their texts, music, and videos online—is only the latest technical culmination of this development. If one understands the "society of the spectacle" as an alienated society that can be made habitable at least for isolated moments by "situationist" tactics of reinterpretation and appropriation, then one might speak of a "society of situationism."

This is a nightmare scenario not only for Situationists, when maximum capitalist coverage—millions of contacts and marketing units—is directly coupled with consumers who adopt the position of situationists, drifting about and taking pleasure in working with the material on offer. Pimp your everyday life! Creatively style everything! Performance to the last pore! Your camera-phone, your life! My website is my bed! But this is only one side—that of commenting on and presenting oneself. The other side is that of commenting on and presenting the world. YouTube.com hosts thousands of short films by people who add contradictory soundtracks to speeches by George W. Bush or edit in a few repeats of his verbal gaffes; the website is bursting with parodic remakes of the greatest hits of the "society of the spectacle."

To Marshall McLuhan's observation that old media become the subject matter for new ones, it should be added that new media also become subject matter for the old—creating a mutual effect of influence and remodeling that predictably results in a merging. Walter Benjamin and McLuhan concur that with every new medium there is an anarchic phase of opportunities and new experiences: a window of utopian opportunity that shuts as soon as the political and economic powers feel it has gone far enough.

But consumers also cultivate a form of pseudo-authority, constantly assuring themselves and others that their consumer choices are not influenced by cheap tricks, that they assess the material on their own terms and treat it in a "situationist" manner. Certain successful artworks manage to give the viewer a body-check in this respect, robbing one of this self-assurance that can actually be deceptive. They play on precisely these expectations of critical distance in spite of enjoyment, frustrating this contrived "situationist" sense of aplomb.

103

104

**Douglas Gordon**
103  24 Hour Psycho, 1993
104  Five Year Drive-By, 1995

In Douglas Gordon's best works, the kind of viewer that is simultaneously critical and obsessive can be sensed in the work itself. *24 Hour Psycho* (1993) stretches Hitchcock's most famous movie to twenty-four hours, each scene running in extreme slow motion and without sound. In the exhibition space, the film is projected cinema-screen size. The almost still image gives it the quality of a painting; and, finally, of a sculpture, as the screen is positioned diagonally in the space. The key aspect of the piece is the technical conditions for its stretching of time. In the early 1990s, when the piece was made, home video recorders that used digital technology to allow almost flicker-free extreme slow motion and stills became affordable for the first time. The point, then, is not merely whether the technological potential for Gordon's works were given. Rather, the point is how the piece emerged from a generally accessible mode of reception. With such a device, it would have been no problem to realize Gordon's work at home, dozing off in front of a TV set showing *Psycho* in super-slo-mo. In a 1996 interview, Gordon explains that he got the idea for *24 Hour Psycho* during a Christmas visit to his family in Scotland when he watched a video of Hitchcock's film recorded off the television, until he came to the moment where Norman Bates (Anthony Perkins) watches through the keyhole as Marion Crane (Janet Leigh) gets undressed: "I thought I saw her unhooking her bra. I didn't remember seeing that in the VCR version and thought it was strange that, in terms of censorship… more would be shown on TV than in the video, so I looked at that bit with the freeze-frame button to see if it was really there… It was as if the slow-motion revealed the unconscious of the film." To which one might add that the slow motion equally reveals the unconscious of a viewer who is not sure of actually having seen such a scene.

The technical possibilities of the video recorder, some of which imitate possibilities of a film editing suite (still, slow motion, and rewind and fast-forward at different speeds), facilitate a kind of film analysis previously only within the reach of directors and the few film scholars with access to such editing suites and film material: a search for the film's fine structure, if not its "unconscious." At least as much as the old medium of cinema, Gordon focuses on the theme of its appearance in the media of television and home video; and thus also on how the experience of cinema shifts and fragments into that of television, which consists in no small part of repeated showings of cinema movies. Not least in his emphasis of the family context in which he made his discovery, Gordon takes on the role of the film fan with an interest in detail, who watches films again and again, who analytically and obsessively manipulates their linear sequence.

Taking a logical step further in the same direction, Gordon made *Five Year Drive-By* (1995), which slows down John Ford's western *The Searchers* (1956) so that watching the whole film would take five years—the time John Wayne spends in the film searching for his niece who has been abducted by the Comanche. Here, as well as the new film's duration dictated by the narrative time of the original, the moving images are slowed down to such a degree that they really do seem to become stills. Here, unlike *24 Hour Psycho*, seeing any kind of movement at all calls for considerable patience. But even this is not the main point, as indicated by the second part of the programmatic title, "drive by." In 1999, the film was shown in Mies van der Rohe's New National Gallery in Berlin, a glass cube framed in black by its roof and supports, located on a busy intersection. Inside, the piece was projected onto a screen in such a way that it was visible through the glass from afar, especially after dark, like a kind of very slowly changing billboard. This suddenly turned the building itself into a huge monitor, a potential with which it seemed to have been equipped from the start but which had never been used in this way before. As a result, the principle audience consisted of those passing in their cars early in the morning or in the evening, who saw something similar or something totally different each time: John Wayne getting off his horse, a view of Monument Valley, etc. The monumentality of this grim movie was further monumentalized—but also reduced to associations with a home TV screen, as if the real architecture had become a model of a monitor. As in the case of *Psycho*, the source is a well-known film which many people saw for the first time not in the cinema but on television. Now it's like in a dream where the TV screen appears in the urban landscape itself. This gives the image a hypnotic effect; it draws one into a surprising vision, generating moments of "immersion," even for someone sitting in a passing car.

It would be silly to attribute a subversive effect to Gordon's work. As well as depending for its impact on the fame and mythical status of the films used, it also doesn't parody their style or the way they tell their story; *Psycho* remains a horror thriller, *The Searchers* an epic western. And above all, instead of mocking the viewer as a blind, mindless consumer, it takes new modes of seeing seriously. Besides his films' formal and conceptual elegance, their achievement consists in rendering everyday consumer usage of media technology productive as a method for the creation of artistic situations. The found material and the "found" reception are left essentially intact, but thought through to the end—and shown through to the end, even if it takes five years.

This clear, compelling quality, this precise awareness of the media and conditions of reception was also promised by *Zidane—A 21st Century Portrait*, the film Gordon made together with Philippe Parreno. The initial idea appears as simple and rigorous as that of earlier works: take a single famous soccer player already surrounded by myth—Zinédine Zidane—and have him filmed by seventeen cameras for the duration of an entire match, without interruption. The resulting material was then edited into a film whose real time is determined by the real time of the player's actions—a familiar length, both on the football pitch and in the cinema, of around ninety minutes. Although the number of cameras is high, it's not unthinkable for the regular transmission of an important soccer match by a major television broadcaster. The difference between this and a regular TV broadcast is that instead of the whole game, only one player is shown. There are no action replays. The match is an ordinary league fixture (Real Madrid, Zidane's team, against Villarreal, on April 23, 2005).

The idea is far from new. In 1970–1971, German experimental filmmaker Hellmuth Costard made *Fußball wie noch nie* (Football Like Never Before), which documented an ordinary league match between Manchester United and Coventry on September 12, 1970, but with eight sixteen-millimeter cameras pointed at the legendary Manchester United player George Best. There are important differences between the two films. Whereas Costard's use of close-ups was limited by his camera positions and the available technology, Gordon and Parreno have cameras with fast telephoto lenses allowing extreme close-ups of Zidane's face or feet, and high-speed cameras capable of capturing fast movements in crystal-clear images. Of course, this corresponds to the development of the sport in the intervening thirty-five years—its athleticization, acceleration, and commercialization. But this aspect remains fairly marginal and is reflected in the film technology itself. What we actually see is, above all, Zidane wiping the sweat from his shaved head with his hand; we hear him uttering brief commands or signals ("Hey," "Yo"); and we see his feet skipping over the grass. In this way, the supposed advantage of state-of-the-art technology emerges as a setback. By suggesting that this technology allows them to show something that usually remains invisible in team sports—the microscopic details of the "magic" that makes a truly great player—Gordon and Parreno achieve the opposite.

105     **Douglas Gordon and Philippe Parreno,**
        Zidane–A 21st Century Portrait, 2006
106a+b **Hellmuth Costard,** Football Like Never
        Before, 1970/71

Not that they should have strayed from the purism of concentrating on a single player to show what any ordinary television coverage shows: the way Zidane interacts with his fellow players. But instead of focusing their fetishizing gaze solely on Zidane's face and feet, as if they explained everything, more attention could have been placed on his body in space—as is unavoidably the case in the George Best film due to technical limitations. Best appears just as isolated as Zidane, who, like Best, spends most of the match trotting around the pitch, clearly saving his energy, appearing almost detached, only to explode into action at key moments to make passes that decide the course of the game. But Best appears as a figure, not just as a face with feet.

Being generous, one could interpret this as a fragmentation of movement in the vein of experimental cinema—the close-ups as affect-images that allow desires to mirror themselves in the protagonist's face without revealing anything about his "inner life," and the fast shots with the feet as pure action-images. But such "experimental" fragmentary images have long since become conventions in commercials for sports equipment and in mainstream action films. Here, athletes are presented as digitally dissected icons who switch between super-slow-motion and high-speed as if between pure soul and pure body; and sport is explained in spiritual terms (the surmounting of barriers, fears, emptiness, a lack of will power, etc.), hence the focus on the face. The problem is that this aesthetic works for the length of a commercial, but not for the length of a feature film. One senses Gordon and Parreno trying to compensate for this with sound effects, music, and narrative elements. The sounds of breathing become well-tempered hisses and snorts; the sound of Zidane's feet on the grass is so heavily laden with effects that it sounds like a herd of bison crossing the prairie. The man responsible for the sound, it was reported, had previously worked on the 2005 remake of *King Kong*—a real mistake. Scottish instrumental band Mogwai accompany the pictures with their rather lifelessly phallic version of an endlessly delayed rock climax, crudely suggesting tension with dense "atmospheric" sounds and crescendos. And then there are the narrative elements which spoil the mix for good. Like in some dire 1980s pop video, at halftime we are shown collaged news footage of the day's events, giving a suggestion of destiny. It becomes clear that it doesn't make sense to read the affect-images and the action-images in isolation from other filmic elements (sound, narrative etc.) to gauge their artistic worth. It's important to consider the work as a whole.

This became clearer still when the film was shown as a large-scale projection at the stadium of Basel FC to coincide with the Basel art fair in 2006. The intention, in itself perfectly acceptable, was obviously to create a framework: all the spectacular trappings of a soccer match in a stadium. Several thousand people, mostly invited guests, sat in one of the two curved sections of the grand-stand. Opposite them was a gigantic screen lying flat on the ground that was pulled upright hydraulically, with a dramatic lightshow, to reveal two members of Mogwai at the mixing desk, playing records ranging from instrumental rock to dance. But the "dance floor"—the screen and the space between it and the barriers—remained empty. After half an hour, people understandably became impatient with this absurd presentation of dance culture as a seated cinema overture. But then things got really bad; an exuberant presenter welcomed the former chairman of Real Madrid, Florentino Pérez, the man who had signed Zidane to the club. In addition, the Moroccan middle-distance runner Hicham El Guerrouj was steered onto the stage, presumably in the absence of Zidane or any other member of the club, as if to say: a famous track-and-field athlete is better than no sportsman at all. One might have taken the whole thing for a brilliant parody had the film that followed not been so obviously at pains to achieve a sense of sublime grandeur.

The notion of the "spectacle" is often used either to brand the artwork in question as merely the expression of the spectacle, or, conversely, as a clever borrowing of *the* spectacle's trickery turned against its own logic. It's quite easy to produce evidence for both arguments. But a value judgment based on such a mechanism is of little more use than a judgment of taste based on immanent criteria of composition or color (good picture because yellow and green are well balanced). It's not enough, at least not under conditions halfway free of censorship, to show whether an artwork has fallen prey to the mainstream or whether it subverts the mainstream's mechanisms. The truth in most cases is that the so-called mainstream welcomes innovations, in particular when they appear in the guise of subversion. The mainstream has also long since developed an appetite for things that were once avant-garde experiments and that are now a "look" or a "sound." Compared with the romanticism of total withdrawal, it's more interesting to get one's hands dirty and keep testing the mainstream's rubbery capacity for absorption to see if things aren't gradually getting transformed in a positive way after all.

When Berlin-based Danish artist Olafur Eliasson created a huge cinematic illusion in the gigantic turbine hall of London's Tate Modern that was a massive popular success (*The Weather Project*, fall 2003), an esteemed curator commented to me that this was nothing short of aesthetic shock and awe in the spirit of Albert Speer or Leni Riefenstahl. By placing an indoor sun in the already extremely high space and doubling it with a reflective coating on the ceiling, the artist had lost all sense of human proportion. My impression was different. Sure, faced with the monumental and simple sight of the sun, the audience response was dominated by a romanticist willingness to dreamily crouch on the floor, instead of showing any interest in the fact that the installation was quite happy to reveal its status as a fabrication. From the upper floors, one could see the gossamer-thin reflective sheeting from the side, and from the ground it was possible to look behind the semicircular yellow shade lit from behind by two hundred street lamps, which only formed a full "sun" with the reflection in the mirrored ceiling, while smoke machines gave the light a hazy dimness. The comparison with Nazi bombast is very superficial, for although the mirror duplicated the space, it cast it back down to the viewers on the ground, to the level on which the individuals in the crowd were moving. As a result, groups repeatedly used the mirror to generate slogans formed out of people: "Go Home Bush" was to be seen there, in the country of America's most loyal ally, in November 2003 during a state visit by the U.S. President six months into the Iraq War. Other people had picnics, gave dance classes, or took photos of themselves and their friends against the backdrop of the artificial sun. As much as it has to do with "the masses" when 2.2 million visitors are delighted by the World's Fair-like staging of a natural phenomenon, it's hardly evidence of receptive ineptitude, let alone totalitarian aesthetics. On the contrary, this was the celebration of a democratic sense of community in a country where community traditionally takes place on precisely this axis between small talk about the weather and explicit statements of political opinion.

The lesson of such a successful large-scale project, as compared with the many failed ones, is that an elaborate production calls (as in the case of movie directors) for a strong sense of coordination and a well developed critical faculty. One must be capable of telling an internationally renowned sound engineer that his clattering sounds like cattle. Otherwise, the viewer ends up having the sobering experience that is possible with any form of art: instead of using a few elements to create something that keeps me interested for a long time, many elements are used to create something that soon leaves me cold. Finally, the artists are the ones who are "seduced," calling on an apparatus that gets beyond their control. But the same thing can happen to those artists who stand in their tiny studio and cobble together sculptures out of scrap metal. Material is as unruly and unpredictable as meaning; one must learn to identify its laws and variables. Admittedly, multipart film and video installations are particularly complex and hard to keep under control. The number of laws and variables is especially high.

# The Flaneur: Why Standing Still Is At Least as Important as Walking
## Rodney Graham, Gary Hill, Gillian Wearing, Peter Campus, De Rijke/De Rooij, Sharon Lockhart

As in the case of architecture, no still image, press release, or one-channel video version can replace the concrete three-dimensional experience of a multi-channel video or film installation, especially if one is interested in how the audience deals with these works. As far as is possible, they should be written about on the basis of direct observation, and a good opportunity for this was provided by the above-mentioned exhibition "Beyond Cinema" (carefully if conservatively curated at Hamburger Bahnhof, Berlin, in the fall of 2006). In Rodney Graham's *Edge of a Wood* (1999), a helicopter's searchlight restlessly scans the tree-line at night. Were I to watch the eight-minute loop as a single-channel video on my screen at home, I would probably see myself in the position of a sovereign viewer, as if I were the pilot, maybe chasing an escaped prisoner. In an exhibition setting, the two different camera angles covering the scene are shown on two separate free-standing screens set up side by side in the space. I am offered a panoramic format that mimics the panorama of the edge of the wood, especially as the picture is flush with the floor. At the same time, it's a stereo image, with a gap of some fifty centimeters between the two screens, duplicating the stereo of the viewer's own two eyes. At Hamburger Bahnhof, the piece was positioned diagonally to face visitors head-on as they entered the exhibition. This reinforced the impression of moving toward the edge of the wood at night and—with the loud sound of rotors in the space—of being surprised by the helicopter. Instead of walking around the screen, as is the case with most freestanding works, most viewers were stopped in their tracks, brought to a standstill. At this moment, rather than pilots at the controls, they were like deer caught in a car's headlamps. The work presents the deeply romantic vision of the edge of a wood at night being "surprised" by technical illumination, observation, and surveillance.

With his work entitled *Viewer* (1996), video installation veteran Gary Hill also denies the viewer the illusion of such a free-floating perspective. The five-channel video projection shows seventeen men, day laborers of various ethnicities recruited by Hill from the area around his studio in Seattle. They are projected slightly larger than life-size and flush with the floor of the space; they barely move, but slight movements tell us that these are not stills but loops without sound lasting roughly ten minutes. It's as if these men have been lined up for a police identification parade. Their silent, staring presence in their working clothes immediately forms a counterpoint—facing them, my status as a "typical" (bourgeois) exhibition visitor is highlighted. Suddenly, I'm the one being looked at. As soon as I start moving along the projections, I feel like a cynical exploiter inspecting his cheap workforce. If I stop in front of one of the seventeen men, I catch myself being relieved that there is no "interactive" element where the man might react to my presence (such interactive elements do feature in other works by Hill). The piece deals with the identity of those portrayed above all with respect to the way it powerfully marks my difference to that identity. There is a work by Gillian Wearing (not part of the Hamburger Bahnhof show) that forms a precise complement to Hill's *Viewer* and that was made the same year: *Sixty Minute Silence* shows twenty-six British policemen and policewomen lined up in three rows as if for a group photo—but the flash and the shutter release don't come, they have to stay still for a whole hour and of course they become increasingly restless. The video is projected in a room of its own, the audience is free to choose how long to watch the scene: whether to simply verify the conceptual idea of the work, or to enter into the details of how the protagonists behave. Either way, unease and amusement are closely related.

Philosopher Louis Althusser explains his vision of the bourgeois subject in the modern state with a simple scene: when a policeman stops a passerby on the street with a cry of "Hey, you there!" then it is this "interpellation" that singles the person in question out and constitutes them as a subject. In the works of Hill and Wearing, this interpellation is made to contradict itself. It is mirrored to both sides; it seems to be the inserted imaging technology itself that performs the "interpellation." This is illustrated especially clearly in a work by Peter Campus entitled *Prototype for "Interface"* (1972/1999). It consists of a video

107

108

107    **Gillian Wearing**, Sixty Minute Silence, 1996
108    **Gary Hill**, Viewer, 1996

projector, a large sheet of glass, and a video camera. The camera films the viewer from the front as he or she steps up to the freestanding sheet of glass, and the image is projected live and life-size onto the glass. The visitor sees him- or herself as an inverted mirror image and, at the same time, "the right way round" in the projection; the two figures overlap. "Interpellation" becomes a technical invocation of ghosts. One afternoon at Hamburger Bahnhof, some visitors reacted with the blitheness of today's media users: one man was using his camera-phone to take pictures of his own reflection and projection on the glass, prompting others to do the same, or to photograph the photographer. "Interpellation" was sent into technology's hall of mirrors.

So what does this kind of seeing and being seen do to the viewer? Instead of standing contemplatively in front of the masterpiece, he finds himself vacillating uncertainly between walking, standing, and sitting, between registering and being registered. So are we dealing here with the famous and often-cited "flaneur"? The question is whether this evokes the right associations—from the bourgeois male city dweller who (as was briefly the fashion in Paris around 1840) strolled through the streets with a tortoise on a leash, protesting against the bustle of industrialization with pronounced leisure (and who could afford to do so), through to the modern bohemian intellectual à la Charles Baudelaire and very much à la Walter Benjamin, who takes the crowds as a backdrop for a perambulatory reading of the city, voyeur and detective at the same time.

Visitors to exhibitions do not usually walk at a brisk pace, of course, so in this sense they are strolling, maybe even contemplatively, occasionally letting themselves drift, pausing here and there in front of exhibits as if in front of shop windows. But the multiple projection spaces certainly don't always leave their viewers with an arresting jumble of impressions like the boulevards and shopping arcades, exposing them instead to a more strongly coordinated orchestration of sensual stimuli. Above all, however, we need to dispense with the notion that a bourgeois, male, nineteenth-century subject is still paradigmatic for people looking at art today. Does the contemporary viewer become a co-director—or a guinea pig, a mouse in a maze, an involuntary walk-on part? Does the daydreaming moviegoer become a dreaming sleepwalker in an exhibition?

In his essay *Leaving The Movie Theater* (1975), Roland Barthes describes the moviegoer first as a kind of silkworm in a cocoon, as a passive-narcissistic body glued to the screen as if hypnotized by its own fascination and desires. Instead of thinking one could avoid this effect by arming oneself with the appropriate counter-ideology, he suggests aiming for a kind of double state: the passive-narcissistic perceiving body, plus a "perverse" body that breaks the illusion by making everything that goes on off the screen—the dark crowd of the audience, the dancing light of the projector beam, the entering and leaving the movie theater—into a conscious part of the experience. In this way, he writes, it is possible to achieve a kind of Brechtian alienation effect, although the resulting distance is actually more "amorous" than intellectual insofar as it is part of our fascination with the film medium.

The same year this text was written, Pasolini's film *Salò or The 120 Days of Sodom* put this double state of the viewing body to an extreme test with its drastic portrayals of the sadistic acts of a fascist clique. Pasolini deliberately drives a large portion of his audience beyond the limits of what can be stomached, and out of the movie theater. But this makes the cultural contract of sticking it out in the cinema all the more apparent: for the duration of the projection, one puts oneself in the hands of what is shown, usually only leaving one's seat to visit the bathroom. And if one leaves for good, this is a way of saying one found what was shown unbearable.

It is this dictate of the cinema that's at work when I feel uncomfortable not watching a film installation right to the end, even when I'm given no indication of what its full length is. But in exhibitions, the conventions of the cinema are absent (fixed times, paying to watch a single screening, trailers, commercials, drinks, and popcorn). At the same time, I'm usually free either to stop watching and to content myself with a brief impression or to study the work in detail, possibly even watching it several times in a row. In any case, the rules are unclear.

At major exhibitions of recent years, such as Documenta and the Venice Biennale, many have complained that art videos have gotten out of control, robbing us of our precious reception time. The proverbial horror scenario is the hours-long avant-garde documentary study requiring twenty minutes to get any idea what it's about and what its conceptual angle might be, if it has one at all—projected in a dark, stuffy box with a bare wooden bench that is already occupied, while those standing around the entrance crane their necks to catch a glimpse of this work that is clearly not to be missed. But this can also be described in a way that applies to every medium. Good art shown badly, bad art shown badly—these things happen even in the best genres.

Often enough, complaints about the absence of fixed presentation conventions are mixed with openly reactionary nostalgia calling for a return to painting and sculpture, at best dressed up in a pseudo-progressive critique of "the spectacle" that needs to be kept out of art. But this absence of established conventions can actually be put to active and considered use. It's ultimately left up to me, for example, how long I watch the piece (a fragment or the full length, which in all fairness should be stated on the wall label) and how often (just once, or repeatedly). And I'm also not always given to understand that I haven't actually seen the work in the true sense if I haven't appreciated the whole duration, least of all by works that are more or less humanly impossible to watch all the way through. One need only think of the above-mentioned films by Douglas Gordon, or of Fischli/Weiss, who in the Swiss pavilion at the 1995 Venice Biennale set up twelve screens showing ninety-six hours of material with scenes of banal Swiss everyday life.

Stan Douglas drives this balance between sense of obligation and waste of time to an almost neurotic standstill. He has made several "recombinant" works composed out of various elements according to a particular mode of permuta-tion in such a way that they can run for days or weeks without ever repeating themselves. *Journey Into Fear* (1998) is loosely based on the spy thriller of the same name, twice made into a movie after a novel by Eric Ambler, though some of the dialog comes from Herman Melville's *The Confidence Man* (1857). One fifteen-minute scene on a container ship, shot in accordance with the conventions of the thriller genre, shows a man and a woman who both seem to be plotting something evil and whose dialog during a cabin scene has something to do with trivialities, dubious deals, and threats of violence. Although the looped scene in the single-channel sixteen-millimeter film installation lasts just fifteen minutes, it is accompanied by five possible dialogues between which a computer can switch back and forth at specific moments, meaning that there are 625 possible varia-tions that would last a total of 157 hours. Ultimately, film idiom and narrative are broken down into a bewildering puzzle that cannot be put back together. Protagonists and viewers alike are confronted with the frustration of finding no conclusion, no resolution—"Sisyphean narrative," as Douglas calls it.

In more general terms, one could say: Douglas makes sure I cannot just bring my television and cinema expectations with me into the exhibition space. Not even my video art expectations. For when films are shown in exhibitions as continuous loops, I'm already accustomed to watching them at least until I've seen the whole thing once and thus "done my duty." In other words: until I've performed the receptive task of translating the film—however fragmentary and

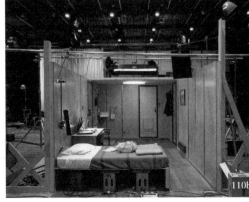

109     **Peter Campus,** Prototype for "Interface," 1972
       (installation view, Mexico City 2003)
110a+b **Stan Douglas,** Journey Into Fear: Pilot's Quarters
       1 and 2, 2001

non-linear its narrative content may be—into a linear story with a beginning, a middle, and an end. In this way, the loop becomes a mere mode of presentation. In the recombinant works, whose loop structure switches unpredictably between different versions, the question of how much time I should invest is deliberately complicated; I can only spend too little or too much time with them. This dilemma is aggravated by the certainty of always knowing either too little or too much about the many allusions and quotations. In each work, Douglas includes a long list of philosophical, literary, or cinematographic references, mostly from different periods (Freud, Proust, Kurosawa, Argento, the Brothers Grimm, Poe, Cervantes, Swift, De Sade, et al.). I know too little because levels of meaning may escape me; too much because in the tight network of references, I may lose sight of what insight and what new experience they are meant to serve (a problem I share, incidentally, with the artist).

There is a tendency, then, to leave it up to me, the viewer, to dictate the beginning and end of my experience of the work—a freedom that can be extremely frustrating or extraordinarily stimulating. Of course, the exact opposite remains a possibility, with fixed screening times and intervals. Dutch artist duo Jeroen de Rijke and Willem de Rooij made several works combining the conventions of documentary film in the ethnographic tradition of "visual anthropology" with three-dimensional artistic presentation of images in the tradition of the white cube. In the gallery space, a soundproofed box for the projector is installed and the film is projected without a frame onto the bare white wall with the audience seated on simple benches—an extremely secularized and sculpturalized mode of cinematographic presentation. It is suggested that one should watch the film from start to finish, but this is not defined by an opening and shutting of doors; in smaller gallery situations, the film is projected on request, but never as a loop. What is projected is an uncut scene, a static long shot of the "external" visual reality of a socially, ethnically, and ethically ambivalent location. *Of Three Men* (1998) shows the interior of a former church converted into a mosque in Amsterdam; *Bantar Gebang* (2000) shows a shanty town built on a rubbish dump at the edge of Jakarta, Indonesia; and *Untitled* (2001) shows a cemetery located in the center of the same city.

One could come up with commercial reasons why such works remain in art spaces. After all, it is the art market and the acquisition budgets of museum collections that provide most of the money for such films, rather than film companies or film funding budgets. But this cannot be the whole answer. For art house

111    **Jeroen de Rijke/Willem de Rooij,** Bantar
        Gebang, Bekasi, West Java, May 2000
112    **Sharon Lockhart,** Pine Flat, 2005

cinemas at least are usually happy enough to be used for screenings of films that are then sold on the art market; and some large museums have movie theaters of their own. Of equal if not greater importance, then, are the conditions under which the works are projected—and which themselves become an active part of the artwork.

In this light, although not really a step outside the art world, it was a gesture of control over the conditions of projection when Sharon Lockhart always insisted—until her *Pine Flat* project (2005)—on screening her films in cinemas and not in galleries (where she showed only her photographs). *Pine Flat*, too, was first shown at the Sundance Film Festival in 2005. I saw it at the Berlin Film Festival in 2006 and in this context, the tensions between cinema and gallery screening were clearly highlighted, especially since the film is designed so that it can be shown as a multipart installation in museum exhibition spaces.

The film begins with an almost static shot of a thick forest in the snow, and I think I hear a child's voice saying: "Where are you?...Ethan?" At some point, a wolf howls. Apart from this, we see no movement other than snowflakes and occasionally a branch jerking upward when its load of snow falls off. After precisely ten minutes, the screen goes black, followed by the next scene: a girl sitting on a sloping meadow reading a book, again for exactly ten minutes. Then, a boy is shown sleeping restlessly on grassy ground in the shelter of a large rock. After six such ten-minute shots comes a ten-minute break during which we only see the word "Intermission" and hear a version of the pop-punk song "Stay Together for the Kids" by Blink 182, played by a boy on a guitar. This is followed by six more scenes, this time with several children: a boy and a girl in the water, obviously looking for something under the surface; and two girls and a boy fighting and smoking in a lush wooded meadow before being surprised by a shower.

All these scenes are film portraits, all set in picturesquely wild and romantic terrain in the foothills of California's Sierra Nevada, in the town of Pine Flat, where the featured characters live. Lockhart holds the California-based avant-garde filmmaker James Benning in high esteem, who in turn follows her work with interest. In formal terms, *Pine Flat* in particular has direct and deliberate parallels with Benning's films *Thirteen Lakes* and *Ten Skies* (both 2004), which also consist of ten-minute static shots of landscape scenes, but without people. Both test their cinema audience with the blend of tense longing and dragging tedium potentially involved in contemplations of nature. An additional factor in Lockhart's film, however, is that tense longing and dragging tedium are two key emotional poles during adolescence. Adolescence is also the time when we inevitably begin to present ourselves to the world more consciously, for love and for work. As a result, each scene is charged with the question of how consciously the young protagonists are acting for the camera and how self-absorbed they possibly remain nonetheless, not least due to the long static shot, which may in turn be one of many takes (Lockhart shot the film over a period of two years). Is the howling of the wolf an added "special effect"? Is the boy really sleeping or just pretending? What's the girl reading, what's she thinking? One asks oneself these questions, but they are overridden by the formal rigor of the film: Can I become absorbed in this—by normal standards—absolutely endless ten minutes, or will I drift off, and if I do, is that a problem? What is the meaning of concentration, distraction, full frame, detail?

At the screening in Berlin, Lockhart was present, and before the film began she told the audience they could go out during the ten-minute intermission to stretch their legs and get a drink. For film fans, it is unthinkable to leave the cinema after just an hour, however long the individual shots last (surprisingly few people did take the opportunity). But it's interesting that she based the film's structure on this criterion, in the knowledge that she would be putting the professional media competency of festival-goers to a tough test—especially as she could not be sure that the majority of those present knew they were about to watch a series of ten-minute static shots. Lockhart's film inevitably has a nostalgic level, since it highlights the "old-fashioned" photographic aspect in the medium of film, as well as negating more recent media technology that certainly also plays a major role in the everyday life of the young people featured—and in that of the audience.

This tension—how much can I expect the viewer to put up with?—is no longer present when the scenes are shown separately in museum gallery spaces as loops. Lockhart's concept here is to show them two at a time—one solo and one group scene—at the same time but in different rooms. Each pair is shown for a whole day, so that by the end of six days all the scenes have been shown and the round begins again. Consequently, most exhibition visitors will inevitably only see part of the overall work, unless they are willing and able to return for at least twenty minutes on each of six consecutive days. Lockhart clearly accepts that not all viewers will manage this quota or have seen the entire film in the cinema, and by looping the sections she also offers the option of viewing the images "episodically," to come and go and switch between the two scenes.

What I see and what I don't, what I look at for a long time or just briefly—the tension between frustration and withholding on the one hand and accessibility and availability on the other characterizes the dynamic not only of the film itself but also of the way the film is shown in the art space. All this points to one key insight: there is a broad spectrum of reception intensities which the work may anticipate, but which, ultimately, have to be decided on by the audience. This in itself is an imposition with which an artist can work.

Whether presented with a constantly recombining puzzle of scenes or simply a repeated loop with a single shot, the viewers are never just viewers, dreamers stuck in their seats as in the cinema or reverently rooted to the spot as in a church. They are also not sovereign flaneurs letting themselves drift, or cyberspace surfers riding the waves of data on offer. Perhaps they are most like stumbling navigators on their way through unknown territory, sometimes more with map and compass, sometimes more without. Or, to describe it in more theoretical terms: they become what Dutch art historian and narratologist Mieke Bal calls "focalizers."

The concept of *focalization* was introduced by French narratologist Gérard Genette and further developed by Bal. It describes the technique used by the author to describe narrative content from the point of view of a person. Perception of an event or object can be achieved via the outside view of an uninvolved narrator (external focalization). In this way, the reader is given the possibility of relating the plot to the modes of thought and perception of the characters (or the narrator), of identifying the differences and similarities. The concept of focalization is borrowed from photography—what occurs at the point in the optical lens where the incoming parallel rays of light are bundled. This makes it suitable for use when thinking about art even where there is no explicitly narrative content. In the case of figurative art, where the individual figures in the pictures take on the role of focalizers, a significant portion of the focalizing is already performed by the viewer, who views the picture in relation not only to himself but also to the context in which it is being shown. In contemporary art, which usually presents narrative as a fragment, if at all, and in a height-ened sense in the case of multipart film/video installations, this viewer-as-focal-izer also becomes a navigator. If one defines narrative as the dynamic between breaks and continuity, between event and plot, then in the case of contemporary art more than other art forms, the viewer is cast as a participant in this dynamic. Either he must reconstruct the event to accompany the plot, or the plot to ac-company the event.

Just as the invention of the telescope and the sextant transformed seafaring with technologies of seeing, one can assume that the increasingly widespread use of digital camera- and video-phones will influence the "performance" of the audience in multipart installations. This is acknowledged even in the banal possibility—as in works by Tacita Dean or Jonathan Monk—that the visitor can flick a switch to start the film. Or, slightly more complex, in the presence of an archival function that allows me to choose a particular work from an assortment—as realized for the "Out of Actions" exhibition (Los Angeles, 1998), where videos and films of performances on DVD were presented in such a way that they could be selected with a barcode-reader pen: the exhibition as a digital archive. All this is possible, and its possibilities have by no means been exhausted.

Peter Weibel—who was already using video as an artist in the 1960s and who is now the influential director of the Center for Art and Media in Karlsruhe—has called the deliberate activation of a media-competent audience by the artist the "technology of allusion." According to Weibel, allusion is replacing previous forms of anti-illusion, which were characteristic of the art of the 1960s and 1970s, and illusion, which was characteristic of the 1980s. Younger artists, like Trisha Donnelly, who use a few minimalist interventions—a sound heard at sporadic intervals, an obscure film still—to evoke in me the viewer entire B-movie genres and stylistic periods, seem to confirm Weibel's point. But this undervalues one decisive aspect: it's not enough to simply name the allusion; the allusion itself must be staged. It continues to depend on the dynamic between illusion (narrative, figuration) and anti-illusion (process, abstraction)—on what Barthes calls "amorous distance." The allusion only comes to life when it is coupled with a concrete aesthetic experience.

# The Viewer—All Eyes, No Ears?
# Alvin Lucier, Janet Cardiff/
# George Bures Miller

When art and art theory turn their attention to technological media, they often tend to ignore the dimension of sound. The silent pictorial tradition is projected onto the world of mass media, but the soundtrack is forgotten; there is much talk of "image theory" and "visual culture," but at the same time, those speaking cut off their own ears by this very choice of terminology, as if we were still living in the age of silent movies (and even they were usually shown with musical accompaniment). Whereas in fact (and this is a fact agreed on by both advocates and opponents of emotive cinema with its strategies of overwhelming), as physical beings, sound and music are what "open us up" for the pictures, or cause us to snap shut. There are few things worse when watching a film than having one's enjoyment totally spoiled by music that's unsuitable, or overly suitable. In an installation with multiple projections, the possibilities for getting something wrong are also multiplied—sequences that are too short or too long; soundtracks that are too loud, too quiet, or just bad; multiple projections whose multiplicity is merely an expression of randomness and conceptual vagueness. Things can get worse still in big exhibitions if various works kill each other by cacophony.

To take a closer look at the role played by sound, it therefore makes sense to put the visual element aside for a moment, before returning to it later. Let's begin with the composer Alvin Lucier, as he is among those who have most explicitly explored the dimension of sound in space, on the border between composition and sound installation. In his *Music for Solo Performer* (1965), an EEG transmits alpha-waves from the performer's brain to loudspeakers and the resulting frequencies in turn generate vibrations in percussion instruments spread around the space. The necessarily immobile performer (often Lucier himself) can thus trigger movement in the space by thinking. The opposite number to this work is *Vespers* (1968). Here, sound coordinates the movements of the performers, who hold echo sounders based on the sonar system of dolphins as they move around a dark room, orienting themselves purely acoustically. From today's point of view, the resulting sounds with their polyrhythmic cricket-like signals—which can only be captured to a limited degree by a stereo recording—are remarkably similar to the electronic music of the late 1990s.

Visitors' switching between standing still and moving around is the basis for the way sound in installations works. Although Canadian artist couple Janet Cardiff and George Bures Miller have in recent years increasingly worked with film, *The Forty Part Motet* (2001) is a sound installation. In it, forty loudspeakers are mounted on stands at average head height, the idea being to translate a forty-person choir performing Thomas Tallis's *Spem in Alium Numquam Habui* (1573) as a three-dimensional physical presence into a recording played on forty separate loudspeakers at the same time. Small fragments of noise and talking between members of the choir before the performance are also inserted, making them seem to us like physically present individuals and not like performers removed in time and space. The crucial thing here is that as a listener, I perceive the singing (that tells in Latin of religious transcendence) as if I were a ghost or a choirmaster walking along the rows of a choir and pausing briefly in front of each singer. The way I move through the recorded material (eight groups of five voices that cover the entire tonal spectrum from male bass to child soprano) makes me both the ghost and the director in my own performance, different each time, the details never precisely repeatable.

Cardiff and Miller create situations where that which is absent in physical terms but present thanks to media technology is overlaid with that which is physically present but distant psychologically. The choir is not physically present or visible, but its voices are embodied in the space in the form of the loudspeakers; the listener is physically present, but he or she is transported away to a different space-time scenario (that of the music recording). This overlaying is not kept secret, the technology is not hidden and sold as magic, but in spite of this, the sound-in-space experience cannot be resolved into analytical distance; it remains suggestive and touching. Just as an insight into elements of one's own psychological makeup does not make them disappear, so the experience of the overlapping of levels of reality can never fully rid them of their affective impact. And if this were possible, it would no longer be an experience, as it would have no phenomenological basis in perception.

For the *Video Walks* (since 1999) and the *Ghost Machine* (Hebbel Theater, Berlin, 2005), Cardiff and Miller worked with standard shop-bought camcorders and headphones that were issued to the individual viewers/listeners. Cardiff's voice invites me to follow her route, to become her doppelgänger. In addition, however, the protagonists of the video footage pre-produced in this same real setting, which I am seeing synchronously at these locations, are now projected into these locations like ghosts. The effect is such that at one moment, alone between two doors, I hear footsteps behind me and am unable to stop myself from turning round. Using modern but entirely ordinary media technology, Cardiff and Miller translate the classical philosophical and religious debate on body and soul as a "simple" dualism into a relationship of intersections and overlapping. The irony is that however philosophically they may be interpreted, the staged video walks have true theme park potential and one wonders why no one has thought of staging camcorder ghost trains in the same way. Art-specific experiment and mass entertainment are astonishingly close together here, without that necessarily being a bad thing.

The dubious pleasure of a profound mental shock brought about by the visual confrontation with a work of art—the "Stendhal syndrome" of former times—is apparently denied us by our heightened media competency and the wealth of filters with which it is equipped. In fact, critical distance has since the nineteenth century been held up as the ideal, as opposed to (supposedly) naïve, unreserved empathy in the face of artworks. But sound is the level on which the controlled distance of the educated art viewer risks coming unstuck. The more audio elements—voices, sounds, noises, music—have come to be used in film and video installations since the 1960s, the greater the fear of loss has become, the fear of losing distance and separateness. The standard art rhetoric of undermining certainty, as served up since the early days of the avant-garde, thus props up the deceptive certainty of my oh-so-self-reflexive understanding of art.

For this reason alone, "illusionistic" strategies of overwhelming are, in principle, perfectly legitimate (not just in film/video installations), since they are the only way to achieve the fascination of a sudden loss of distance in the moment of non-comprehension (what's happening to me?), a fascination which is potentially countered by my distancing insight into the mechanisms responsible for creating this non-comprehension in the first place. In other words, I must operate in the gap between illusion and anti-illusion, distance and loss of distance, image and image. But what if the greatest illusion of all makes itself at home in precisely this gap?

# Beyond the Viewer, the Flaneur, the Black Box, the Spectacle:
# Doug Aitken, (Feat. Pablo Ferro, Jean-Luc Godard, Dan Graham), Marcel Odenbach, Eija-Liisa Ahtila

The breathless rhythm of a ticking clock dominates the multiple images created by commercial filmmaker, opening credits designer, and film editor Pablo Ferro for the thriller *The Thomas Crown Affair* (1968). In the 1950s, he was already using the quick cut technique in short television commercials. For *The Thomas Crown Affair*, he placed the film stock over a grid pattern of black stripes and treated it like a mobile mosaic of moving images that constantly reassembles

113 **Janet Cardiff**, The Forty Part Motet, 2001 (installation view, Bregenz)

114a-c **Janet Cardiff/George Bures Miller**, Ghost Machine, 2005

itself—the first time anything of the kind had been seen on cinema screens. Mike Figgis adapted this technique, which is based on the editing suite time code that allows images and sounds to be synchronized. He used the time code as a rigid organizing principle—four pictures on a single screen—for otherwise unedited real time video footage, also naming the film accordingly: *Time Code* (1999). The television series *24* (first shown in 2001) uses this same mode of presentation to show the simultaneity of events taking place in real time so that an hour of broadcasting corresponds to an hour of plot (including the commercial breaks, that is).

Instead of demonstrating simultaneity in the mode of a mosaic or kaleidoscope, the pictures in the work of Jean-Luc Godard and Dan Graham—to name two further schools of editing that are relevant in this context—appear in the mode of overlapping levels of time and meaning. In Godard's films, the various facets of society and of life are layered and made to confront one another based on the principle of the conjunction "and." As a result, editing and dramaturgy generate not a dialectic contrasting or a whole as the sum of combined parts, but rather permanent, continuous variation. In *One Plus One* (1968), documentary scenes of the Rolling Stones working on the song "Sympathy For The Devil" stand side by side with allegorical acted sequences in which the Black Panthers execute white virgins, or quotes from *Mein Kampf* are recited in an adult bookstore. The glaring contradictions appropriate for the year 1968 add up, but without forming a whole. According to Godard, one plus one remains one plus one and does not become two. In the works by Dan Graham discussed above, his interest in and enjoyment of pop, cliché, and the wide world of entertainment initially appear separate from the "serious" elements of the architectural, performative, and sculptural—but they do so as in a puzzle. Graham's principle is not that of "and" but that of a slash. The oblique stroke creates a parallel, a shared space, an axis around which force fields turn: enjoyment/analysis, pop/theory, Dean Martin/Bertolt Brecht, rock/architecture (Graham was a close friend of Robert Smithson, whose work revolved around "place/non-place"). Or as Graham himself has aptly put it: "Hybrids with interference." Graham's fondness for "mass entertainment" is not something he presents demonstratively, revealing it only in the structure of his work—the same way the material shown on the front garden screens in *Video Projection Outside Home* would be dictated not by the artist but by the inhabitants.

One artist who has absorbed all of this and who has developed his own language in the spatial orchestration of moving images and sounds is Doug Aitken.

With his book published in 2006, he gave an impressive indication of what the potential new quality of projections in installations could be. The book is called *Broken Screen*. The twenty-six filmmakers, artists, architects, and designers whose conversations with Aitken make up the book—including Pablo Ferro and Mike Figgis—have one thing in common: by breaking down linear narratives, if not totally atomizing them, they attempt to follow the way contemporary auditory and visual experience is going, at the same time as moving ahead, and opening up spaces for further development. But what almost all of them also share is the belief that the audience becomes part of the work because it must contribute to this game of breaking down linearity by performing intellectual and affective construction work—including potential frustrations and pitfalls.

At certain moments in some of Aitken's conversations, this has the slightly unpleasant taste of a hollow postmodern invocation of plurality and disoriented perception that avoids the question of whether it might actually be important to wrest back a more rigorous sense of meaning precisely from a fragmented perception of reality—this time with the active assistance of the audience. Or in other words, broken, negated narrative and perspective are only interesting when they are not just failed linear narrative and perspective but really something different.

As an example of something really new happening, Aitken described his experience of seeing Andy Warhol and Paul Morrissey's *Chelsea Girls* (1966) in the cinema for the first time: "As the two reels rolled through the projectors simultaneously, images in real time slowly moved across the screen. Very little happened in them, proving Warhol's doctrine to create 'not a plot but an incident.' As … the scenes played out in a narcoleptic stupor, we somehow saw deeper into the collective shadows of the on-screen characters and into what it truly means to want to be looked at. An hour or so into the film, my eyes left the screen and scanned the audience, where I saw that others were silently looking around too. It was as if in that moment, we were all realizing that the audience was as much the subject of the film as its celluloid characters."

Unlike Warhol, Aitken does work with precisely timed simultaneities and contrasts in his installations. They are elaborate, well thought out, perfect. As in the case of Charles and Ray Eames, the images are juxtaposed with algorithmic precision, not just put together intuitively or at random. At the same time, the camera eye becomes bodiless, ubiquitous in macro- and micro-spheres, switching back and forth between satellite and microscope, telescope and surveillance camera, as if it were a matter of channeling all these images to a war room where reality is being observed in all its dimensions. This has sometimes led Aitken to be accused of borrowing manipulative techniques from the cinema as a way of overpowering his audience's critical faculties with the sheer volume of impressions. This critique focuses exclusively on the question of whether he uncritically imports the media technology of capitalism into art, or whether, on the contrary, he is making a critical commentary on capitalism. But this seems to miss the point of his approach. In 1993, Aitken fittingly adapted the old Situationist idea of critically unmasking and parodying found material from Hollywood movies or other sources by reiteration and re-appropriation. *I'd Die for You* brings together John Wayne's fourteen on-screen deaths—shot, drowned, burned alive: the paradigmatic Wild West hero caught in an endless moment of death. But since then, his approach has been more of an atomization of the material, out of which he then generates new pictures and sounds. Instead of legitimizing his use of sophisticated "entertainment technology" by parodying appropriation, he now actively lays claim to it as a legitimate machinery for art, before dismantling it in a delicate, digitally splintered, architectural manner. He simply assumes that his viewers, like Warhol's cinema audience, are aware and emancipated, no longer naively glued to the screen.

*Eraser* (1998) resulted from a visit to the Caribbean island of Montserrat one year after the devastation caused by a volcanic eruption. This work, too, was recreated as part of the "Beyond Cinema" show at Berlin's Hamburger Bahnhof. The walls are painted navy blue, and the sequence of spaces is so meandering that one goes round at least four corners, able to see two, four, or five screens at once, but never all seven. First, two pairs of double screens are installed in a corner. Visitors can either position themselves diagonally at a point between the two or concentrate on one of them. This arrangement, which has a crystalline quality, deliberately contradicts Aitken's concept of crossing the volcanic island with his camera in as straight a line as possible. One of the two double projections shows lush vegetation and water, scanned by the camera with restless but precise pans, left to right, right to left. The other shows fragments—some static, some from a subjective, walking camera—of a deserted settlement. A telephone, an observation post, and a general store are all covered in a heavy coat of dust. The singular, romantic panorama of the volcano in all its grandeur and dangerousness becomes stirred up and agitated; there are close-ups of solitary aerials and rusty satellite dishes. Various possible zooms and shots—close-up, long shot—are played through as if to scan the terrain. The sound atmosphere is full of static, crackling electrically; at one point, we hear, as if from a distant radio, Louis Armstrong's "We Have All The Time In The World" accompanied by a snatch of rhythm. Transmission and recording technologies seem to plague these natural locations like ethereal ghosts. This place depopulated by the forces of nature is visited not as a way of getting as far from "Western civilization" as possible, but to find its ghostly, resonating echoes. In the third area, three screens show a walk across the lunar landscape of lava; the sudden appearance of a herd of cows is like a flash of post-apocalyptic life. The mood is a mixture of Robinson Crusoe and *Omega Man* (1971), the science fiction film in which Charlton Heston plays the only survivor of a terrible epidemic by which everyone else has been either killed or reduced to a zombie-like, half-dead state.

The girl in *I Am In You* (2000) is maybe ten or twelve (her exact age doesn't seem important). Right at the beginning, totally absorbed in her own concentration, she whispers two sentences: "You got to run as fast as you can all of the time," and "You got to be sharp!" The you she addresses soon becomes me, the navigating-focusing viewer, as I really do have to hurry to at least halfway follow the fast-paced orchestration of the visual action unfolding around me—light, humming noises, and pictures fading into each other. Not chaos, however, but a rhythm that I haven't quite locked into yet. My rattling synapses try to keep up, as it becomes clear that the layout of the five screens (imagined from above) is like the "S" on an LED display. The girl—like me the viewer—is engaged in pattern recognition, hungry for learning. I see, alternately, her and structures of thick lines that are beamed up in a precise, stroboscopic staccato, as if the child were registering the structures like a scanner. In the midst of this initially confusing action, it soon becomes clear that a kind of osmosis is taking place between the central freestanding screen and the four others around it. It is as if the ensemble of these screens is made to pulsate by the editing that is precisely synchronized between all five projections: a glowing jellyfish of vectors, pumping itself elegantly through a dark sea. Or, to use a different image: a modular architecture, something like a folding chair laid on its side and multiplied around its own axis.

This filmic-architectural osmosis generates a kind of constant inversion of perceptive space. The screen in the middle is not just the "inside," the mind of the girl, just as the surrounding screens are not just the "outside world." And it's not just the other way round, either. Instead, it's a rhythmic movement of expanding

115a

115b

115a+b **Doug Aitken,** I am in You, 2000

and contracting. The work's title is to be understood in this sense: one moment, the line between me and you blurs, and the next it stands out clearly.

In theory, all of this could be organized on a single screen—crystalline, rhythmical structures within a sequence of cuts. But it's only the spatial dimension that draws me into the process—I can no longer adopt a position of either detached autonomy or submissive passivity to avoid the decision of what to focus on, when, and in what direction. It's as if the space-time continuum as such is expanding and contracting. This impression can be linked to the urban experience of streets and architecture, the metabolism of a great city. In early 2007, Doug Aitken realized a huge series of seven projections on the facades of the Museum of Modern Art in New York City, entitled *Sleepwalkers*. It features, among others, Donald Sutherland tap dancing on the roof of a taxi, Tilda Swinton working in an office and playing the violin, and songwriter Chan Marshall, also known as Cat Power, sorting letters at a mail depot—synching the urban hum of a city like New York, and its special rhythm of drivers and pedestrians, workers and consumers, to the broken beat of celebrity and isolation.

Marcel Odenbach's interest in the video medium stretches back to the mid-1970s; the "star" of his early videotapes was himself, the location mostly an ordinary monitor. *Sich selbst bei Laune halten oder die Spielverderber* (To Stay in a Good Mood or The Spoilsports, 1977), contrasts newspaper clippings on events leading up to and during the wave of left-wing terrorism in Germany in the fall of 1977 with pictures of the artist's hands struggling with toy puzzles (number games, magnetic balls), while in the background we hear a Western blaring out on a TV set and the inexorable ticking of a metronome. In the face of intense confrontation between the state and terrorism, further intensified by breathless media coverage, there is no room left for analysis—just for inexorable ticking and nervous fidgeting.

Odenbach has repeatedly created a direct link between the wider political climate and his own feelings—increasingly in the form of multipart video installations. *Ach wie gut, dass niemand weiß* (Oh How Good That No One Knows, 1999) is an eight-minute mini-drama that unfolds on four parallel freestanding screens. One of the outer screens shows footage of the demonstrations that followed the assassination of Martin Luther King, Jr. on August 4, 1968. At the other end, we see the riots after the killing of the young demonstrator Benno Ohnesorg by a Berlin policeman on June 2, 1967. And between them are pictures of a black basketball player and a white pole vaulter. The use of such symbolically loaded material from both sides of the Atlantic coupled with the fetishized bodies of black and white sportsmen might have resulted in a crude equation: black Civil Rights movement meets white student protest; black basketball elegance meets white Olympian physical prowess that could have been dreamed up by Leni Riefenstahl. Initially, Odenbach pretends to accept this dualism of cultural stereotypes of the male body and the politics of "races," but then he twists them around their own axes several times in time and space. Meaning is created not merely by the combination of elements, but in the way the elements are set in motion and dramatized. Firstly, the historical footage is literally shaken up. Like the sportsmen, it jumps up and down (Odenbach strapped small digital cameras to the athletes and had them film the historical material while jumping up and down on trampolines). Secondly, for at least half the time the two sportsmen leap out of their own screen and into the other, so to speak, switching places and thus political-cultural contexts. But, thirdly, sound is the decisive element in dissolving fixed symmetry and shaping the choreography of the work. The score unfolds around us while the athletes remove their track suits and tie their laces. Glenn Gould's *Goldberg Variations* overlap and merge with Miles Davis's *Sketches of Spain*, and a rippling, fluid simultaneity flows through the space. But then we see the close-up of a needle skidding across the record and hear the corresponding loud crackling sounds. The jumping begins in slow motion and the sound of the trampoline is like the dull heartbeat of a galley, while the historical footage to the left and right now staggers along at the same tempo, almost inducing seasickness. The rotating brushes of a carwash wipe over a windshield and water blurs the view, until the piano melody and the calm flow of the rap in Gang Starr's hip-hop elegy "Moment of Truth" resolve the tension into melancholy and mourning. The feeling of an ending, of final credits, is just setting in when suddenly a short passage from Hitchcock's *The Man Who Knew Too Much* (1956) appears—the scene with the orchestra when, at the very moment the percussionist clashes the cymbals, a piercing scream is heard that anticipates the shot waiting to be fired. The piece ends with a close-up of door handles and the harsh sound of door latches clacking shut. It's as if over the course of the work, the polyharmonic, polyrhythmic fabric of the music triggers the ups and downs of a political struggle that is overwhelmed and brought under control by an inexorable metronomic beat and finally brought to an end by a bang. But the loop continues and the mini-drama fills the space once again.

**Marcel Odenbach**

116    Oh How Good That No One Knows, 1999 (installation
view, Cologne)

117a+b To Stay in a Good Mood or The Spoilsports, 1977

Eija-Liisa Ahtila's video installations are usually also realized in a short film version, offering a second means of access to her work. The cinema version is the one that takes me by the hand and guides me through a scenario that is far from linear and in which the levels of image, sound, characters, narrators, plot, story, and language—always shot in Finnish, with English subtitles—shift and interlock tectonically. A family speaks with the voice of the father, a woman with that of her husband (*Me/We*, *Okay*, and *Gray*, 1993). Or the grandfather's accidental death is told from the point of view of his granddaughter and from that of his son, but also from that of an older woman who might be the widow or the granddaughter grown older, decades later (*Today*, 1996/97).

Whereas these two films do not try to recreate multiple projection in the cinema version, the short film of *If 6 was 9* (1995) also splits the screen into three in the style of Pablo Ferro. This provides a good example of playful but conceptually rigorous handling of the resulting possibilities. The film features adolescent girls between thirteen and fifteen talking about their ideas and experiences concerning sex. In one scene, a girl sits in an armchair—she is shown in the right-hand picture (the other two remain black at first)—and talks as if to herself, into film space, telling how as a child she always used to play doctors and nurses all on her own under the covers. Then she lifts her head slightly, and at this precise moment—as she says, "I was a patient and the doctor examined my bottom"—two more girls appear in the left-hand picture, also sitting at a living room table, passing a bag of potato chips back and forth between them. And while the first girl says: "I had to open my asshole while they all stood around… the doctor, a nurse, and maybe someone else," the middle frame is filled with another two girls. In panoramic format, we now see a domestic scene with the five girlfriends (the scene is shot simultaneously with three cameras) sitting round the table. The four who are listening seem to be rather detached or distracted, an impression that is reinforced by the rock music playing in the background. And as if reacting to this slight disinterest, the girl talking turns to "her" camera so she is now speaking to "us" and says: "The doctor cured me by injecting me in the ass, right in the middle, right up the hole." With this dry description of a childish fantasy, shame, pleasure, and obscenity are played off against each other; the girl appears serene, grown-up, with a sense of humor. She adds: "I twisted and turned under the covers, sweating all over. At that stage, I knew nothing about the pussy." And as she says this, one of the girls from the left-hand frame walks through the middle one to join her in the right-hand picture, sitting down beside her as if in a gesture of solidarity.

In this short scene, the spoken word and its contents are directly related to the dramaturgy of the acting and its distribution across the three pictures. As soon as she describes the presence of a doctor in her fantasy, prompting her (mostly older) listeners to start feeling uncomfortable about being used as the audience for a girlish fantasy, two of the other girls can be seen; and as soon as she mentions the possibility of others being present, they are joined by two more. The confessional report of embarrassing or funny doctors and nurses games is situated step by step in the teenage clique, in the social context, in the now of a shared evaluation of experiences, of dawning awareness of oneself as an autonomous sexual subject. This is achieved primarily by the dramaturgy of cuts across the three screens—with the viewers as "focalizers" between them.

The parallel projection of Ahtila's *Consolation Service* (1999) on two screens is a direct metaphor for the story it tells, the story of a young couple separating shortly after the birth of their child. But the split screening doesn't just stand for separation or schizophrenia. Instead, it is a double view both of the central scenario and of its atmospheric, affective manifestations in glances, chairs, lamps—a constant asymmetrical stumbling that is duplicated again in the relation between the Finnish language and the English subtitles. It's as if a rather sleepy educational broadcast on divorce therapy has been hijacked in the spirit of Godard as a way to shake up the routine rhetoric of peacemaking and jump into the void that cannot be explained away when a love dies. This is already noticeable in the stoic intro during which the narrator explains, as she watches a neighbor taking his dog for a walk, how the story will be structured—a first section about how best to separate, a second about the separation itself, and a third about reconciliation. The couple who visit a psychotherapist to get help with their divorce are advised to try to express their feelings for each other without words. In a tragicomic turn, they start barking at each other (people-as-dogs is a typical Ahtila theme). The ritual is supposed to initiate mutual acceptance, and it brings to light pent-up anger that soon collapses into a vacuum. The same evening, the husband is celebrating his birthday. The therapist asks what he'll do with the baby during the party—he answers that a neighbor will be babysitting, the one "who's writing this story." The same night, this story-writer will make the couple and their guests fall through the ice of a frozen lake, and even if this is only a subject of party small talk among the group, it is also an allegory for the way the couple's love has gone cold. Finally, the husband, who has been separated from mother and child, appears like a ghost in the hallway of the apartment; as soon as they approach him, he bends forward, shrinks to the size of a small child, and splinters into thousands of pixels, before reappearing again for the separating couple's ritual of reconciliation—a deep bow to each other. This special effect recalls computer animations of the early 1990s; Michael Jackson appearing and disappearing in a very similar way, as if made of magic pixel dust, before the pharaoh's throne in the video for *Do You Remember the Time* (1992). At first, this reminiscence seems kitschy and inappropriate, but it becomes touching with repetition. The animation has to be kitschy to be touching. It shows how instead of self-assuredly grasping the "real" social significance behind all the mass media portrayals of painful relationships and separation when they are going through one themselves, people remain caught up in all the ridiculous, stereotypical, endlessly repeated gestures. The "therapy" consists in realizing that in spite of this, through and beyond the media-multiplied relationship and therapy kitsch, they can communicate and show each other respect.

In *The House* (2002), too, the special effects are related in a particularly direct manner to both the narrative content and the division of the projection into three. Just as the film sequences expand into the exhibition space as a large triptych across a corner, the film's theme is the invasion of the protagonist's domestic and mental space by sensory impressions—or, to be more precise: the way a woman is literally pursued by sounds. She parks her car in front of the house, but the humming of her fridge grows into the humming of her car, and now a "real" car, but in miniature, suddenly drives threateningly across the striped wallpaper, almost as threatening as if it were a fat rat. The same happens to her with sounds of the docks and the city that do not stop at the gates of her beautiful lakeside house in the country. The next moment it's the ringing of a cow's bell on the television, and before she knows it, the cow is walking through her living room. The nightmarish situation of her quasi-psychotic state is balanced out by peaceful scenes in which she floats weightlessly through the woods like an astronaut—wearing just socks, no shoes. Back in her apartment, she decides to black out all the windows so as not to have to see the images in addition to the unavoidable sounds; so she can imagine she really is on a ship, at the shops, on the beach.

In all of Ahtila's works that exist in both cinema and installation versions, the fraying and overlapping of the borders between characters and narrative points of view is multiplied in the installation form. As in Aitken's work, there is a

118

119

**Eija-Liisa Ahtila**
118   The House, 2002
119   If 6 was 9, 1995

continuous switching of focus between the screens, which is additionally varied by repeated viewings and which, like a tissue of memory, lays itself over what I have seen. (When and how did I see which scene? It's almost impossible to give a precise answer.) But where Doug Aitken's works require navigation (the viewer's physical movement through a space structured by pictures), most of Ahtila's works, limited to double or triple projections, involve constant changes of viewing direction from a stationary position—while the narrative level makes high demands in terms of focusing. In *The House* this focusing itself becomes a subject, a psychosis, as the protagonist suffers from and is defeated by her inability to filter and focus sensory impressions.

As she vacillates between composure and tension—standing as if rooted to the spot one minute, then pacing up and down the room again—the main character reflects my own uncertainty as a focusing viewer. Although I am not proto-religiously intimidated as by monumental art, I am equally unable to fall back on the deceptive role of the sovereign viewer who inspects the window displays of art like a strolling shopper. This uncertainty is not necessarily an intellectual one—I am perfectly able to perceive, name, and classify all of what I see. Instead, to use a buzzword from recent discussions of cinema and installation art, it is an "affective" uncertainty. Affect is a kind of missing link between perception and cognition, an emotional state that is explicitly related to indeterminacy (in contrast, for example, to the absolute nature of passion or drive). For affect, at least if one doesn't define it as merely a reaction to a stimulus, is an adequate term for "the range of mental states where an agent's activity cannot be adequately handled in terms of either sensations or beliefs but requires attending to how he or she offers expressions of those states," as literary and art theorist Charles Altieri puts it. In other words: I enter a state in which what I perceive latently incites me to communicate and to act, but which also prevents me from doing so by holding my attention. Affect thus extends like an electric field between frustration and fascination. I am neither the sovereign flaneur in a sensory paradise nor the mouse in a labyrinth. I do not remain distanced, nor am I completely immersed. But this tension can only be maintained if it is generated not by structural weaknesses but by structural strengths. The spatial organization and the sequence in time must add up to what Mieke Bal calls an "affective syntax," they must have a dramaturgy that stimulates my affects, for example by surprise and contrast (behind the next door lurks an artwork, after something huge comes something very small, etc.);

equally, however, it might be a stupendous frustration of precisely this expectation of "surprise" and "contrast."

As we have seen in the case of painting within installations, affective syntax can be created without moving images. But if the medium of the exhibition incorporates the medium of video/film, then it multiplies the "affective syntax" like an echo chamber, except that the original signal seems to become not quieter and weaker, but louder and stronger. On the part of artists and their audience alike, this calls (and not just where sound is involved) for a musical sense of three-dimensional rhythm. From the choice between metrical synchronization and intuitive accumulation, between loop and linear sequence, the development progresses to syncopation sequenced in time and space. In music, syncopation is a shifting of the rhythmic emphasis that seems to contradict "natural" meter and which is exciting for this reason. It's like a stutter that's repeated as a deliberate pattern (in jazz, for instance, sustained syncopation becomes an offbeat). Artists like Aitken, Ahtila, or Odenbach use this technique not only with sound, but also with moving images, in the way they follow on, contrast, or overlap in the space.

In a conventional single-channel film, whether in the cinema or at home on TV, there are gaps "between the pictures" into which the viewer can slip. The usual example of this is the use of shot/counter-shot for dialog. When J. R. and Sue Ellen trade hostilities over a glass of whiskey in the Ewings' living room, two camera positions alternate, each showing one character over the other's shoulder; the viewer finds himself in an imaginary blind spot, so to speak, between the two intersecting visual axes. In film theory, this gap is referred to using Jacques Lacan's notion of a "suture," the surgical term for a seam created when a cut is stitched up. The operating theater here is the editing suite (or the computer). Wherever the seam between illusion and anti-illusion may run, there is always a gap "between the images" which allows the viewer to identify with something in the film. But of course, besides multiple projections, single-channel film, too, has access to all kinds of syncopation and other rhythmic techniques in editing, camerawork, narrative, and subject matter, to ensure that this process of identification doesn't take place too smoothly. Ahtila shows this with her cinema versions, and it is also demonstrated by film directors like David Lynch (whose movies could be imagined as installations), or Isaac Julien, Apichatpong Weerasethakul, Chantal Akerman, and Harun Farocki, all of whom have also made installations. But however clearly they break the illusion of a unity of time and place in what they show, they at least leave the viewer *one* option for sovereign identification—with the position of the director who has decided to structure what I am seeing in this particular way and not in any other.

But when the gaps "between the pictures" are joined by actual physical gaps between the screens, a shift occurs. And the imaginary attempt to inhabit the gap between the pictures is joined by the concrete physical act of navigating between the screens. These two processes are not identical, and the result is a double-bind: I am affectively caught between active navigation and passive integration. The concept of the double bind was first developed in connection with schizophrenia, which explains why, in Ahtila's *The House*, the position of the viewer seems to coincide with that of the protagonist; both are affectively caught between what they hear and what they see.

Artists can try, as Bill Viola does, to make the gaps in the space and the gaps between the pictures coincide by means of monumentality and simple themes, thus generating a premodern experience of the sublime and creating a continuum with the immersive worship environments of religion (and with science fiction's fantasies of virtuality). Or they can not do this, playing instead with the "gaps between the gaps," stretching them like chewing gum or compressing them as in a pressure chamber, adding them up like Jean-Luc Godard or splitting them up like Dan Graham, reflecting and fragmenting them, dancing with the pictures and their viewers—dancing polkas, waltzes, and sambas—dancing all night long.

# Art *versus* Market The Logic of Unseizable Gratification

## "Throw' em out, they break my heart"

She, relatively unknown, borrows original silkscreens from him, very well known, in order to make exact copies of his work, putting them on display as her own; he's perfectly happy with this... A document includes a clause stating that the person acquiring it has to offer a reward for the capture of a wanted bank robber... She transfers money to her two sponsors; later, they transfer more money back, and she keeps the difference... He, quite successful and well known, organizes an exhibition at a renowned museum featuring only "leftovers," works his numerous galleries haven't yet managed to get rid of... Chairs from the café of a London art institution are shipped to Karachi, Pakistan, where they are left on the street to be taken away for free by anyone who feels so inclined... She trades places with a prostitute for four hours; the latter appears on her behalf at the opening of her show at a renowned institution, while she herself sits in the window of a brothel in the red light district for the duration... As soon as a gallery visitor moves toward the exit, the gallery assistant stands up, walks a few steps, falls to the floor and begins to feverishly recite the exhibition press release... Dozens of people stand in line in front of the art society for hours on end, even though there are no sought-after concert tickets or bargains to be had...

All of these are genuine art works with dates and titles. And all of them aim to derive critical potential and aesthetic innovation from precisely those processes and mechanisms which—supposedly—rob art of its capacity for critique and aesthetic originality: from copying and business transactions; from selling, distributing, and consuming; from exploitative labour and the role models it entails; and from media announcements and ordinary work routines.

All of this begs one fundamental question: Isn't the idea of a critically engaged and aesthetically challenging work of art within the realm of the marketplace—be it in the context of an art fair, an exhibition of works for sale, or a project funded by an international company like Unilever or BMW—a contradiction in terms? Over the years of the current art boom, during which the art world has developed into a full-blown industry with connections extending to the entertainment and mass culture sectors, many artists have doubtless asked themselves this question more than once. And they have felt a need to justify their entry into this "impure" realm—even if only to gain a clear idea of why they renounce the widely held view that art and critical thought can only flourish in autonomous zones, aloof from the vulgarity of commerce.

According to this view, artists are faced with a fairly simple choice. Either they make critically and aesthetically viable works that reject the market and its mechanisms, such as educational work in a particular social environment, fleeting poetic interventions in everyday life, or performances registered by very few people. Or, alternatively, they jump headfirst into the bubbling whirlpool of the art market, producing pretty stuff that asks no questions and that everyone understands (preferably figurative painting). In other words, the choice is between the instant gratification of commercial success and the deferred gratification of institutional and academic recognition that accrues over time—if you're lucky.

This binary model is oversimplified; I'm merely stating what is often lazily assumed as a basis for discussion. But neither can it be a question of merely defining compromises in between—painting with unexpected pockets of resistance, or challenging performance for more than a handful of spectators. Instead, we need to consider those artistic approaches which twist and turn and break this either/or. Any gratification that an artist may reap is related to the gratification—instant or delayed—derived by the audience from looking at (and, where applicable, buying) his or her work.

Umberto Eco was one of the first to clearly name this showdown between condemning and embracing the market and mass culture, at the same time as attempting to formulate a way out of it. In his essay "Apocalyptic and Integrated Intellectuals: Mass communications and theories of mass culture" (1964), he identifies the most intelligent manifestations of the "apocalyptic" school of thought in the writings of the Frankfurt School, whose general thrust is a categorical rejection of the commodification of artistic utterances in the realm of the culture industry. Based on their reading of Karl Marx and Immanuel Kant, Theodor Adorno, Max Horkheimer, and Herbert Marcuse argue that such commodification destroys a work's aesthetic value, in turn resulting in the alienation of the aesthetic experience. As an Italian semiologist familiar with Adorno and his writings, Eco had no desire to champion the "apocalyptic" cause. But he was equally unimpressed by that of the "integrated" intellectuals, the U.S. sociologists and cultural theorists—including Daniel Bell and Gilbert Seldes—who, according to Eco, defended "mass culture" with claims including: that it made high culture accessible to broader sections of society, thus facilitating the possibility of wider education; that a broader spread of cultural information did not automatically mean a decrease in quality; and that instead of being merely a perpetuation of cultural conventions, "mass culture" actually allowed the proliferation of new forms of expression and communication. In Eco's view, however, the "integrated" camp's chief reason for promoting "free trade" in cultural products was their belief that mere intensification of circulation was inherently beneficial for the advancement of an enlightened, civilized society.

Against this background, it is all the more ironic that Eco's "integrated" intellectuals finally turned "apocalyptic" themselves. As early as 1924, Gilbert Seldes became one of the first to emphasize the achievements of popular culture in his seminal book *The Seven Lively Arts* (by which he meant comic strips, movies, music hall, vaudeville, radio, popular music, and dance). But in 1957, Seldes stated that "with the shift of entertainment into the area of big business, we are being engulfed into a mass-produced mediocrity." Going much further in his 1976 book *The Contradictions of Capitalism*, Daniel Bell lamented the demise of traditional values and arts as well as the retreat of religion. With quotes from Friedrich Nietzsche's *Will to Power*, he aimed to prove that organic ties to the soil and what Nietzsche called "the inalienability of property" had been well and truly ruptured. Without these links, Bell stated in a clearly apocalyptic tone, the Western world had degenerated into a "commercial civilization." Modern capitalism, he continued, had undermined itself by abandoning the original Protestant ethic of productive work and deferred gratification that had made it flourish in the first place. Bell's Armageddon was California, especially the liberal Hollywood of the 1970s: the land of sexual liberation, individualism, hedonism, and the immediate gratification of all desires. Bell distorts Max Weber's analysis of the connection between the rise of capitalism and the Protestant work ethic of deferred gratification (work, work, work, then a little bit of pleasure in recompense—but not too much!) by turning it into a manual of internalized obedience and a pious lament. (Reading Bell makes you want to smoke crack.)

To top the irony of the integrated becoming apocalyptic, the formerly apocalyptic intellectuals in turn become perfectly integrated—a development foreseen by Eco in 1964. The apocalyptic critique of the culture industry became an integral part of that culture industry, a conventional "expert opinion" expressed in countless mass market paperbacks, newspaper commentaries, and TV talk shows. Eco's assertion is that "a laboriously veiled frustrated desire" is at work within those who play this elitist role, speaking elsewhere of a "betrayed love or a repressed sensuality." The intellectual who feels engulfed by the sentimental, vulgar products of commerce suddenly "resembles the rich man who, feeling beset by a pleader, bids his manservant: 'Throw the guy out, he breaks my heart!'" With their sentiments thus aroused, the apocalyptic intellectuals, Eco claims, fail to even attempt a concrete analysis of the products in question and the way they are actually consumed. Instead, for them "the central criteria seems to be the artwork's non-dissemination, even the impossibility of its dissemination." (The fact that, during his lifetime, Guy Debord severely restricted and ultimately banned distribution of his films is a striking example of this.)

Seth Siegelaub was a new kind of art dealer who in the 1960s aimed for the exact opposite: he turned the dissemination of a work into its central, integral criterion. Almost single-handedly, he set the stage for the group of New York conceptual artists whom he represented (Joseph Kosuth, Robert Barry, Douglas Huebler, Lawrence Weiner). He went so far as to declare that the possibility of the dissemination of an artwork is its only "physical reality." The invitation card or the catalogue could be the "actual" exhibition. He organized shows, publications, and symposia that undermined traditional notions of what constituted a show, a publication, or a symposium. Or, rather, he blurred the line between the three. In this way, he transformed the way idea-driven art was circulated, how it was received, and how it was bought. "How can a collector possess an idea?" he asked rhetorically in 1973, two years after quitting the art world for other pursuits.

All this pointed to a fundamental schism within Conceptual art: it refused the fetish of the object, but it also needed to define a market for itself. It was no mere caprice of art history that some of the most important early manifestations of Conceptual art—then among the most experimental and challenging work being made—took place in "commercial" contexts such as the "Prospect 69" show at Kunsthalle Düsseldorf (subtitled "an international preview of art from the world's galleries"). Nor that this art was represented by dealers like Siegelaub and the Düsseldorf gallerist Konrad Fischer.

Selling ideas was a paradox. Once they were out in the world, uttered or displayed by the artist, how—apart from the artist's own claim to intellectual property—could they be "owned" by anyone? Often enough, what was available to the collector was little more than a trace or an object related to the work, but not the work itself; after all, it was reasonable to ask what "ownership" meant when Robert Barry released inert gases into the atmosphere or when Lawrence Weiner stated that "the work does not have to be built."

This goes to the heart of the economic transaction. It would be too easy to assume that collectors simply become patrons. This is not what Conceptual artists longed for. Rather, the buying and selling of Conceptual art signified a "destruction of wealth" in the spirit of potlatch, the ceremonial feast of presenting gifts among native peoples of the Pacific Northwest coast of North America. Generous gifts become competitive transactions, and vice versa. For isn't it a strangely unseizable gratification which the collector obtains by spending a great deal on "nothing," on an idea that he cannot "possess"? The wider audience shares in this experience of *unseizable gratification*. Even if the idea-based work is defined as a "service," as something that is consumed in the moment of its production, this consumption doesn't necessarily produce a tangible result (like a new haircut does, or a massage). This element of unseizable gratification is among the most important aspects of Seth Siegelaub's activity as a dealer, and of Conceptual art in general. Instead of diluting the heritage of Conceptual art with a few halfhearted marketing strategies, Siegelaub changed the parameters for ownership of works, rendering Conceptual art more conceptually consistent and interesting in the process. The Protestant ethic of rejecting immediate gratification (hedonism, pleasure) in favor of deferred gratification (salvation, higher goals) is undermined by an unseizable gratification that oscillates between the two. Conceptual art is often a comical but logical game, and the same is true of the economic transaction envisioned by Siegelaub.

In a text published in 2004, Siegelaub wrote that he experienced his return to the art world after more than thirty years—prompted mainly by increased art historical interest in his earlier activities—"like a sort of Rip van Winkle," the protagonist of Washington Irving's eponymous story of a man who wakes from two decades of sleep to find the world radically changed. He noted a dramatic increase in contemporary art's proliferation, its prestige, its central role in society, and of course its links to the commercial sector. From this he concluded that cultural and monetary values had become interchangeable, or even identical. But he also noticed that "these changes have also brought with them contradictory and positive aspects as well, especially the 'democratization' of art making to include the sensibilities of nonwhite middle-class men, many more women, 'minorities'… and artists who are not necessarily living in NATO countries."

Many interesting artists today are very much aware of the "contradictory aspects" of the art world's expansion. Whether they develop and show their work in galleries or exhibition situations, at art fairs or biennials, they operate deliberately between immediate and deferred gratification, and thus between a "satisfying" and a "frustrating" experience of art—for frustration is a fundamental component of unseizable gratification.

# Circulation I: Money, or How Gratification Remains in Circulation
## Robert Barry, Hans Haacke, Robert Morris, Douglas Huebler, Maria Eichhorn, Eva Grubinger

Robert Barry's *Invitation Piece* (1972–73) illustrates unseizable gratification in the form of circulation. Barry's exhibition at Paul Maenz Gallery in Cologne consisted of an invitation card that directed visitors to a show at Art & Public in Amsterdam; there, an invitation card advised them to go to London—and so forth, until, in 1973, a gallery in Toronto sent avid Barry viewers back to Cologne. This merry-go-round of reference dissolved art into its means of mediation. It gave instant access to the circle, while at the same time denying the possibility of actually visiting an exhibition. The addressee entered a semiotic loop; instead of simply replacing gratification with frustration (or vice versa), these sentiments were played off against each other.

A few more words on the notion of "circulation." Originally, it was used to refer to the metabolic distribution and redistribution of fluids and matter. As a metaphor, it has been used with respect to urbanization, population flows, and traffic in the city. From about 1750, money began to "circulate" (the likes of Baron Montesquieu and Jean-Jacques Rousseau used the term in connection with cash flow and labor); after the French Revolution, ideas, newspapers, and rumors "circulated"; and from 1880, so did traffic, air, and electricity. For Marx, "circulation" was the sphere of supply and demand, where distribution enables the exchange of goods and money. The kind of "circulation" Lenin had in mind when, with his 1902 pamphlet, he confidently asked, "What is to be done?" was the circulation of revolutionary propaganda via newspapers and party apparatuses. This emphatic, forward-looking, linear will to circulation was perhaps most vividly embodied in the spiral structure of Vladimir Tatlin's *Monument to the Third International* (1919).

Today the question "What is to be done?" has a slightly idiotic or presumptuous ring to it (as if it were a question of art world players heroically spearheading movements for political emancipation), while any return to "spreading the message" from the top down seems quite preposterous. Which is why today's version of "What is to be done?" is a healthily skeptical "What, How and For Whom?" (the name chosen by a curatorial collective from Zagreb in 2000, based on their rereading of *The Communist Manifesto*). Yet this question, which ultimately asks about the audience, is not an innocent one; it could come straight from the mouth of a marketing executive thinking aloud about new products for future target groups.

But cultural knowledge is not a commodity like any other, however much the market tries to reduce it to its exchange value. Cultural knowledge is not *only* a product, otherwise it would not be knowledge. The criteria that co-regulate the immaterial production of this knowledge—aesthetic potential, political relevance, scientific value—can satisfy the market's hunger for innovation, but also disrupt its mechanisms. Italian philosopher Maurizio Lazzarato concludes from this that the widespread notion of culture as a lofty, autonomous sphere removed from the market must be turned on its head. In other words, the criteria governing the cultural sphere are not beyond the economic sphere, but should be applied to it. This has obvious disadvantages. What in the one sphere may be

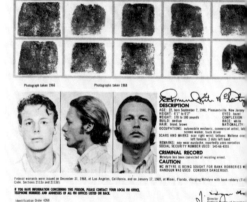

**Maria Eichhorn Aktiengesellschaft (2002)**

Documenta11, Kassel

**Medien, Materialien, Vorgänge:**
- Notarielle Gründungsverhandlung und konstituierende Aufsichtsratssitzung
- Aktiengesellschaft
- Gründungsurkunde
- Satzung
- Niederschrift über die erste Sitzung des Aufsichtsrats
- Bericht der Gründerin über den Hergang der Gründung
- Bericht der Mitglieder des Vorstands und des Aufsichtsrats über die Prüfung des Gründungshergangs
- Gründungsprüfungsbericht
- Anmeldung der Gesellschaft zur Eintragung im Handelsregister
- Handelsregisterkarte
- Öffentliche Bekanntmachung der Registereintragung
- Vertrag zur Übertragung aller Aktien an die Gesellschaft
- 50.000 Euro in 500er Banknoten
- Bankschließfach
- Safe
- Sitzbank
- Konsole
- Publikation *Maria Eichhorn Aktiengesellschaft*
- Text „Maria Eichhorn Aktiengesellschaft. Aktiengesellschaft. Entwicklung, Funktionsweisen, Struktur und Bedeutung der Aktiengesellschaft. Kapitalaufnahme, Kapitalmobilität, Börse. Konzernverantwortung. Handel/Spekulation. Gesetz. Veröffentlichungsgebot, Mitbestimmung. Selbstbestimmung. Frage nach dem Wertbegriff. Wertbegriff. Geld, Ware. Kapitalgewinn durch Kapitalzerstörung (-auflösung). Wertakkumulation (-zuwachs, -steigerung)/Wertreduktion (-verlust). Öffentlichkeit/Zugänglichkeit eines Werkes. Handelbarkeit/Nichthandelbarkeit, Besitzverhältnisse eines Werkes, Copyright. Wissensbesitz. Bedingungen des künstlerischen Theorie und Praxis, Aufheben der Bedingungen."
- Körperschaftssteuererklärungen
- Jahresabschlüsse
- Lageberichte
- Aufsichtsratssitzungen
- etc.

**Orte, Institutionen:**
- Notarkanzlei Klaus Mock, Berlin
- Mittelweg 50, 12053 Berlin (Sitz der Maria Eichhorn Aktiengesellschaft)
- Amtgericht Charlottenburg Handelsregister, Berlin
- Industrie und Handelskammer
- documenta GmbH, Kassel
- Documenta11
- Finanzamt für Körperschaften III, Berlin

120a

120

121

120a+b **Maria Eichhorn,** Presentation of Maria Eichhorn
Public Limited Company, Fridericianum Kassel 2002
121 **Robert Barry,** Invitation Piece, 1972/73
122 **Douglas Huebler,** Duration Piece no. 15 Global, 196

idealism can, in the other, quickly become exploitation. But this doesn't automatically devalue the idea of "unseizable gratification," an idea that sustainedly confronts the market with cultural standards.

Hans Haacke's works of the 1960s and early 1970s mark the transition of "circulation" from physical phenomenon to economic metaphor—from water in transparent cubes (*Condensation Cube*, 1963–65) and tubes (*Circulation*, 1969) to the provenance of a painting, its "history of circulation" in *Manet PROJEKT '74* (1974) for which he established a link between Manet's *Bunch of Asparagus* (1880) and the chairman of the curatorial board at Cologne's Wallraf Richartz Museum, the "de-Nazified" Deutsche Bank spokesman Hermann Josef Abs. *Manet PROJEKT '74* was a full-frontal attack on the veiling of economic and historical links within an art institution, and resulted in the cancellation of the work's display. To put the revelations (information concerning Abs's biography and his activities during the Nazi period, plus the fact that he was among the painting's previous owners) into circulation, Haacke used conceptual means of presentation (text works). As a result, as well as being the talk of the town, the piece was shown in other locations (including Paul Maenz Gallery)—anywhere but the gallery walls where it was originally to have been exhibited.

Rather than providing information about economic processes and their political implications, as Haacke had done, artists also began working directly with the economic processes themselves. In 1969, as his contribution to the "Anti-Illusion: Procedures/Materials" exhibition at the Whitney Museum in New York City, Robert Morris invested fifty thousand dollars on the stock market—money loaned from a trustee of the museum. He kept the interest generated over the course of the exhibition, while delegating the decision on how to present the piece in the group show to the curators. The work thus took the title of the exhibition literally, in three steps: as an "anti-illusion," it pointed to the dependency of the museum on private donors; during the "procedure" of the accrual of interest, their money generated a little money for the artist; and this was made visible without further artistic shaping or comment in documentary "materials." Yet where did the work reside? In the documentation? In the artist's initiative? In the economic process itself? The locus of the work remained beyond grasp, as the visible elements of the process were explicitly not subjected to formal artistic treatment.

From the appropriation of an economic process as art (Morris), the next logical step leads to altering the logic of this process itself. With his *Duration Piece #15, Global* (1969), Douglas Huebler offered a reward of 1,100 dollars for information leading to the arrest of a bank robber for whom the FBI had already issued wanted posters: one Edmund Kite McIntyre. As with other *Duration Pieces*, the work was manifested in the form of an illustrated certificate, the illustration in this case being the wanted poster. The catch was, however, that a collector buying Huebler's work for the stated price of $1,000 would also be responsible for paying the reward—although the buyer would be reimbursed any reward money paid out, up to a maximum amount of the sale price of $1,000. To further complicate matters, Huebler stipulated that the reward would be reduced by $100 from month to month, from the start date of January 1, 1970, until the end of the year when there would be no more reward. In other words, the artist would only profit from his work if the reward did not have to be paid at all, whereas the collector would have to pay an extra $100 at most, should the reward be claimed during the first month of the offer. The only person who definitely did not stand to gain from this strangely vacillating gratification in the sphere of art was Mr. McIntyre.

For the Documenta in 2002, Maria Eichhorn made a work where the amount of money involved could be seen as a hidden reference to the fifty thousand dollars invested by Robert Morris in 1969. This time it was 50,000 euros that went into founding the Maria Eichhorn Public Limited Company, whose statutes expressly prohibited the growth of this capital. Frozen in this way, the money was taken out of circulation and put on display behind glass in Kassel instead.

In that work, Eichhorn forbade gratification, whereas Eva Grubinger proceeded more in keeping with the old rogue's motto of "take the money and run." The "Art & Economy" group exhibition at Hamburg's Deichtorhallen included a series entitled "Economic Visions," for which each artist was to realize a joint work with a partner from the business sector. This implied a creative exchange between equals, but although such a scenario may be conceivable in individual cases, there is usually a huge gulf in terms of power between a company and a single artist. Grubinger ironically took this supposed parity at its word and made a work entitled *1:1* (2002). Shortly before the introduction of Europe's common currency in January 2002, she transferred a total of 30,000 deutsche marks to the accounts of her two partners, Deutsche Bank and Siemens. Soon after, she received 30,000 euros in return. The difference of roughly 15,000 euros corresponded to the projected budget for the realization of the work, and Grubinger pocketed it as "profit." In all, then, there were three counts of impertinence here. First, the artist began by transferring a "donation"

123    Eva Grubinger, 1:1, 2002

to two big companies acting as patrons. Second, she imposed a modality that made them look rather foolish (as if they had confused the currencies in the two transactions). And third, at least part of the difference that was intended as her budget went into her own pocket. In spite of this, although the amount transferred might represent a tidy sum for an individual, measured against the financial power of the two companies in question it was less than peanuts.

# Circulation II:
# Copies, Package Deals, and Leftovers
# Warhol/Sturtevant, Louise Lawler,
# Swetlana Heger/Plamen Dejanov,
# Nedko Solakov, Matthieu Laurette

Conceptual pieces consisting of nothing but a transaction and maybe some documentation are not the only works that leave one wondering who can claim "ownership," and how. Just as the flourishing trade in holy relics in the Middle Ages was fuelled by all manner of bogus shrouds and chicken bones, so too in art one must always reckon with forgeries and with the question of what constitutes an "original" and what is "merely" a reproduction. At some point in the early 1980s, a guest at a lunch with Andy Warhol made a show of trying to sell Salvador Dalí prints of questionable authenticity, mischievously alluding to the way Factory screenprints were arguably often made by assistants without Warhol actually being present. Warhol grabbed a white slice of bread, signed it with a felt pen, and threw it across the table at the obtrusive questioner saying, "Here, sell that!" The laughs might have been on Warhol's side, but the joker did have a point.

Warhol actively promoted this confusing proliferation of works, and Dalí later in life happily signed blank sheets of paper, contributing to the trouble with countless forgeries of his work flooding the market after 1985. At the artist's own instigation, this gives a false taste to the question of authenticity of works. This question is posed religiously in the spirit of the old notion of authorship: Who is the one true creator? But what's at stake is quite profane: scarcity and boosting prices on the art market.

The Catholic Warhol played his games with this pseudo-religious logic of scarcity and price boosting. His *Time Capsules* are monthly archive boxes

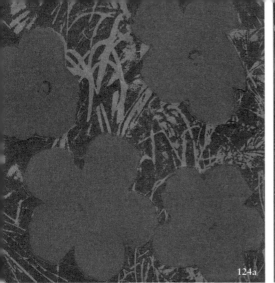

124a

124b

124c

124a-c **Sturtevant,** Warhol
Flowers, 1969–70

filled with the flotsam and jetsam of his life as an artist. Anything and everything that was lying around at the Factory ended up in these boxes, from
Clark Gable's shoes to an Air France cutlery set from the Concorde to the
newspaper article from which Warhol cut the picture of Jackie Kennedy in
mourning. At first, one may view these boxes through the eyes of an archivist,
since they contain untold clues to the genesis of major Warhol works. But
sooner or later the question is bound to pose itself: Are these footnotes to his
work, or works in their own right? The answer is surprisingly mundane. The
status of the *Time Capsules* as works is documented by the Warhol Foundation with a journal entry dictated by Warhol over the phone to his evangelist
Pat Hackett shortly before his death: "Took a few time capsule boxes to the
office. They are fun—when you go through them there are things you really
don't want to give up. Some day I'll sell them for $4,000 or $5,000 apiece.
I used to think $100, but now I think that's my new price." Water to wine!
So this is the deeper meaning of the "transfiguration of the commonplace,"
as Arthur C. Danto called it (inspired by Warhol's *Brillo Boxes*, his screen-
printed replicas of the packaging for a leading brand of scouring pads). The
mysterious transformation occurs simply by naming a price.

Sturtevant took things one step further by making exact copies of copies.
In 1964, she had a decisive idea: she would repeat selected works by her contemporaries, surprisingly soon after their creation. In this case, repeating did
not mean copying as exactly as possible, like a forger, nor did it mean making
works "in the spirit of" like in a master class. Instead, it meant plunging right
into the Bermuda Triangle of idea, method, and execution—be it readymade,
replica, or plaster cast; screen printing or painting based on serial originals;
film or video. She asked Andy Warhol to lend her his "original" printing
screens to make replicas of his *Flowers*, themselves based on a Kodak advertisement. Warhol agreed. Sturtevant's work is titled *Warhol Flowers*, which
doesn't always rule out confusions. It's as if Sturtevant takes the know-it-all
"I could do that" that has always accompanied modern art and turns it into
a brilliant questioning of that art's methods: Could I do this? If so, how?
Where would it take me? And what does it mean for the artwork? What is
its "essence" if it's not the physical original itself? This has consequences for
both the market and the museum. In 2005, Frankfurt's Museum of Modern
Art cleared the house for a show of 140 Sturtevant works from four decades.
An uncanny encounter with the art of the twentieth century in the work of a

125

126

125  **Louise Lawler,** An Arrangement of Pictures
      (installation view, Metro Pictures,
      New York), 1982
126  **Swetlana Heger/Plamen Dejanov,**
      Plenty Objects of Desire, 1997/98

single artist, with iconic works by Duchamp, Beuys, Johns, Lichtenstein, and Kiefer. The fact that no museum, even in the United States, had ever dared host a major Sturtevant exhibition is due primarily to the perceived affront of being asked to look at repetitions of famous originals. But one certainly doesn't have the feeling of being presented with "cheap" imitations. In terms of both texture and iconography, Sturtevant's flag paintings, for example, are every bit as good as those by Jasper Johns (his famous first version is from 1954). She made them in 1965–66, and, like Johns, she used a technique borrowed from the mummy portraitists of ancient Egypt: encaustic (or hot wax) painting. By painting the stars and stripes not flying in the wind but front on, as if it were one with the canvas, the American flag is turned into an irritating double presence where there ought to be a clear message: a flag is a flag. So this is what a flag is like then… Where does this lead? Repetition is always affirmation and parody at the same time. Repetition is a celebration of contradiction. This was already true for Johns. But when Sturtevant repeats Johns's repetition of the flag, the doubling redoubles itself, a virus invading every certainty. For example, it invades the certainty of gender: Why plain Sturtevant without her first name, Elaine? Why only repeat male colleagues, many of whom, like Johns or Warhol or Felix Gonzalez-Torres, are gay? Does she deny the feminine in modern art? No, she emasculates the masculine. Here, too, she remains true to her method, eroding the unspoken equation of masculinity and creative power by repetition, thus reducing its value. Walking from work to work through the museum, however, one also realizes that Sturtevant's oeuvre itself is also a museum. The startling thing is the prophetic way she repeated the most iconic works in the heat of their early reception, when responses from art criticism and fast market value had not yet been galvanized into art-historical and institutional recognition, when the present had not yet become history—except, it would seem, for Sturtevant.

Like Sturtevant, Louise Lawler plays on the value of other artists' works, not by repeating them, but simply by showing them: she is closer to the role of an art mediator than a copyist. When she had her first solo show at Metro Pictures gallery in New York in 1982, she did nothing more than what curators do for money and collectors for pleasure: she put together works by artists of the gallery (including Cindy Sherman and Robert Longo) and offered the result for sale under the title *An Arrangement of Pictures*, including a ten percent commission. Later, she began photographing works sold by the gallery in the homes of collectors. She combined one of the strategies of Appropriation Art (placing works by other artists in a new context like a readymade) with those of Institutional Critique (laying bare the economic and social structures "behind the pictures").

This same combination was adopted from the mid-1990s by Swetlana Heger and Plamen Dejanov, who shifted the focus even more strongly onto business transactions, to hiring, buying, and selling. In exhibitions, they hired space on platforms of their own design to interested companies or private individuals, from a women's card playing club, to a medium-sized engineering company, to a bank. The money raised in this way (between a few hundred and several thousand deutsche marks per client) was then invested in young contemporary art and classic designer objects, which, in turn, they arranged on platforms and presented as part of a whole (*Plenty Objects of Desire*, 1997–98). To the heightened market value of scarce luxury goods such as art and design, they added the dimension of incorporation into the micro-cycles of the two artists' own value creation system. This short-circuiting of the "foreground" of showing work with the "background" of business transactions took on board the predictable animosity toward such a "selling out" of artistic autonomy. In a series of works entitled "Playtime," begun in 2002, Swetlana Heger stages herself, with the help of advertising professionals, as a model for brands like Hermes, Adidas, and Wolford. In theory, the photographic result might have looked pretty much the same even without this transfer to the art context. However, accusing the Berlin-based Czech artist of selling artistic autonomy to upmarket brands is a little tedious. The fact that she makes no explanatory reference to her status as a migrant should not be taken as an invitation to reserve the right to lead a luxurious lifestyle only to those who already have it at their disposal—while encouraging "immigrants" to be modest.

The brutal switch from socialism to turbo-capitalism forced many Eastern Europeans—not least well-educated intellectuals and artists—into a "suitcase economy." They spend their weekends traveling around Europe on buses and trains, offering their services or selling stuff out of suitcases at markets in faraway cities. In the process, their already meager profits are further diminished by the amount of time spent traveling and by the price of tickets and bribes. There's a piece by Bulgarian artist Nedko Solakov that reflects attempts to cope with such absurd exploitative and value-destroying aspects of so-called cultural exchange. Invited to realize a project in Denmark, he changed a one-thousand-crown bill into dollars, then the dollars back into crowns, and so forth until the money was eaten

127

128b

Matthieu Laurette
*El Gran Trueque (The Great Exchange)*, Bilbao.
2000.
(detail) video stills from *El Gran Trueque* TV programme presented by celebrated TV presenter Alicia San Juan on *Canal Bizkaia TV*, Bilbao from January to April 2000. The programme was aired daily 6 time a day and reaches more than 50,000 households every day.
Courtesy Matthieu Laurette / www.laurette.net - Consonni, Bilbao ß Blow de la Barra, London.
© Matthieu Laurette / ADAGP.

Matthieu Laurette
*El Gran Trueque (Le Grand Troc)*, Bilbao.
2000.
(détail) extraits du programme tÈlÈvisÈ *El Gran Trueque* prÈsentÈ par líanimatrice vedette Alicia San Juan sur la chaÓne *Canal Bizkaia TV*, Bilbao de Janvier ‡ Avril 2000. Le programme Ètait diffusÈ quotidiennement 6 fois par jour et Ètait captÈ par 50.000 foyers chaque jour.
Courtesy Matthieu Laurette / www.laurette.net - Consonni, Bilbao ß Blow de la Barra, London.
© Matthieu Laurette / ADAGP.

128a

128c

128d

127    **Nedko Solakov**, A Life (Black & White), 1998–2001
       (installation view Venice Biennale, 2001)
128a-d **Matthieu Laurette**, The Big Exchange, 2000

up by exchange rates and fees (*The Deal*, video, 2002). In 2005, Solakov made an ironic comment on the desperate selling off of anything that moves when he announced a solo show at Kunsthaus Zürich with the title "Leftovers." In the exhibition space stood a rough-hewn shelf unit containing works not yet sold by Solakov's various galleries, crudely lined up with labels detailing their provenance. In fact, however, the works on show actually included some of his best, like *A Life (Black and White)* (1999–2000), which exists in an edition of three and which consists of an action whereby two housepainters continually paint and repaint the walls of the gallery space white and then black for the duration of the show. In "Leftovers," Solakov staged a collision between the venerable convention of the one-artist retrospective and the atmosphere of a clearance sale, between deferred and immediate gratification.

Like Solakov, Matthieu Laurette has also replaced the principle of value creation with that of value destruction. From an art project budget in Bilbao, Spain, Laurette bought a car and realized a series of programs on Basque TV called *El Gran Truque* (The Great Exchange, 2000). In a phone-in auction, people could offer objects in exchange for the car. The highest offer was accepted and the object in question was presented the following week for exchange in the same manner, and so on. After a few months, the series of trades ended with the presentation of six blue glasses. Not a trace of economic growth there. What began with a car of some value ended with something that could have come from a flea market. A million pesetas turned into two hundred. The laws of the market were shaken up. Of course, the people calling in wanted a good deal on their trades, but the rule that elevated demand increases the value of the item on offer was stood on its head.

# Circulation III:
# Sold, Lost, Given Away, Short Supply
# Katya Sander, Aleksandra Mir,
# Jens Haaning, Dan Perjovschi

For her work *Capital Failure (Sold)* (2006), Katya Sander sent out a number of assistants to stick thousands of red stickers marked "SOLD" over the price tags on wares in stores in downtown Copenhagen. She put something into circulation, then: a kind of unauthorized product recall designed to disturb the flow.

Interrupting one kind of circulation to facilitate another was also the idea in *Monument for Image Production and Image Consumption* (2004), this time in the sphere of a mass medium. Asked to propose a monument in Copenhagen, she realized the piece in collaboration with Denmark's second-largest daily newspaper *Politiken*. In the summer of 2004, one edition of the paper appeared in two versions. The second—handed out free and with no prior announcement or further explanation with each copy of the "original"—was purged of everything but the pictures and the front-page logo. The piece can be read as a sanctimonious lesson about the mindless production and consumption of media images, but it can equally be seen as a monument to their fleeting, extensive circulation.

In his book *The Intellectuals and the Masses* (1992), John Carey makes the case, based on works and statements, that much of early modernist literature and art (from the late nineteenth and early twentieth centuries) was driven not least by a deep-seated upper-middle-class sense of superiority over the new mass readership created by the first illustrated newspapers. This elitist sentiment survives within the art world to this day. Artists are heroes, producing unique works in a solitary struggle against mass culture. At the same time, at least since the 1960s, there is growing discontent with precisely this view. Without in any way abandoning their critique of the media's ideological manipulations, artists are now making work that addresses their own fascination with mass media.

On September 11, 2002, New York-based artist Aleksandra Mir (who now lives in Palermo) self-published the first and only edition of the tabloid newspaper *Daily News*. She did this to celebrate her birthday, which the year before had coincided with the terrorist attacks on New York and Washington. More than a hundred friends were asked to submit pieces, from crossword puzzles to political manifestos to recipes. The aim was to reclaim the artist's date of birth, and the main headline on the front page screamed "Happy Birthday!" At a time when it was increasingly considered "unpatriotic" to dissent, the newspaper celebrated the ideal of freedom of opinion by publishing every single submission. The fact that the paper appeared as a one-off edition of one thousand copies, for free, highlighted the fact that this vision of free circulation was utopian, deferred gratification at grassroots level, indulged in by the artist not least as an act of immediate gratification. A photograph shows her drinking coffee on a New York fire escape, reading a copy of her very own newspaper.

# WE ARE NORMAL
## Pink Tank
STORY INSIDE

# DAILY ⊡ NEWS
www.nydailynews.com — Wednesday, September 11, 2002

# HAPPY
# BIRTHDAY!

KID I'M GOING TO GIVE YOU A SHOW.

- How to Ride the Bus
- Bring on the Clowns
- Punching through the Clouds
- She's so Good at being Bad

129a

---

# Editorial

Dear friends. Today is my 35th Birthday and this is a good year in the estimated 'middle of life' to reminisce one's past and catch future. But what a year it has been! I have spent most of mine on the road and in the sky, making art and new friends along the way, many of whom have now contributed to this special edition of the Daily News. I thank you dearly for these gifts.

Reclaiming my birthday from the fixation of 9-11 reconsideration, seemed tremendous already...

I would further like to dedicate this space to the memory of my paternal grandmother Ghana Klansking, who migrated to settling in a Swedish nunnery home on December 30, 2001...

Yours, Aleksandra Mir

Aleksandra Mir, Nina Manandhar and Shanta Khanna, London, August 2002.
Photo: Polly Staple.

## HAPPY BIRTHDAY FROM THE LIGHTHOUSE
### By Peter Hill

I was one of three Dickensian characters — the best of times and the worst of times. It stretched over a twelve month period, between 1973 and 1974, 18 hours working as a lighthouse keeper off the West Coast of Scotland...

Glasgow and Belfast.

One last summer's day two photographic students were brought out by fishing boat...

## To the Editor:

Ghost

The rumbling weather has an attitude. In September, at least, the unexpected, dreadful, stormings, suburban, for highest vertices...

BEASLEY
ART & TRUCKING

129b

---

Aleksandra Mir:
129a+b New York City, September 11, 2002

130a+b **Jens Haaning**, Redistribution (London-Karachi), 2003

Just as Mir celebrated her own birthday with the *Daily News*, she has to date celebrated the remarkable lives of four otherwise unknown people in *Living & Loving*, a newspaper-format journal distributed for free and published in cooperation with Polly Staple. *Living & Loving # 2—The Biography of Zoe Stillpass* (2004) reconstructs the biography of the daughter of an art collector from Cincinnati solely through interviews with her parents. First distributed at the Frieze Art Fair in London in 2004, the expectations raised by a handout at such an event contrasted sharply with its intimate account of the life of someone only very indirectly related to the art market. Yet this allowed Mir to offer an intimate insight into the social sphere were art collecting is situated in terms of gender, family, age, and popular culture: From baby's pacifier being occasionally dipped in Dom Perignon to calm her down, to the teenage girl's habit of constantly losing her Prada wallets and Fendi bags, as if countering her father's activity of collecting with the activity of losing.

As a contribution to the "Publicness" show at London's ICA, Danish artist Jens Haaning had all of the chairs from that institution's popular café sent to Karachi in Pakistan, where they were left in the street for anyone to take for free (*Redistribution London–Karachi*, 2003). Faced with such a work, it's easy to lose oneself in nebulous statements about globalization, cultural exchange, and cultural difference. But the interesting thing here is the concrete when and where of the work: the political, economic, and historical relationship between Great Britain and its former colony, inevitably complicated by developments since September 2001, is boiled down to a simple transaction that turns a "theft" into a "gift."

At first glance, Dan Perjovschi's works have little in common with artistic takes on the circulation of products, images, information, or opinions. His cartoons seem to come from the same planet as those of David Shrigley or Olav Westphalen, but they are different in the way that their radical simplification in terms of both style and content is their main point. The invitation card for an exhibition in Cologne described the sorry state of the German economy from the viewpoint of an artist accustomed to the tough conditions of a country like Romania, as follows: five beer glasses, two of which have been crossed out (*Recession*, 2004). Another invitation card for a group show in Berlin offered an alternative theory as to why Communism was bound to fail: a group of people has gathered under the word "Commun-" while a single solitary person remains under "ism" (*Commun-ism*, 2004). Perjovschi's jokes are about supply bottlenecks: too little

131    **Marina Abramović,** Role Exchange, 1975
132    **Adrian Piper,** Funk Lessons, 1983
133    **Dan Perjovschi,** Recession, 2004

beer in the economy, too few people in society, too few rockets for the war. But he has also devised a specific form of "supply" for his own working method. Instead of sending finished drawings to a given exhibition venue, he usually travels there in person with his sketchbook and copies directly from his notes onto the wall. The drawings are more like graffiti than newspaper caricatures (not to mention meticulous art drawings); they allude directly to profane circulation via public toilets and house walls. This results in very specific "conditions of performance." The drawings cannot go on tour without their creator; they cannot be sold straight off the wall as works on paper; they remain a passing apparition for the duration of a single exhibition. For a show at Zeche Zollverein in Essen in 2003, Perjovschi drew with chalk straight onto a rough industrial interior that only had to be hosed down afterwards.

# Circulation IV: Delegated Action
# Adrian Piper, Marina Abramović, Andrea Fraser, Gianni Motti, Tino Sehgal, Santiago Sierra, Roman Ondák

Humor is amusing and promises immediate gratification through laughter; teaching is demanding and promises deferred gratification through education. In the early 1980s, first-generation Conceptual artist Adrian Piper did a series of performances in which she kept the two in an electrified equilibrium as an effective way of putting subcultural knowledge into circulation. In her video *Funk Lessons* (1983), which documents one of these performances at the University of Berkeley, we see her showing the predominantly white audience how to dance to funk music. The typical assumption is that such dances cannot be taught because they occur spontaneously, but in *Funk Lessons* the teaching is successful and this is achieved by isolating individual movements such as the "shoulder shrug." While those present practice the new steps with an enthusiasm bordering on slapstick, words like "sexually expressive" flash up on the screen, blinking rhythmically—an ironically alarming "Watch out! Watch out!" The point is not just that a lesson is taught, but also how it is taught.

Nicolas Bourriaud has coined the term "relational aesthetics." Based on the assumption that a fundamental "scrambling of boundaries between consumption and production" has taken place in art (a view shared by Boris Groys), he comes to the conclusion that artists no longer view aesthetic objects as their goal (to present them as readymades, for example), making them instead in order to establish "relations between people and the world," ultimately considering "interhuman exchange an aesthetic object in and of itself." "The artist models and disseminates disconcerting situations," Bourriaud continues, and strives "to shatter the logic of the spectacle." But in whose name does he or she do this? And who is actually involved in the ensuing "interhuman exchange"? Is the "relational" artist a modernist hero fighting a lonesome battle against commercial culture, "relationally" linked to a kind of support group of viewers who cheer him or her on? "Interhuman exchange" suggests direct contact between artist and viewer. Combined with the alleged fusion of production and consumption, this amounts to consumer society's appeal—boosted by the advent of e-commerce—to "cut out the middleman." But even if Bourriaud does also mean indirect, mediated forms of exchange, it remains unclear what makes the relation between artist and audience a "relational" one. This may be because, by claiming that production and consumption have merged, Bourriaud makes the sphere of circulation—the actual sphere of dissemination and exchange—simply disappear. All that remains is either "interhuman exchange" or "spectacle."

With this in mind, when artists work with individuals who they involve in a form of exchange or circulation of activities, I would like to speak not of "relational aesthetics" but of "delegated action." This term makes clear that besides a relationship being established, there is also sharing or total relinquishing of responsibility for actions, handing over partial control either to the participants or to the process itself. Piper's *Funk Lessons* is based on the need for her to demonstrate the movements, but at some point her students begin to dance themselves, "on their own." "Delegated action" shifts constantly between performance and choreography, between the wish to control and the loss of control, between personal action and "impersonal" dissemination (and not least between immediate and deferred gratification).

In 1975, Marina Abramović created a piece called *Role Exchange* that involved her trading roles with a prostitute for four hours. The woman took the artist's place at the opening of her exhibition at De Appel in Amsterdam, while Abramović spent four hours sitting in a window in the red light district. "We both take total responsibility for our roles," concludes the dry description of the piece in the style of a Conceptual instruction. This apparently simple idea throws up a whole host of complex contradictions, which are only amplified by historical distance (that is, for all those who were not part of the immediate audience). What does this responsibility entail? How can the prostitute take over Abramović's role when she doesn't look even remotely like her, and when the exhibition included, for example, the video *Freeing the Voice* (1975) in which the artist can be clearly identified as a different person? And what about Abramović's "responsibility" in the red light district? The black-and-white photographs documenting the action allow no conclusion to be drawn as to whether or not she took care of any actual business. All of these uncertainties, however, do not compromise the piece; in fact they constitute its quality. They bring to light the intricate networks of fact and speculation, information and rumor that surround every social context. The "role exchange" is like a castling move in chess, changing not only the relation of the two figures involved, but also the whole situation on the board. Abramović emphasizes the real status of the body of the artist in relation to the imaginary status of her work.

Abramović's work establishes a polemic link to the idea of "art as prostitution," a notion already fielded by Baudelaire and one that was taken to extreme lengths by Andrea Fraser in her work *Untitled* (2003). From the mid-1980s, she had both used and questioned the ideological conditions of the art context in her performances, research projects, and video works. *Official Welcome* (2001) is the performance of a speech first given at the home of a collector couple who helped make the work possible. In it, Fraser switches seamlessly between acting numerous art world types (artist, gallerist, critic, collector, etc.) as if possessed by demons, without excluding herself from the tangled web of struggles for authority, recognition, and gratification. As Fraser has stated: "My own artistic position is included, as is my body and my biography. That is why I decided to take my clothes off, and also to weep in the performance: I wanted to close the gap between myself and what appears to be *not* me." *Untitled*, realized two years later, involved the following: as a commissioned piece for a collector, she had sex with this same collector, who remains anonymous, in a hotel room, filmed by a video camera with no sound from a surveillance position and shown as a single-channel DVD on a small screen. Any pornographic lust is thus more frustrated than satisfied, but there remains the feat of the artist risking her integrity for a pointed demonstration of the relationship between artist and collector. According to Fraser, however, the work is "not just a critique of art by way of prostitution as a metaphor for the reduction of all human interaction to relations of economic exchange. It also moves in the other direction, transforming an

134

135a

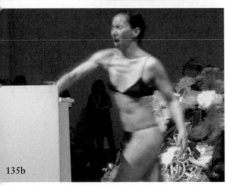

135b

**Andrea Fraser**
134    Untitled, 2003
135a+b Official Welcome (MICA Performance), 2001

economic exchange into a very human relationship." But the artist keeps the precise details of this transformation of exchange into relationship to herself, from the price paid by the collector to the specific agreements that preceded and accompanied the realization of the work.

The works of both Abramović and Fraser seem to be constituted in equal parts by what one is told about them and by what one is not told. In the case of Gianni Motti, what one is not told actually seems to be the *main* element. In other words, it is first and foremost a rumor. At his "retrospective" at Zurich's Migros Museum in 2004, his work could not be seen, but only heard about in the form of stories. Guides wore T-shirts printed with the words "Plausible Deniability," a mordant hint at the truth content of everything they said, including anecdotes about Motti staging his own funeral, or about him creeping into a session of the UN disguised as an Indonesian delegate.

Of course, putting anecdotes and stories into circulation only works as long as the artist can manage, at the same time, to prevent the circulation of "real" documentation (photographs and official descriptions of works). This is also a key element for Tino Sehgal. His work manifests itself in people who move, talk, sometimes dance, sometimes sing—all this in art exhibition spaces. Sehgal himself is never involved as an active participant. As in the case of several other young artists today, he delegates action to amateurs who are paid by the hour, or to people with specific functions (gallerists, museum attendants) who help perform the work in addition to their usual duties. The work manifests itself, for example, in gallery assistants who, as soon as a visitor moves toward the exit, stands up, walks a few steps, falls to the floor, and begins to feverishly recite the exhibition press release (*This Exhibition*, 2004); or in a woman and a man in everyday clothes lying on the floor of an empty exhibition space, slowly writhing and kissing like a couple of sloths trying out positions for sex, until at some point the woman says "Tino Sehgal" and the man says "Kiss" and the woman says "2004" (*Kiss*, 2004). Sehgal's work is located in the bodies and voices of those who perform it; in its reception and in memory; and in the time and space that it occupies. His works are actions enacted throughout the opening hours of an exhibition, so they are not performances. They are explicitly not recorded in photographs, videos, wall labels, or even in written contracts of sale. What's astonishing is the number of precursors and ingredients from the 1960s that can be identified in Sehgal's approach. These include elements of artists like Ian Wilson (who in 1968 made a work consisting of a verbal discussion that was not recorded or otherwise documented, although its duration and location were certified) or Yvonne Rainer (whose dance choreographies moved seamlessly from complex, highly conceptualized patterns to repetitions of mundane movements that could be performed by absolutely anyone). But the sum of possible influences doesn't explain what happens to us when we encounter Sehgal's works; these works are neither simply physically present choreographies and sustained performances, nor a further footnote on the "dematerialization" of conceptual art, which in Sehgal's case extends even to the absence of documentary photographs, explanatory accompanying texts, and certificates (anyone buying one of his works does so in the presence of a notary but with no written proof of purchase). Instead, it is precisely the combination of a manifest physical level in the performance of the work by the trained "interpreters" (as Sehgal calls them) and the complete absence of other physical "carriers" (down to the lack of wall labels), which lends his work its special, unique character. Besides the action itself, the work exists only in its reception, in rumors, and in art criticism. It is an expression of the same kind of idea of conceptual unity and elegance that prompts mathematicians to speak of "beauty" when referring to a simple formula that describes something highly complex. It is an idea which manifests itself physically but which cannot be completely "consumed" as a product. It remains, by definition, forever in circulation. This is something that infuriates both those who think conceptual art is humbug and those who consider themselves to be its guardians. The former find Sehgal too puritanical in his rejection of objects and illustrations, while the latter find him too vulgar in his love of the direct physicality of dance and the celebratory affirmation of pop.

There are often conflicting reports concerning the exact nature of a particular work by Sehgal, not least because its concept is varied enough to avoid being reduced to its "basic" idea. Take *This objective of that object* (2004), realized in 2006 at the ICA in London. On entering a room, one found oneself facing five people standing with their backs to the entrance. After a while, they began saying the following sentence in unison: "The objective of this work is to become the object of a discussion." The only problem was that any attempt to establish eye contact for such a discussion resulted in the five turning away. During my visit, someone asked a question nonetheless; the answer given by one of the interpreters sounded rather precocious, like someone trying to shine in a university seminar by means of endless talk. But this didn't detract from the fascination of the work; it merely highlighted the fact that the performers were choosing their own words within the framework laid down by Sehgal. Only later did I find out what would have happened if no one had asked a question. Then, the five interpreters would have "died" and dropped to the floor, as if failing to become the object of discussion had also robbed them of their status as an art object. The viewers were given no written indication whether or not they "got it right," and that wasn't the point. The work consists of the fascination of an unmediated interaction with a person trained according to as-yet-unknown rules, plus the frustration of possibly only having experienced a fragment, a random sample of the possible manifestations of these rules. Truly unseizable gratification.

The collecting and "exhibiting" of people in art exhibition spaces brings to light a characteristic feature of the market economy: while objects can almost seem to become living things, living things become objects. The value of human labor is the focus of the work of Santiago Sierra. The way most of his works function is that for the duration of their realization, unskilled workers, junkies, prostitutes, or asylum seekers—in other words, people who will do anything for money—are taken out of their usual exploitative context and transferred to the sphere of art. He "contaminates" the sublime abstractions of Minimalism and the clinical space of the White Cube with the concrete reality of obscene exploitation—at the same time as deliberately profiting from it. He pays no more than the participants would usually earn, and sometimes less.

Santiago Sierra is talked about on account of his reputation for unparalleled and ruthless directness in moving the barbarity of exploitation inside the aesthetic "special zone" of art. All the more surprising, then, that he repeatedly gives the impression of being someone who works very precisely in formal terms, and rather sloppily and contradictorily in terms of content. In 1999, Sierra hired 465 "mestizos" (men of mixed ethnic origin) through an employment agency to stand around for three hours at a museum opening in Mexico City. Their number was calculated to ensure a density of five people per square meter. Sierra's description of the work makes no mention of the reaction of the presumably rather taken aback museum visitors, but it does say that the agency, as he later discovered, had clearly not paid most of the men, as well as asking friends and entire school classes to turn up for free. Whereas here Sierra at least addresses these facts, in other cases he doesn't even mention them: *Polyurethane Sprayed on the Backs of 10 Workers. Lisson Gallery, London, U.K., July 2004* is the descriptive title of another work; we are told nothing about how much the men were paid.

Sierra has a historical precursor in the Argentinean artist Oscar Bony. In 1968,

Bony hired a family of workers to stand on a kind of podium in their Sunday best for an exhibition. For the duration of the show, he doubled the father's meager hourly wage as a sheet metal worker. Through this act of exhibiting, the family was "doubled"—but so was their pay. In Sierra's work, the reverse is the case; he doubles the exploitation. The four decades from Bony to Sierra describe the distance between evenhanded matter-of-factness and high-handed disillusionment. The problem is not that Sierra acts "immorally," but that, on the contrary, he obviously attributes a moral position to himself as someone who pushes the ills of society into the abstractions of art. One might of course argue that Sierra is forcing the privileged people who have time and money for art to face the material presence of the exploitation from which they indirectly profit. But he lets them off the hook surprisingly easily, as he makes not the slightest effort to point to the concrete political causes of this exploitation. In his work, poverty appears as a mysterious destiny.

When dealing with the delicate issue of putting human labor into circulation "as art," it becomes important how the artist behaves toward those who become his "material." He or she doesn't have to be a saint, but the aesthetic gain achieved by the artwork ought to stand in a productive relationship to the ethical implications it raises. The problem in Sierra's case—and in that of Vanessa Beecroft, who makes women in Gucci stilettos stand around in exhibitions rather than junkies or prostitutes—is that he acts as a manipulator in the background who is concerned primarily with shock and awe rather than with worrying about conceptual coherence—for example in terms of a work's alleged political implications.

The work of Roman Ondák is very different in this respect. Although he doesn't appear as a performer himself, it's as if he's on a level with those performing his delegated actions, treating them as equal partners in a game in spite of his instructions. No one lets you know in advance that he's planning, at a particular point in time, to have a line of several dozen people standing outside Kölnischer Kunstverein (Cologne's Art Society) for hours, even though there are no sought-after concert tickets or bargains to be had. As a passerby in the busy city center, even if one notices that this is a performance—perhaps because someone has already mentioned it—one almost automatically asks oneself whether there's something here to which one has no access. In the case of Ondák, who lives in Bratislava and grew up in Czechoslovakia, the history of such queuing as an expression of shortages in planned economies is certainly

136a-f **Santiago Sierra**, Polyurethane Sprayed on the Backs of 10 Workers (London 2004)

relevant. But this form of "deferred gratification" also recalls the typical market economy fear of missing out on some gratification you didn't even know you wanted.

# Against the Instrumentalization of Art

Pop Art was the movement that made perhaps the most effective use of the contradiction between the direct impact of mass culture and its long-term effects on history, memory, and reflection. The more interesting protagonists of the Pop tradition know how to uphold this contradiction, negating the Protestant work ethic of endlessly deferred gratification, but without simply buying into a sanitized form of controlled hedonism. This contradiction can only be resolved at the price of Pop Art losing its interest and becoming a dead relic. The idea of unseizable gratification—fluctuating between performative presence and speculative absence, between factuality and myth—can be seen in relation to Freud's concept of the "belatedness" of a traumatic core of experience (on which art historian Hal Foster's understanding of the "return of the real" in twentieth-century art is also based). The "instant pleasure" of commodity consumption and market gratification has a delayed impact (for better or often for worse) on the subsequent historicization and reevaluation of the art experience. There may be "integrated" art world business types who believe the future value of art can be controlled, and there are the "apocalyptic" intellectuals who see a mafia of market manipulators at work. But most artists have long since realized that instant gratification cannot be extended forever, while deferred gratification inevitably produces an everyday work reality that is empty, alienated, and disciplined. Works of art whose outstanding feature is unseizable gratification expose and reflect this dilemma.

Against this background, three major misunderstandings emerge—misunderstandings that are constantly reiterated in discussions of the nature of project-based artistic production. The first misunderstanding, as mentioned above, is to think that art should be about bypassing the culture of the spectacle by triumphantly negating broad or open distribution and circulation—for the sake of "unmediated" exchange within a social group created by context-based art practice. In such discussions, however, notions of who the audience is are often highly inconsequent. There is a tendency to keep one's circle closed, celebrating "community" and "group" over supposedly passive or anonymous "audience" (that is, people you haven't met yet); or favoring non-art audiences (grassroots political groups, "ordinary people," etc.) who can be more or less relied upon not to apply the aesthetic criteria of art discourse.

The second misunderstanding is to think that fluctuating situations automatically have something to do with opportunism: that artistic decision-making on a case-to-case basis—participating in certain cases, but not in certain others—means there are no underlying aesthetic or ethical criteria. Whereas in fact, criteria such as conceptual coherence, critical potential, aesthetic merit, freedom of access, and the dismantling of privilege are the requisite yardsticks for arriving at such decisions.

The third misunderstanding is based on the assumption that art can only fulfill a valuable (ethical) function if it dispenses with its aestheticism. This is the "ethical" version; the "aesthetic" version of the same misunderstanding holds that the ethical element is merely a sanitization and disciplining of the aesthetic potential of artistic production. This showdown is worthy of Punch and Judy: Gandhi versus Oscar Wilde (both as caricatures, of course). I agree with the "aesthetic camp" that "uselessness"—art's freedom from "application" and instrumentalization in the realms of politics, economics, etc.—is precisely the use of art. But one should not forget that this kind of "uselessness" inevitably implies possible uses in other situations and future scenarios. This potentiality is the bugbear of those who see in popular culture the harbinger of the apocalypse—hence the obsession with artworks that cannot be distributed or reproduced, using pure circulation to secure them against future corruption and co-optation.

In an essay from 1996 entitled "What's intangible, transitory, immediate, participatory and rendered in the public sphere? Part II: The critique of artistic autonomy," Andrea Fraser outlines a more complex position: "Far from functioning only as ideology critique," she argues, the Conceptual art of the 1960s and 1970s "aimed to construct a less ideological form of autonomy, conditioned not by the abstraction of relations of consumption in the commodity form, but by the conscious and critical determination, in each particular and immediate instance, of the uses to which artistic activity is put and the interests it serves." The simplistic idea of artistic autonomy as somehow detached from uses and interests did not gradually erode; it was flawed from the outset. Even if one accepts the existence of co-opting, interests, and entanglements, the idea that the artist could gain complete control over these factors remains an illusion. The concept of unseizable gratification allows art at least to keep this issue in limbo, to prevent anyone—be they viewer, participant, or owner—from getting away easily with attempts to "eternalize" any interest they may wish to invest in it.

Ultimately, the paradox of art's uselessness is that it can only be upheld if artists allow themselves to be exposed to situations where this very uselessness is put to the test.

# Glowing Prospects

Where might things go from here? Just to briefly recap: slapstick is the method that saves art from becoming frozen in dogmas and schools, including the dogmas and schools of slapstick itself; the slapstick method addresses the fantasy of an automated, flexible, and accelerated life by making it halt and stumble. As a status symbol for the powerful and as a medium for reflections on the everyday use of images, painting exemplifies the contradictory position of art within society. As a result, interesting painting, flickering between two- and three-dimensionality, acts as a sounding board for the milieus and spaces where these factors collide, switching between suspension of the space-time continuum and spatio-temporal experience of a modular visual system. The interesting film/video projection spaces in contemporary art push precisely this aspect of contemporary paint-ing further toward rhythmicized fragmentation and simultaneity. Rather than providing holistic, quasi-religious experiences or carefully ordered information about the state of things, they involve their audience in a productive double-bind between active navigation of the exhibition and passive integration into the rhythms of image and sound sequences. And finally, in successful cases, the art forms that take a conceptual approach to the circulation of actions, objects, and information offer a way out of the traditional conflict between immediate gratification in the market and deferred gratification in the museum and other sites of institutional recognition and preservation. They content themselves neither with the comedown after the fast kick, nor with the long depression on the way to eventual recognition. Instead, they put their audience in a situation that transforms the torture of Tantalus (the eternal frustration of abstinence in the face of ripe fruit and spring water) into a playful pleasure—like not simply stuffing cherries into one's mouth straight away, but throwing them high in the air first.

This is all very well, I hear myself saying, but aren't these all forms of artistic production that constantly undermine their own laws to the point of collapse? And doesn't that make them arbitrary? But that is the point. Arbitrariness would occur precisely if they did attempt to "enshrine" ultimately arbitrary formal criteria. The interesting art of today makes fools of those who cannot resist the temptation (and everyone falls into this trap, again and again) of trying to pin it down with prescriptive, normative standards. Which doesn't mean—just to make this clear—that art which undermines its own standards is exempt from criticism, such as the kind that compares the implicit claims of such undermining with the actual effect of the resulting works.

I have tried, in my account, to do without the existing categorizations of artistic strategies that constitute my own daily bread as a professional art viewer: all the talk of Appropriation Art, Neo-Modernism, Docufiction Art, etc. For, among other things, art is always an argument with all these normative models that have accumulated in the course of its history. And insofar as the light shed on art in this book has any kind of normative character, the artists in question have long since moved on. First, because their hunger for experiment drives them across the dividing lines of genre—artists like Rodney Graham and Rosemarie Trockel, who have been making art for decades, could rightly appear in three if not all four chapters of this book. And second, because young artists are taking much of what is described here as the basis for new dizzying leaps into the unknown. Aleksandra Mir, for example (some of whose works are discussed in chapter four), has since moved on to make projects that include a book printed using the highly sophisticated technique of potato printing (*The Meaning of Flowers*, 2006), a strikingly real-looking life-size interplanetary rocket built out of junk (*Gravity*, 2006), and transforming a gallery into a studio to churn out, for the duration of a show, large drawings based on more than ten thousand *Daily News* and *New York Post* covers (*Newsroom 1986–2000*, 2007).

Other artists initially appear to be "just" revisiting the works of early pioneers in order to pay tribute and declare their interest, but this pilgrimage is then used as a site for something new and distinctive. Like young Korean-Canadian artist Tim Lee: *Untitled (The Pink Panther, 2049)* (2007) is a series of three photographs in which we see Lee photographing himself plus his reflection in several of Dan Graham's outdoor pavilions—works that make eloquent use of layerings of mirror and glass reflections, and thus gazes mirrored, diverted, and multiplied. With his title, Lee in turn layers this kind of regress with a semiological one: Blake Edwards's *The Pink Panther,* starring Peter Sellers, was made in 1963, while Steve Martin's remake is from 2006—forty-three years later—and thus the "2049" in Lee's title (another forty-three years on) is a projection into the future of yet another remake of the remake. But that's not where it stops: Lee continues with a pair of photographs—*Untitled I (The Pink Panther, 2092)* (2007)—as if, yet another forty-three years on, the next conflation of *The Pink Panther* and Dan Graham's modernist language of mirror-reflection was due. The first of the two images shows Lee photographing himself between two facing mirrors (or so it seems), with multiple reflections receding into the distance. The second shot, showing Lee in profile, also features receding multiple reflections, thus revealing itself as a manipulation of some kind (the picture obviously cannot have been taken with the camera we see him holding). Lee visualizes the anxiety of an increasingly isolated position of the artist today vis-à-vis the long line of predecessors, and an audience—geographically and socially diversified, fragmented—that he seldom encounters face to face. But that's where the comedy role model of the loser-jerk who inadvertently becomes a hero (whether played by Peter Sellers or Steve Martin) comes into play. Lee is paying homage to all the cultural ghosts he summons, and yet he's always the lone impersonator at the center of his hall of mirrors, turning problems of authority from the past, by sleight of hand, into imaginary solutions for the future. And thus, incidentally, these and other works by Lee conflate the methods of slapstick and modular reflection and fragmentation of images in space outlined in the first and third chapters of this book.

One obvious critique leveled at the kind of art that uses such trickery to locate itself more between objects than in them is that it anticipates—either involuntarily or with cynical intent—the tendencies of economic and political power that aim to subject people to a restless search for potentials of utilization. Conceptual art, for example, with its aesthetic of text, instruction, documentation, etc., has on various occasions been accused of mirroring the spheres of authoritarian state administration or neoliberal marketing, where information and communication are similarly subjected to control and exploitation. In the same vein, the "fluid" modes of representation in film and video installations are often suspected of involuntarily or deliberately mirroring the neoliberal call for ever-increasing flexibility of the workforce and for rigorous self-management. Not that this might not actually be true in certain cases, but as a generalization it becomes a normative concept of aesthetics that takes formal similarities as proof of identical nature. But with art as with mushrooms, the following simple rule applies: what looks very similar can have very different effects.

The idea of multitasking, for example, has long since become a running gag of our times: the Internet is full of amateur slapstick filmlets in which crazed employees trash their computers with their telephones, or vice versa, because they can no longer stand the simultaneity. But this mad frenzy is due not to "information overload" per se, but to its quality and the uses to which it is put. Technologies and media are only ever as good as the interests to which they are harnessed in the long term. If everything is dictated by exploitation and heartlessness, then multitasking is a curse. If we're talking about the excitement of perceiving and comprehending complexities and connections, then it's a blessing.

Accordingly, there can be no formulas for developing taste in the assessment of art. To describe someone as "having taste" would be fair enough if it were merely convenient shorthand for that person having acquired the knowledge, the perceptive faculties, and the confidence to arrive at aesthetic judgments that make a constructive contribution to the discourse in question. But mostly, someone is described as "having no taste" as a convenient way of signaling to that person that they do not fit into the social group or cultural niche of the person making the statement. Judgments of taste concerning art, including its makers and viewers, are thus repeatedly rendered absurd because they are instrumentalized as tools in the proxy war over power and recognition within society, or—worse still—as a form of investment consulting. Of course, it's a great thing when all manner of people invest their love, their critical thinking, or even their fortune in art for all kinds of reasons. But art as nothing but an investment is a contradiction in terms, and a highly unproductive one at that. There remains one criteria that is always an indicator of good art, and that is that it retains a healthy mistrust of the schools it forms itself. It can't be put any more simply than that.

# Selected Bibliography

Earlier writings by the author on artists and themes dealt with in this book, which have appeared in *frieze* (see online archive: www.frieze.com), *Süddeutsche Zeitung* (www.diz-muenchen.de), and several other publications, are only listed below in cases where they provided a substantial basis for the chapter in question.

## Pathos *versus* Ridiculousness Art With Slapstick

I am indebted to Thomas Girst, Pash Buzari, and Rolf Walz for valuable comments on Duchamp.

*Bas Jan Ader: Please Don't Leave Me.* Catalogue, Museum Boijmans van Beuningen. Rotterdam, 2006.

Bergson, Henri. *Laughter: An Essay on the Meaning of the Comic* (Le rire, 1901). New York, 1911.

Le Bon, Laurent, ed. *DADA.* Paris, 2005.

*George Brecht: Events. Eine Hetero-spektive.* Catalogue, Museum Ludwig. Cologne, 2005.

Dale, Alan. *Comedy is a Man in Trouble: Slapstick in American Movies.* Minneapolis, 2000.

Daniels, Dieter. *Duchamp und die anderen.* Cologne, 1992.

Duve, Thierry de. *Pictorial Nominal-ism: On Marcel Duchamp's Passage from Painting to the Readymade* (1984). Minneapolis and Oxford, 1991.

Elias, Norbert. *The Germans: Power Struggles and the Development of Habitus in the Nineteenth and Twentieth Centuries* (Studien über die Deutschen, 1989). Cambridge, 1996.

Elger, Dietmar. *Der Merzbau von Kurt Schwitters. Eine Werkmonographie* (1984). Cologne, 1999.

*Urs Fischer: Kir Royal.* Catalogue, Kunsthalle Zürich. Zurich, 2004.

*Fischli/Weiss: Flowers & Questions: A Retrospective.* Bice Curiger, ed. Catalogue, Tate Publishing. London: Tate Publishing, 2007.

*Martin Gostner: Of Milk and Honey.* Catalogue, Museum Folkwang. Essen, 2003.

Graw, Isabelle. "Mein erster Verriss. Genese einer Voreingenommenheit – Sarah Lucas." *Texte zur Kunst* 45, March 2002.

Heiser, Jörg, ed. *Funky Lessons.* Catalogue, BAWAG Foundation, Vienna and BüroFriedrich, Berlin. Vienna and Frankfurt, 2004.

Hermes, Manfred. *Martin Kippenberger.* Cologne, 2005.

*Georg Herold: X. Baracke 1986.* Catalogue, Galerie Max Hetzler. Berlin, 2005.

Higgie, Jennifer. "Under the Influence: Rebecca Warren." *frieze* 72, Jan/Feb 2002.

Keller, Christoph and Werner Feiersinger, eds. *Werner Feiersinger. Skulpturen.* Frankfurt, 2004.

Kintisch, Christine. "Nothing But Pleasure or Hardly Any Pleasure At All." In Kintisch, ed. *Nothing But Pleasure.* Catalogue, BAWAG Foundation. Vienna, 2006.

Koether, Jutta. "Ein Interview mit Martin Kippenberger." *Texte zur Kunst* 3, Summer 1991.

Kosuth, Joseph. *Art After Philosophy and After. Collected Writings 1966–1990.* Cambridge, Mass., and London, 1991.

Kuenzli, Rudolf, ed. *Dada (Themes and Movements).* London, 2006.

*Lee Lozano. Win First Don't Last. Win Last Don't Care.* Catalogue, Kunsthalle Basel. Basel, 2006.

Meyer-Hermann, Eva, and Susanne Neuburger, eds. *Nach Kippenberger.* Vienna, 2003.

Molesworth, Helen. "Work Avoidance: The Everyday Life of Marcel Duchamp's Readymades." *Art Journal*, Winter 1998.

Molesworth, Helen. "Rrose Sélavy Goes Shopping." In Leah Dickerman and Matthew S. Witkovsky, eds. *The Dada Seminars.* Washington D.C., 2005.

Naumann, Francis M. "Marcel Duchamp: A Reconciliation of Opposites." *The Definitively Unfinished Marcel Duchamp.*

Thierry de Duve, ed. Cambridge, Mass., and London, 1991.

*Richard Artschwager. The Hydraulic Door Check* (catalogue, MAK Vienna). Vienna and Cologne, 2002.

Robbins, David. "Concrete Comedy: A Primer." *Artforum*, Nov 2004.

Rugoff, Ralph. "Falling with Style." In *Sudden Glory: Sight Gags and Slapstick in Contemporary Art.* Catalogue, CCAC Wattis Institute. San Francisco, 2002.

Sanders, Barry. *Sudden Glory: Laughter as Subversive History.* Boston, 1995.

Schwarz, Arturo. *The Complete Work of Marcel Duchamp.* Fourth revised and expanded edition. New York, 2000.

Seifermann, Ellen, and Jörg Heiser, eds. *Romantic Conceptualism.* Catalogue, Kunsthalle Nürnberg and BAWAG Foundation, Vienna. Bielefeld, 2007.

Stauffer, Serge. *Marcel Duchamp: Interviews und Statements.* Stuttgart, 1992.

Stern, Steve. "Tomorrow Never Comes: Mike Kelley." *frieze* 97, March 2006.

Taschen, Angelika, and Burkhard Riemschneider, eds. *Kippenberger*, Cologne, 1997.

Tomkins, Calvin. *The World of Marcel Duchamp.* New York, 1966.

Tomkins, Calvin. *Duchamp: A Biography.* New York, 1996.

Trainor, James. "Ain't no such thing as Superman: William Pope L." *frieze* 83, May 2004.

*Rosemarie Trockel: Post-Menopause.* Catalogue, Museum Ludwig. Cologne, 2005.

Verwoert, Jan. *Bas Jan Ader: In Search of the Miraculous.* London, 2006.

Weiss, Jeffrey. *Picasso, Duchamp, and Avant-Gardism.* New Haven and London, 1994.

# Bodiless Elegance
## *versus*
## Pungent Physicality
## The Painting of Decisions

The sections on Gerhard Richter and Glenn Brown are based in part on the text: "Master and Minion," published in *PARKETT 75*, 2005; and the section on Dana Schutz on "Bling Bling, Grrr Grrr: Pop and Painting Eat Themselves," in *Dana Schutz*, catalogue, The Rose Art Museum, Waltham, MA, 2006.

Beyer, Susanne, and Ulrike Knöfel. Interview with Neo Rauch, "Zeit der zarten Bitternis." *Der Spiegel*. 38/2006.

Bois, Yve-Alain. "Painting: The Task of Mourning" (1986). Reprinted in Douglas Fogle, ed. *Painting at the Edge of the World*. Catalogue, Walker Art Center. Minneapolis, 2001.

Crimp, Douglas. *On the Museum's Ruins*. Cambridge, MA, and London, 1993.

*Charline von Heyl*. Catalogue, Secession. Vienna, 2004.

*Maria Lassnig*. Catalogue, MUMOK Wien et al. Klagenfurt, 1985.

*Maria Lassnig: Körperporträts*. Catalogue, Museum für Gegenwartskunst Siegen. Siegen, 2002.

McCloud, Scott. *Understanding Comics: The Invisible Art*. New York, 1993.

Murakami, Takashi. "A Theory of Superflat Japanese Art." In Douglas

Fogle, ed. *Painting at the Edge of the World* (op. cit.).

Obrist, Hans-Ulrich, ed. *Gerhard Richter: 100 Pictures*. Ostfildern-Ruit, 2002.

*Exposition Albert Oehlen: Peintures—Malerei 1980–2004*. Catalogue, Musée Cantonal des Beaux Arts Lausanne. Zurich, 2004.

*Laura Owens*. Catalogue, Kunsthalle Zürich. Zurich, 2006.

*Sigmar Polke. Bilder Tücher Objekte*. Catalogue, Kunsthalle Tübingen et al. Tübingen, Düsseldorf, and Eindhoven, 1976.

*Sigmar Polke. Die drei Lügen der Malerei*. Catalogue, Kunst- und Ausstellungshalle der Bundesrepublik Deutschland. Bonn, 1997.

*Neo Rauch*. Catalogue, Museum der bildenden Künste Leipzig. Leipzig, 1997.

*Neo Rauch. Neue Rollen. Bilder 1993–2006*. Catalogue,

Kunstmuseum Wolfsburg. Cologne, 2006.

Reise, Barbara M. "Who, What is 'Sigmar Polke.'" *Studio International*, part I and II, July/Aug 1976, part III Sept/Oct 1976, part IV Jan/Feb 1977.

*Daniel Richter. Grünspan*. Catalogue, K21 Düsseldorf. Bielefeld, 2003.

Richter, Gerhard. *The Daily Practice of Painting, Writings 1962–1993*. London, 1995.

Roberts, James. "Magic Mushrooms: on Takashi Murakami." *frieze* 70, Oct 2002.

*Wilhelm Sasnal—Night Day Night*. Catalogue, Westfälischer Kunstverein und Kunsthalle Zürich. Ostfildern-Ruit, 2003.

Staple, Polly. "The Finishing Touch: Gillian Carnegie." *frieze* 64, Jan/Feb 2002.

Storr, Robert. *Gerhard Richter: Doubt and Belief in Painting*. New York, 2003.

Verwoert, Jan. "Emergence: On the painting of Tomma Abts." In Daniel Buchholz and Christopher Müller, eds. *Tomma Abts*. Cologne and London, 2004.

# Illusion
## *versus*
# Anti-Illusion
# Film/Video in Exhibition Architectures

*Eija-Liisa Ahtila. The Cinematic Works* (book and DVD). Helsinki, 2003.

Aitken, Doug. *Broken Screen: Expanding the Image, Breaking the Narrative. 26 conversations with Doug Aitken*. New York, 2006.

*Doug Aitken (Contemporary Artists Series)*. New York and London, 2001.

Altieri, Charles. *The Particulars of Rapture. An Aesthetics of the Affects*. Ithaca and London, 2003.

Bal, Mieke. *Introduction to the Theory of Narrative*. Toronto, 1997.

Bal, Mieke. "Affekt als kulturelle Kraft." *Affekte*. Antje Krause-Wahl and Serjoscha Wiemer, eds. Bielefeld, 2006.

Barthes, Roland. "Leaving the Movie Theater." *The Rustle of Language*. Berkeley, 1989.

Beil, Ralf, ed. *Der Schwarzraum in der Kunst*. Catalogue, Kunstmuseum Bern. Ostfildern-Ruit, 2001.

*Janet Cardiff. The Walk Book* (artist's book, TBA 21). Vienna, 2005.

Colomina, Beatriz. "Enclosed by Images: the Eameses' Multimedia Architecture." *Grey Room* 2. Winter 2001.

Debord, Guy. *The Society of the Spectacle*. Trans. Donald Nicholson-Smith. New York, 1994.

Deleuze, Gilles. *Cinema 1: The Movement-Image. Cinema 2: The Time-Image*. Minneapolis, 1986/1989.

Godfrey, Mark. "Light Year: Mark Godfrey talks to Anthony McCall." *frieze* 99, May 2006.

Graham, Dan. *Works 1965–2000*. Düsseldorf, 2001.

Gunning, Tom. "Illusions Past and Future: The Phantasmagoria and its Specters." http://193.171.60.44/dspace/bitstream/10002/296/1/Gunning.pdf (accessed March 31, 2008).

Husch, Anette, Joachim Jäger, and Gabriele Knapstein, eds. *Beyond Cinema: The Art of Projection*. Catalogue, Hamburger Bahnhof. Ostfildern-Ruit, 2007.

Iles, Chrissie, ed. *Into the Light: The Projected Image in American Art, 1964–1977*. Catalogue, Whitney Museum of American Art. New York, 2002.

Johnson, Steven. *Everything Bad is Good for You: How Popular Culture is Making Us Smarter*. New York, 2005.

Manovich, Lev. *The Language of New Media*. Cambridge, MA, 2001.

Marx, Karl and Friedrich Engels. *The German Ideology*. Buffalo, NY, 1998.

Marx, Karl. *Capital, Book I: The Process of Production of Capital*. London, 1992.

Michalka, Matthias, ed. *X-Screen*. Catalogue, MUMOK Wien. Cologne, 2003.

Sanborn, Keith. "Return of the Suppressed: on the films of Guy Debord." *Artforum*, Feb 2006.

Spector, Nancy. "This is all true, and contradictory, if not hysterical." Interview with Douglas Gordon in *Art from the UK. Sammlung Goetz*. Catalogue. Munich, 1997.

Spector, Nancy. "Only the perverse fantasy can still save us." *Matthew Barney. The Cremaster Cycle*. New York, 2002.

Stemmrich, Gregor, ed. *Kunst/Kino*. Cologne, 2001.

Tobin, Amy. "Douglas Gordon." *Spellbound: Art and Film*. Philip Dodd and Ian Christie, eds. London, 1996.

*Jeff Wall. Catalogue Raisonné 1978–2004*. Göttingen, 2005.

Weibel, Peter. "The Allusive Eye: Illusion, Anti-Illusion, Allusion." *Fast Forward: Media Art Sammlung Goetz*. Catalogue, ZKM Karlsruhe. Ostfildern-Ruit, 2006.

# Art
## *versus*
# Market
# The Logic of Unseizable Gratification

This chapter draws largely on: "Throw 'em out, they break my heart: Artists' projects, the market and the logic of unseizable gratification." Melissa Gronlund and Polly Staple, eds. *Frieze Projects Artists' Commissions and Talks 2003–2005*. London 2006; and on "Good Circulation," *frieze* 90, April 2005.

Abramović, Marina. *Artist Body: Performances 1969–1997.* Milan, 1998.

Bell, Daniel. *The Cultural Contradictions of Capitalism.* New York, 1976.

Bourriaud, Nicolas. *Postproduction.* New York, 2002.

Bourriaud, Nicolas. *Relational Aesthetics.* Paris, 2002.

Eco, Umberto. "Apocalyptic and Integrated Intellectuals: Mass communications and theories of mass culture." *Apocalypse Postponed.* Robert Lumley, ed. Bloomington, 1994.

Fraser, Andrea. *Works 1984 to 2003.* Catalogue, Kunstverein in Hamburg. Cologne, 2003.

Fraser, Andrea. "What's Intangible, Transitory, Mediating, Participatory, and Rendered in the Public Sphere? Part II: The Critique of Artistic Autonomy." *October* 80, spring 1997.

Fraser, Andrea. Interview. *Funky Lessons*, op. cit. Jörg Heiser, ed. Vienna and Frankfurt, 2004.

Groys, Boris. "Der Künstler als Konsument." *Shopping. Kunst und Konsum im 20. Jahrhundert.* Christoph Grunenberg and Max Hollein, eds. Catalogue, Schirn Kunsthalle Frankfurt et al. Ostfildern-Ruit, 2002.

Hackett, Pat, ed. *The Andy Warhol Diaries.* New York, 1989.

*Douglas Huebler. "Variable,"* etc. Catalogue, FRAC Limousin. Limoges, 1993.

Kämmen, Michael. *The Lively Arts: Gilbert Seldes and the Transformation of Cultural Criticism in the United States.* New York, 1996.

Lazarrato, Maurizio. "European Cultural Tradition and the New Forms of Production and Circulation of Knowledge." www.nettime.org/Lists-Archives/nettime-l-9810/msg00113.html. 1998. Accessed

March 31, 2008.

*Adrian Piper seit 1965: Metakunst und Kunstkritik*. Vienna and Cologne, 2002.

Siegelaub, Seth. "The Why and What of the Context of Art/The Art of Context." *The Context of Art/The Art of Context*. Roswitha Fricke and Marion Siegelaub, eds. Trieste, 2004.

Swyngedouw, Erik. "Circulations and Metabolisms: (hybrid) natures and (cyborg) cities." www.ru.nl/socgeo/colloguium/science.pdf. 2004. Accessed March 31, 2008.

# Picture Credits

## Pathos
## *versus*
## Ridiculousness

| | |
|---|---|
| 1a–c | © Atelier Franz West. Photo: Jürgen Schmidt, Cologne |
| 2 | © Archiv Franz West. Photographer unknown |
| 3 | © Succession Marcel Duchamp/VG Bild-Kunst, Bonn 2008 |
| 6 | © VG Bild-Kunst, Bonn 2008 |
| 7 | © Succession Marcel Duchamp/VG Bild-Kunst, Bonn 2008 |
| 8 | Courtesy Francis M. Naumann Fine Art, LLC, New York |
| 9 | © Man Ray Trust, Paris/VG Bild-Kunst, Bonn 2008 |
| 10 | © VG Bild-Kunst, Bonn 2008. Photo: Kurt Schwitters Archives in the Sprengel Museum, Hanover. Photo: Wilhelm Redemann, Hanover. Repro: Michael Herling/Aline Gwose |
| 11 | © VG Bild-Kunst, Bonn 2008 |
| 12 | © Marian Goodman Gallery, New York and John Baldessari. Courtesy bdv (bureau des vidéos), Paris |
| 13 | © VG Bild-Kunst, Bonn 2008 |

| | |
|---|---|
| 14 | © Courtesy the Estate of Gordon Matta-Clark and David Zwirner, New York. © VG Bild-Kunst, Bonn 2008 |
| 15 | © VG Bild-Kunst, Bonn 2008 |
| 16, 17 | Courtesy the artist and Regen Projects, Los Angeles |
| 18 | Courtesy Ronald Feldman Fine Arts, New York |
| 19 | Courtesy Monika Sprüth/Philomene Magers Galerie, Cologne/Munich/London. © Rosemarie Trockel, VG Bild-Kunst, Bonn 2008. Photo: Bernhard Schaub, Cologne |
| 20 | © Martha Rosler |
| 21–23 | © Estate Martin Kippenberger, Galerie Gisela Capitain, Cologne |
| 24, 25 | Courtesy of Galerie Krinzinger. © VG Bild-Kunst, Bonn 2008 |
| 26 | Courtesy Castello di Rivoli, Museo d'Arte Contemporanea, Rivoli-Torino. Thanks to Galleria Giò Marconi, Milan, Galleria Franco Noero, Turin. Photo: Matthias Vriens |
| 27 | Courtesy the artist and Hauser & Wirth Zürich London |
| 28a+b | Courtesy Contemporary Fine Arts, Berlin. Photos: Jan Bauer, Berlin |
| 29 | © VG Bild-Kunst, Bonn 2008 |
| 30, 31 | © the artist. Courtesy Sadie Coles HQ, London |
| 32 | Courtesy Maureen Paley, London |
| 33 | Friedrich Christian Flick Collection. Photo: Nic Tenwiggenhorn. © VG Bild-Kunst, Bonn 2008 |
| 34–40 | © Peter Fischli David Weiss. Courtesy Galerie Eva Presenhuber, Zurich, Matthew Marks Gallery, New York, Monika Sprüth Philomene Magers, Cologne/Munich/London |
| 41 | Courtesy Gabriele Senn Galerie. Photo: Rainer Iglar |
| 42 | © Mike Kelley. Private collection. Courtesy Jablonka Galerie, Cologne/Berlin. Photo: Nic Tenwiggenhorn |
| 43a+b | Courtesy Gabriele Senn Galerie. Photo by the artist |
| 44 | Courtesy Galleria Emi Fontana, Milan, and West of Rome Inc., Los Angeles. Photo: Fredrik Nilsen. © VG Bild-Kunst, Bonn 2008 |
| 45 | Courtesy Galerie Daniel Buchholz, Cologne. Photo: Rainer Iglar |
| 46 | © Bas Jan Ader Estate. Courtesy Mary Sue Ader Andersen and Patrick Painter Editions |
| 47 | © Urs Fischer. Private collection, New York. Courtesy Galerie Eva Presenhuber, Zurich, Contemporary Fine Arts, Berlin |
| 48 | Courtesy 303 Gallery, New York, Donald Young Gallery, Chicago |

# Bodiless Elegance
## *versus*
## Pungent Physicality

# Illusion
## *versus*
## Anti-Illusion

104       Courtesy Douglas Gordon and Gagosian Gallery. *The Searchers*, 1956, dir. John Ford, CV Whitney Pictures/Warmer Brothers © Whitney Pictures/Warner Brothers

105       © 2006 Douglas Gordon/Philippe Parreno/Anna Lena Films, Paris

106a+b  © Studio 1 Filmproduktion

107       Courtesy Maureen Paley, London

108       Courtesy Donald Young Gallery, Chicago

109       © Peter Campus. Courtesy Leslie Tonkonow Artworks + Projects, New York

110a+b  Courtesy David Zwirner, New York

111       Courtesy Galerie Daniel Buchholz, Cologne

112       © 2005 Sharon Lockhart. Courtesy Gladstone Gallery, New York, Blum & Poe Gallery, LA, neugerriemschneider, Berlin

113       Courtesy the artist, Galerie Barbara Weiss, Berlin, Luhring Augustine Gallery, New York. Photo: Markus Tretter

114a–c  Courtesy Galerie Barbara Weiss, Berlin

115a+b  © Doug Aitken. Courtesy 303 Gallery, New York, Galerie Eva Presenhuber, Zurich

116       Marcel Odenbach. Courtesy Galerie Crone, Berlin, and Anton Kern Gallery, New York. Photo: Boris Becker. © VG Bild-Kunst, Bonn 2008

117a+b  Marcel Odenbach. Courtesy Galerie Crone, Berlin, and Anton Kern Gallery, New York. © VG Bild-Kunst, Bonn 2008

# Art
*versus*
# Market

118, 119  © Crystal Eye Ltd, Helsinki. Courtesy Marian Goodman Gallery, New York

120 a+b  © VG Bild-Kunst, Bonn 2008. Photo: Werner Maschmann. Courtesy Galerie Barbara Weiss

121       Collection of MOCA The Museum of Contemporary Art, Los Angeles. Courtesy Galerie Bugdahn und Kaimer, Düsseldorf

| | |
|---|---|
| 122 | © ARS Estate of Douglas Huebler. VG Bild-Kunst, Bonn 2008. Photo courtesy Darcy Huebler |
| 123 | © VG Bild-Kunst, Bonn 2008 |
| 124a–c | Courtesy Sturtevant and Galerie Thaddaeus Ropac |
| 125 | Courtesy of the artist and Metro Pictures |
| 126 | Collection FRAC Nord Pas de Calais, Lille. Courtesy the artists |
| 127 | Collections of Peter Kogler, Vienna, Susan and Lewis Manilow, Chicago, Sammlung Hauser und Wirth, St. Gallen, Museum für Moderne Kunst, Frankfurt am Main. Photo: Andrea Stappert. Courtesy the artist |
| 128a–d | Courtesy Matthieu Laurette/www.laurette.net—Consonni, Bilbao—Blow de la Barra, London. © Matthieu Laurette, VG Bild-Kunst, Bonn 2008 |
| 129a+b | © the artist |
| 130a+b | Publicness, ICA London, Great Britain, 2003. Courtesy Galleri Nicolai Wallner, Copenhagen |
| 131 | © VG Bild-Kunst, Bonn 2008. Photo: Ulay. Courtesy the artist |
| 132 | © Adrian Piper Research Archive, Berlin |
| 133 | Courtesy the artist |
| 134 | Courtesy Friedrich Petzel Gallery, New York |
| 135a+b | Courtesy Friedrich Petzel Gallery, New York |
| 136a–f | Courtesy the artist and Lisson Gallery, London |

The publisher has made every effort to identify the holders of rights. In some cases, this was not possible. Legitimate claims will of course be reimbursed in line with the usual agreements.

# Index